Mania: New Research and Treatment

CLINICAL INSIGHTS

Mania: New Research and Treatment

Edited by
ALAN C. SWANN, M.D.

Associate Professor of Psychiatry,
University of Texas Medical School at Houston

AMERICAN PSYCHIATRIC PRESS, INC.
Washington, D.C.

Note: The authors have worked to ensure that all information in this book concerning drug dosages, schedules, and routes of administration is accurate at the time of publication and consistent with standards set by the U.S. Food and Drug Administration and the general medical community. As medical research and practice advance, however, therapeutic standards may change. For this reason and because human and mechanical errors sometimes occur, we recommend that readers follow the advice of a physician directly involved in their care or the care of a member of their family.

Manufactured in the U.S.A.

The paper used in this publication meets the minimum requirements of American National Standard for Information Sciences—Permanence of Paper for Printed Library Materials, ANSI Z39.48-1984. ∞™

Library of Congress Cataloging in Publication Data

Main entry under title:

Mania: new research and treatment.

(Clinical insights)
Includes bibliographies.
1. Manic-depressive psychoses. 2. Manic-depressive psychoses—Chemotherapy. I. Swann, Alan C., 1946- . II. Series. [DNLM: 1. Manic Disorder—diagnosis. 2. Manic Disorder—drug therapy. WM 207 M2775]
RC516.M35 1986 616.89'15 86-10911
ISBN 0-88048-098-X (alk. paper)

Contents

Contributors

John M. Davis, M.D.
Gilman Professor of Psychiatry, Illinois State Psychiatric Institute, University of Illinois at Chicago

David S. Janowsky, M.D.
Professor of Psychiatry, University of California at San Diego, La Jolla, California

Martin M. Katz, Ph.D.
Professor of Psychiatry, Montefiore Hospital and Medical Center, Albert Einstein College of Medicine, Bronx, New York

Stephen H. Koslow, Ph.D.
Chief, Neurosciences Research Branch, National Institute of Mental Health, Rockville, Maryland

Katherine M. Noll, Ph.D.
Assistant Professor, Department of Psychology, Elmhurst College, Elmhurst, Illinois; Research Consultant, Illinois State Psychiatric Institute, University of Illinois at Chicago

Robert M. Post, M.D.
Chief, Biological Psychiatry Branch, National Institute of Mental Health, Bethesda, Maryland

David R. Rubinow, M.D.
Chief, Unit on Peptide Studies, Biological Psychiatry Branch, National Institute of Mental Health, Bethesda, Maryland

Steven K. Secunda, M.D.
Consultant, Clinical Research Branch, National Institute of Mental Health, Springfield, Pennsylvania

Rajiv Sharma, M.D.
Assistant Professor, Department of Psychiatry, Illinois State Psychiatric Institute, University of Illinois at Chicago

Alan C. Swann, M.D.
Associate Professor of Psychiatry,
University of Texas Medical School at Houston

Thomas W. Uhde, M.D.
Chief, Unit on Anxiety and Affective Disorders, Biological Psychiatry Branch,
National Institute of Mental Health, Bethesda, Maryland

Susan R. B. Weiss, Ph.D.
Staff Fellow, Biological Psychiatry Branch,
National Institute of Mental Health, Bethesda, Maryland

Introduction

The manic syndrome can be considered a medical–psychiatric disorder par excellence. It tends to occur episodically in otherwise healthy people; effective treatments are available; and if it is not treated effectively, the results can be disastrous.

Before the serendipitous discovery that lithium was effective, treatments for mania included hydrotherapy, rotating chairs, and surprise dunks in cold water (the *bain de surprise*). Lithium has supplanted these treatments and is presumably more effective. It is fair to ask what progress has been made since lithium in the understanding of mania and how that progress might be used to improve treatment.

Although lithium remains the mainstay of antimanic treatment, a number of other agents have been found to be effective, particularly phenothiazines and related neuroleptics. In their chapter, Drs. John Davis, Katherine Noll, and Rajiv Sharma summarize the psychopharmacology of mania as it stands now. As is also discussed in later chapters, the identification of the minority of patients who will not respond to lithium is important. A growing number of agents have been found potentially useful for these patients. It is now necessary to develop a systematic, rational means for choosing the optimal treatment for a given manic patient.

The provocative behavior of manic patients is one of the more destructive aspects of the disorder. Drs. Davis, Noll, and Sharma discuss some of the characteristics of mania that can undermine its treatment and isolate the patient from potential sources of support. Some of these interpersonal characteristics appear to be specific for manic episodes, as do the classic affective symptoms.

Acetylcholine was one of the first recognized neurotransmitters. There is increasing evidence relating this transmitter to major psychiatric syndromes and to related aspects of normal behavior, including mood, sleep, motor activity, memory, and attention. If acetylcholine had a stable, specific, and readily measurable metabolite, cholinergic hypotheses of affective disorders might dominate the field. Dr. David Janowsky summarizes the evidence linking acetylcholine to mania—effects of cholinergic agents, rebound effects, and acetylcholine–catecholamine interactions. Although there are practical problems to overcome, this work suggests that manipulating the cholinergic–noradrenergic balance can provide a promising approach to antimanic treatment.

There are tantalizing resemblances between characteristics of affective disorders and the neural phenomenon of kindling, in which after a series of discrete stimuli insufficient to produce a response, an additional stimulus produces a local seizure. This can be produced or facilitated by certain stimulant drugs in addition to electrical stimulation. The most sensitive parts of the brain are those involved with emotion. Drugs, particularly carbamazepine, that are effective in suppressing kindled seizures also are effective in treating episodic affective syndromes. In their chapter, Drs. Robert Post, Thomas Uhde, David Rubinow, and Susan Weiss describe the principles involved, the clinical effects of carbamazepine, and the complex effects on neurotransmitter systems. Regardless of the roles of kindling in the pathogenesis of mania, drugs that suppress it appear to be promising antimanic agents, especially in groups of patients responding poorly to lithium.

As many as 40 percent of manic patients have concurrent depressive symptoms. Kraepelin first observed that they could be among the most severely ill manic patients. Drs. Steven Secunda, Martin Katz, and Stephen Koslow and I discuss the relatively poor response of these patients to lithium treatment and the possible significance of the paradox of mixed mania in the understanding of affective disorders. It has been suggested that these patients may respond relatively well to carbamazepine, but this remains to be proved.

The catecholamine hypothesis of affective disorders has absorbed a bit of abuse since the discovery of many additional transmitters and peptides. Yet it can account for many of the phenomena of mania and its response to lithium. As Drs. Secunda, Katz, and Koslow and I discuss in the final chapter, excessive noradrenergic activity can identify manic patients as a group and correlates with manic severity, but it cannot predict or entirely account for the antimanic response to lithium. Reduction of elevated noradrenergic indexes appears necessary but not sufficient for response to lithium. Effects on at least one other transmitter (acetylcholine?) appear to be required for a successful response to lithium.

Research in mania has so far produced treatments that supplement lithium but do not replace it. Neuroleptic drugs or electroconvulsive treatment can be effective in the most severely ill patients. Anticonvulsants, such as carbamazepine or clonazepam, as discussed by Drs. Post, Uhde, Rubinow, and Weiss, are potentially useful in groups of manic patients known to be relatively lithium resistant or in patients who cannot tolerate lithium. A cholinergic–adrenergic treatment strategy might eventually produce an elegant and rational treatment for mania.

Several problems remain to be addressed in future research. Although 70 to 80 percent of manic episodes respond to lithium and this drug is often effective in reducing the number and severity of subsequent episodes, there is surprisingly little information on the prophylaxis of mania and its failure. The rather addictive quality of recurrent manic episodes in some patients is of practical and theoretical interest, as are possible relationships between manic episodes and stressors. Longitudinal studies, perhaps focusing on adaptive function in addition to specific affective symptoms, may address this problem. It is also necessary to investigate methods for early identification of lithium nonresponders. So far there are no objective predictors of nonresponse that are better than presence of a severe or mixed episode or presence of rapid cycling.

The fortuitous discovery of lithium provided a useful treatment for mania and a basis for research. This must be used to develop the basis for a rational approach to the treatment of mania. The information summarized in this monograph shows that there are interesting leads and more treatments, but the opportunity to develop a rational basis for treatment remains.

Mania is underdiagnosed and underresearched. That is unfortunate, given its potential treatability and the severity of the consequences if it is not treated appropriately. Patients with mania, however, are difficult research subjects. Research in mania, like its treatment, is a challenge but can be a rewarding one.

Alan C. Swann, M.D.

1

Differential Diagnosis and Treatment of Mania

John M. Davis, M.D.
Katherine M. Noll, Ph.D.
Rajiv Sharma, M.D.

1

Differential Diagnosis and Treatment of Mania

DIFFERENTIAL DIAGNOSIS

Distinguishing Mania from Schizophrenia

The classification of disorders has many purposes, but three are generally acknowledged to be central to the value of diagnosis as a tool. These are a) to help elucidate the etiology, b) to indicate the most effective and specific treatment, and c) to improve prediction of the probable course. The value of a diagnosis in directing treatment of an illness is seen by many as its most essential function. Appropriate distinctions in classification of illness are crucial for the determination of the causes of various disorders, which in turn can be hoped to lead to safer and more effective treatments.

Efforts to divide the psychoses into meaningful groups have been made for centuries (Altschule 1976), but none so far has appeared to satisfy all three of the criteria for valid diagnosis. Kraepelin's carefully reasoned effort to divide the major psychoses into *dementia praecox*, with early onset and a progressively deteriorating course, and *manic-depressive psychosis*, with generally later onset and a circular but nonprogressive course, often including significant periods of symptom remission, provided as part of its definition some prediction of the patient's future condition.

Then, as now, however, the etiology of the psychoses was generally unknown, and in Kraepelin's time, no treatments with more than temporary efficacy were available. Bleuler's (1911/1950) reclassification on the basis of thought disorder as the defining symptom of "the group of schizophrenias" may, for all its elegance, not be decisive because current evidence suggests that thought disorder is present in mania as well as schizophrenia (Marengo and Harrow 1985). Similarly, the distinction provided by Schneider's *first-rank symptoms* of schizophrenia, now incorporated into the *Diagnostic and Statistical Manual of Mental Disorders (Third Edition) (DSM-III*; American Psychiatric Association 1980), also do not appear to have provided fail-safe distinctions in diagnosis, because manics may have first-rank symptoms. Lewis and Piotrowski (1954) concluded, "Even a trace of schizophrenia is schizophrenia" (p. 37), and little effort was made to distinguish psychosis of any etiology from schizophrenia. This is the mirror image of some contemporary thinking.

With the sudden explosion in choice of treatments that occurred in the 1950s, however, the issue of classification again acquired major importance. Though antipsychotic drugs were helpful in bringing many of the symptoms of mania under control, the risk of tardive dyskinesia emerged. Lithium not only has been a more effective treatment but also has, on balance, fewer undesirable side effects. Because new treatments in the affective psychoses are rarely beneficial in classic schizophrenia, diagnosis becomes more important.

Although it has long been recognized that the affective psychoses appear to have a less debilitating outcome than schizophrenia, the 30- to 40-year follow-up study in progress at the University of Iowa supports this clinical observation with data collected on a large number of patients and control subjects (Tsuang et al. 1979). Using operational criteria of outcome for marital status, residential status, occupational status, and presence of psychiatric symptoms at follow-up, they found that although both schizophrenic and affective patients showed some long-term impairment compared with surgical controls, outcome was substantially better for affective patients on all four measures. There was no difference in outcome between patients initially hospitalized for depression and those with an initial diagnosis of mania. Roff (1975) reported that the presence of affective symptoms in a group of patients diagnosed as schizophrenic and followed for an average of 22 years predicted a good long-term outcome and an episodic rather than chronic course.

Another group for which the distinction between mania and schizophrenia is nebulous is patients with paranoid psychosis. Roff (1975) found these patients in his sample to have the best outcome of all patients diagnosed as schizophrenic. Persecutory delusions are found with high frequency in manic patients (Taylor and Abrams 1973b). Both Kraepelin and Bleuler (1911/1950) included the paranoid psychoses among their categories of schizophrenia, although Bleuler noted that many of these patients did not have a chronic and deteriorating course. Individuals with paranoid delusions in the absence of widespread psychotic decompensation are now classified in a separate diagnostic group in *DSM-III*, but the co-occurrence of paranoia with psychosis is still usually adequate to earn a patient a diagnosis. Kendler and Hays (1981) and Kendler and Davis (1981) found that relatives of paranoid schizophrenic patients showed no increased risk of schizophrenia, unlike relatives of patients with other schizophrenic diagnoses. Whether this suggests that these patients were actually manic, however, is less clear. These authors felt that they had not found evidence to link this disorder genetically with affective illness.

One new approach to the schizophrenia–mania distinction is discriminant function analysis (Brockington et al. 1979; Fowler et al. 1980a; Kendall and Brockington 1980), which uses available data from both symptoms and life history. This approach appeared to be quite successful in discriminating schizophrenic from affective patients in a large group of mixed psychotic patients. However, application of the function to patients with schizoaffective symptoms failed to show a clearly bimodal distribution (Brockington et al. 1979; Fowler et al. 1980b; Kendell and Brockington 1980).

This introduces the issue of the distinction of schizoaffective disorder from schizophrenia and mania. The changes in the status of this disorder during the development of *DSM-III* may serve to illustrate the difficulties encountered in the attempt to classify it appropriately. The Washington University group, who developed the Research Diagnostic Criteria (RDC; Feighner et al. 1972), investigated not only symptom patterns but also life course and pedigree data and found that most schizoaffective patients had a life course more consistent with an affective disorder than with schizophrenia; in addition, these patients had more relatives with affective disorders than with diagnoses of schizophrenia. These patients were also reported to respond to treatment with lithium (Prien et al. 1972a). Some have suggested that schizoaffective disorder is an affective disorder and should be subsumed entirely under that heading in the preliminary draft of *DSM-III*. Others have pointed out that a significant proportion, between 10 percent and 40 percent of patients with this diagnosis, had a more schizophrenialike course and outcome. Thus, its status has remained essentially undetermined, and it is included in *DSM-III* as a separate, somewhat undefined diagnostic category.

The issue is not yet resolved. A majority of researchers seem to agree that simply returning schizoaffective disorder to its original status as a subtype of schizophrenia would not be satisfactory, but agreement ends there. Several researchers found no identifiable differences between patients diagnosed as schizoaffective by RDC or *DSM-III* criteria and manic or bipolar patients (Abrams and Taylor 1976b; Pope et al. 1980; Rosenthal et al. 1980). Other researchers, however, found a great deal of heterogeneity in this group and concluded that these patients are neither manic nor schizophrenic in terms of symptoms, outcome, or genetic distribution in pedigrees (Baron et al. 1982; Brockington et al. 1979; Brockington et al. 1982; Fowler et al. 1980b; Mendlewicz et al. 1980).

Evidence that schizoaffective disease may have an affective component is provided by the fact that lithium plus haloperidol is slightly more effective in treating schizoaffective disease than is haloperidol alone (Biederman et al. 1979), although the appropriate cautions of circularity should be kept in mind in that lithium response may not necessarily be a marker of affective or bipolar disease.

One of the characteristics of bipolar affective disorders that makes the distinction important is that most of these patients show periods of virtually complete remission, during which they function essentially normally. Himmelhoch et al. (1981) suggested that the presence of continuing thought disorder during periods of apparent symptom remission in schizoaffective patients predicts a more schizophrenialike course, no matter how prominent these patients' affective symptoms may be during the acute phase of the illness. Nevertheless, in contrast to the earlier overinclusiveness of the diagnosis of schizophrenia, many authors currently suggest that the presence of significant alterations of mood or affect in psychotic patients should exclude a diagnosis of schizophrenia (Haier 1980; McGlashan and Carpenter 1979; Roff 1975). Disagreement remains over whether these patients should then be seen as having a type of mania or as belonging to a different category entirely.

One group of patients whose inclusion in either the schizophrenic or affective categories has become frequently questioned, is those having *acute* or *good-prognosis* schizophrenia, most of whom currently receive a diagnosis of *schizophreniform illness* (Taylor and Abrams 1984; Taylor et al. 1974). This group was distinguished with a specific set of criteria by McCabe et al. (1971, 1972), following the suggestions of Robins and Guze (1970). They specified an illness of less than six months' duration, absence of a preexisting diagnosable psychiatric illness other than affective disorder or good-prognosis schizophrenia, and evidence of a good premorbid personality. For good premorbid personality, the individual must have had at least one of the following for one year before the onset of symptoms: successful marriage, full-time work, or school attendance. If not married, the individual must have had either social contacts with the same sex outside work and school or at least monthly contact with the opposite sex. Patients previously ill with either an affective disorder or good-prognosis schizophrenia must have recovered to their premorbid level of functioning and not been treated with neuroleptics for at least nine months. For this diagnosis, at least one of the following symptoms was required: catatonic traits, delusional depersonalization, passivity, symbolic disturbance, haptic hallucinations, special types of auditory hallucinations, other clear delusions that may not have shown clear symbolic disturbance, marked confusions with hallucinations, or marked thought disorder. These patients were more likely to meet criteria for mania or depression and to have visual hallucinations, perceptual disorders, and confusion and were less likely to have affective blunting or a combination of special types of auditory and haptic hallucinations. These researchers found this group of patients to have a high family loading for affective disorders, unlike poor-prognosis schizophrenic patients, who came from families with more schizophrenic illness.

Biological Differences Between Mania and Schizophrenia

Garver and his colleagues have addressed the problem of good-prognosis schizophrenia or schizophreniform disorder at some length. Though lithium has generally been reported to be ineffective in treating symptoms of schizophrenia, some researchers have suggested that a subpopulation of patients with schizophrenic symptoms might show a significant clinical response to lithium and worsen on withdrawal (Alexander et al. 1979). These patients appeared to have a pattern of symptoms and course resembling McCabe et al.'s (1971, 1972) good-prognosis schizophrenia and were also unusual in that they appeared to respond to lithium earlier than classically manic patients (Alexander et al. 1979). In an initial study started at the Illinois State Psychiatric Institute, researchers found that 80 percent of a sample of patients who met the criteria of McCabe et al. (1971, 1972) for good-prognosis schizophrenia showed substantial remission of symptoms, including many classic schizophrenic symptoms, in a two-week trial of lithium alone (Hirschowitz et al. 1980).

Edelstein et al. (1981) found that this lithium response in schizophrenic patients could be predicted by an improvement in thought disorder in response to an infusion of physostigmine, a cholinergic drug, because manic patients but not schizophrenic ones responded to physostigmine. Further studies associated this response with unusually high or unusually low incorporation of lithium into erythrocytes (Garver et al. 1984b, 1984c) and unusually rapid onset of therapeutic response, compared with classically manic patients (Zemlan et al. 1984), in accord with the finding of Alexander et al. (1979). Pedigree studies of first-degree family members of lithium-responsive and unresponsive patients with mood-incongruent schizophrenic symptoms showed virtually total absence of schizophrenic spectrum disorders in lithium-responsive patients' families (Sautter and Garver 1985). Although studies of monoamine oxidase activity in these and manic patients have produced somewhat equivocal results (Hitzemann et al. 1984b), several researchers have suggested that lithium-responsive schizophrenic patients differ from other schizophrenic patients in a variety of dopamine-dependent functions. They showed a growth hormone response to apomorphine stimulation seven times as great as did patients with the more classic mood-congruent psychotic symptoms characteristic of mania (Garver et al. 1984a; Zemlan et al. 1984), and female patients with this diagnosis showed a marked drop in plasma prolactin levels in response to apomorphine, suggesting a true dopamine supersensitivity (Hitzemann et al. 1984a). These patients also showed a rapid remission of symptoms in response to neuroleptics (Garver et al. 1984a; Mavroidis et al. 1985), suggesting that their psychotic symptoms were possibly more attributable to dopaminergic than to other mechanisms. Other authors have reported a similar group of apparently schizophrenic patients to be much more likely than other schizophrenic patients to improve during a 30-day drug-free period and to show even greater improvement on neuroleptic doses substantially lower than the clinically recommended doses (Marder et al. 1979).

These studies raise the question of what relationship these patients have to manic patients. In various respects, these patients can resemble manic patients, resemble schizophrenic patients, or differ from both. This group of patients has been shown to have both a significant deficit in erythrocyte membrane phosphatidylcholine (important not only as a membrane component but also as a precursor of acetylcholine, a neurotransmitter that a number of studies have suggested is deficient in mania) and a marked decrease in $Na^{+}-K^{+}$ counterflow. The decrease in $Na^{+}-Li^{+}$ counterflow would account for abnormal erythrocyte lithium levels. In a group of patients with *DSM-III*-diagnosed schizophrenia, mania, and schizophreniform disorder, phospholipid methylation was significantly below control values for all three groups (Hitzemann et al. 1985). Patients from the schizophrenic and schizophreniform groups who responded to lithium showed significantly lower methylation activity than did nonresponders (Hitzemann et al. 1985). Because methylation activity among manic patients was higher, this finding again suggested a separation of this group of good-prognosis, dopamine-supersensitive, lithium- and low-dose-neuroleptic-responsive, mood-incongruent, schizophreniform patients from the classic schizophrenic and classic manic diagnoses. Whether this group is a third psychosis or a variant is unclear.

Other researchers studying *DSM-III*-diagnosed schizophreniform patients have reported conflicting conclusions when comparing this group with manic and schizophrenic patients, which is perhaps concordant with the finding of Garver and his colleagues. Coryell and Tsuang (1982) noted the intermediate position of these patients on a number of measures, but when patients who had received various forms of convulsive therapies during the index hospitalization were removed from the sample, those who remained had outcomes not significantly different from those of schizophrenic patients. Exactly what this means may be difficult to determine, however, because the patients most likely to be given and to respond to convulsive therapies appear to be those with the most affective symptoms and, as has been suggested more recently, those with supersensitive dopamine receptors. The schizophreniform patients studied by Fogelson et al. (1982), however, resembled affective patients and differed from schizophrenic patients in terms of psychiatric history, family history, acute treatment response, short-term course, and dexamethasone suppression test results. Taylor and Abrams (1984) compared a group of patients, manic by their criteria and also meeting *DSM–III* schizophreniform disorder criteria, with other manic patients; their findings essentially agreed with those of Fogelson et al. (1982).

Taylor and Abrams and their colleagues have questioned the inclusion of these patients in the category of schizophrenia for some time (Taylor et al. 1974). Current *DSM–III* diagnosis follows the traditional pattern of excluding a diagnosis of mania in patients who also have Schneiderian first-rank symptoms. These researchers have considered the symptoms of mania to be prepotent and have classified patients as manic if they have met the RDC and *DSM–III* criteria for mania regardless of the presence of Schneiderian symptoms. Their justifications of this in their initial paper on the subject (Taylor and Abrams 1973b) were reports by a) Mendlewicz et al. (1972) that in a well-defined sample of bipolar patients, about 50 percent had previously been misdiagnosed as schizophrenic; and b) Carlson and Goodwin (1973) that in a longitudinal study of patients with classic manic–depressive disorders, symptoms suggestive of schizophrenia occurred frequently during the development and course of classic mania despite efforts to exclude patients with histories of first-rank symptoms or previous diagnoses of schizophrenia.

Two-thirds of Taylor and Abrams's sample had initially been diagnosed as paranoid schizophrenic, and symptoms of catatonia were also well represented (Taylor and Abrams 1973b). Despite the high representation of schizophrenic features, such as auditory hallucinations, catatonia, and first-rank symptoms, the majority showed an excellent response to either lithium alone or lithium in combination with neuroleptics. In extensions of this work (Taylor and Abrams 1975a, 1975b; Taylor et al. 1974), they found that very few of these patients presenting with hyperactivity; rapid or pressured speech; euphoric, expansive, or irritable mood; and no evidence of coarse brain disease met rigorous research criteria for schizophrenia, although many later met strict criteria for mania. Most showed complete remission of symptoms with treatment and were more likely than schizophrenic patients to have relatives with affective disorders or alcoholism. In these and other studies

(Abrams and Taylor 1976a, 1976b, 1981; Taylor and Abrams 1973a, 1975a, 1975b, 1977), they noted that the presence of such typically schizophrenic symptoms as first-rank symptoms, catatonia, auditory hallucinations, and persecutory delusions did not appear to have predictive value if the patient also met the criteria for mania. A major review by Pope and Lipinski (1978) concurred, particularly when symptoms were observed alone and in cross section without reference to personal and family history.

Taylor and Abrams also noted heterogeneity in patients meeting criteria for mania. In addition to the classic lithium-responsive bipolar affective disorder, they described another group of patients presenting with manic symptoms. They noted that onset of symptoms after age 30 was more often associated with a unipolar manic course and fewer first-degree relatives with affective and associated conditions (Taylor and Abrams 1973a). Though a further study (Abrams and Taylor 1974) failed to show a significant distinction between bipolar patients and those with unipolar mania, a "more sophisticated replication" (Abrams et al. 1979) found a striking excess of men, approximately 80 percent of the total sample, and an increased risk of unipolar depression in first-degree relatives of patients with unipolar mania. They concluded that there was significant evidence for more than one type of mania.

Jampala et al. (1985) studied a subgroup of patients who, while having symptoms of the full manic syndrome, also demonstrated emotional blunting. This subgroup appeared to resemble schizophrenic patients substantially more than other patients with manic symptoms in terms of demographic, clinical, and family variables. These patients, however, also had histories indicating greater prior treatment with neuroleptics. Although this might have been a result of their more schizophrenialike pattern, the authors also suggested the possibility that the emotional blunting might have been secondary to neuroleptic use and suggested further exploration of the relationship between long-term neuroleptic use and emotionality. The Taylor and Abrams manic group would include Garver's lithium-responsive good-prognosis schizophrenia. Again, the question remains: Is this a variant of mania or a third psychosis?

CLINICAL CHARACTERISTICS OF MANIA

Classification of Mania

Klerman (1981) described no less than six distinguishable subtypes of bipolar disorder. Classic cycling manic–depressive disorder would, in accord with current usage, be called Bipolar I. A second variety of apparent bipolar illness, first described by Dunner and his co-workers (Dunner et al. 1976a; Dunner et al. 1976b) and characterized by periods of depression and of hypomania (in which the patient experiences elation, talkativeness, reduced need for sleep, and often some grandiosity but intact reality testing) would be designated Bipolar II. This is in accord with the usage of Dunner and colleagues (Dunner et al. 1976a), who observed that these patients appear to share more characteristics of bipolar than of unipolar patients. Klerman (1981) also proposed Bipolar III (patients who become manic or hypomanic when given tricyclic antidepressants but have not had spontaneous episodes), Bipolar IV (individuals with cyclothymic personality, in which neither the mood lows nor highs reach clinical significance but who often respond very well to lithium), Bipolar V (those with a family history of bipolar illness but who have not themselves shown significant symptoms), and Bipolar VI (Abrams and Taylor's [1974; Abrams et al. 1979] unipolar manic patients). Even this classification system leaves out *rapid-cycling bipolar illness*, which appears to be pharmacologically different from other forms of bipolar illness (Bunney 1978; Dunner et al. 1977; Potter et al. 1982; Ross et al. 1983) and manias secondary to other physical illnesses or drugs (Groat and MacKenzie 1980; Josephson and MacKenzie 1980; Krauthammer and Klerman 1978; Price et al. 1984; Thienhaus and Khosla 1984).

Thus, there appear even now to be a great number of manias, manialike disorders, and schizophrenialike disorders distinguishable from each other in a variety of meaningful ways. Some show different symptoms from other forms but respond to the same treatments, and others show symptoms very similar to other forms but fail to respond to the same treatments. The division between schizophrenia and mania, if indeed it is appropriate to presume that these are the only primary functional psychoses, remains elusive. It seems likely that findings regarding differential diagnosis will become more confusing before the three goals of diagnosis are met for these disorders.

Time Course of Relapse

Schou et al. (1970a, 1970b) presented data on the time course of relapse among bipolar patients. We calculated the rate of relapse for manic-depressive patients maintained on placebo, and our results indicated an exponential curve, with the rate of relapse being approximately 15 percent per month; therefore, the half-life of untreated patients in remission is approximately four and one-half months. Although the number of relapses may not seem very high in the first month, the number of relapses becomes impressive when they occur at this rate month after month. Shou and Baastrup also compared the relapse rates of patients from their double-blind clinical trial (Baastrup and Schou 1967) and those from their naturalistic study (Baastrup and Schou 1968a, 1968b) and found them to be essentially equal.

Symptoms of Mania

The symptoms of mania, including rapid thought and speech, euphoric mood, and grandiosity, have been well described. It is our clinical opinion that mania is characterized also by certain styles of interpersonal behavior. Styles of interpersonal behavior are often thought to be enduring character traits. We have noted that manics may at times flatter and may at other times attack another person's vulnerabilities. They project responsibility in such a way as to make others feel responsible for their actions. They test the limits of a situation to a sometimes ridiculous degree. Janowsky et al. (1974) developed the Manic Interpersonal Interaction Scale to test the hypothesis that manics have a characteristic interpersonal style of behavior. Patients were evaluated on the following items: testing of limits, projection of responsibility, sensitivity to others' soft spots, attempts to divide staff, flattering behavior, and ability to evoke anger. All of these items intercorrelated highly. We evaluated 9 schizophrenic, 10 schizoaffective, and 10 manic patients. Schizophrenic patients constituted the control group. The results are shown in Table 1. The manic patients were markedly abnormal on all of these variables. The schizoaffective patients were substantially abnormal, but manic patients were about twice as abnormal as schizoaffective patients. There was a major difference between schizophrenic patients and patients with affective disease, whether schizoaffective or classic mania.

The next question we asked was, Are these enduring personality traits of manic patients, whether sick or well, or are these limited to the acute manic episode? In other words, are these state or trait? For that reason, we evaluated manic patients when sick and recovered. In Table 2, we compare scores of acute manic patients with those of the same patients in remission.

Table 1. Interpersonal Characteristics of Psychiatric Patients

Symptom	Schizophrenic	Schizoaffective	Manic
Testing of limits	1.16 ± 0.36	4.53 ± 0.84	7.16 ± 0.34
Projection of responsibility	1.35 ± 0.46	4.64 ± 0.95	6.49 ± 0.74
Sensitivity to others' soft spots	0.53 ± 0.39	2.36 ± 0.55	5.86 ± 0.63
Attempts to divide staff	0.09 ± 0.06	1.32 ± 0.44	3.33 ± 0.77
Flattering behavior	0.58 ± 0.28	1.97 ± 0.57	4.25 ± 0.90
Ability to evoke anger	0.58 ± 0.35	3.61 ± 0.81	5.76 ± 0.48
MIIS	4.29 ± 1.51	18.01 ± 3.35	32.85 ± 3.36

Note. MIIS = Manic Interpersonal Interaction Scale (Janowsky et al. 1974).

Table 2. Interpersonal Change With Remission of Manic Patients

Symptom	Acutely 11	Remitted	% reduction
Testing of limits	7.67	1.44	81.2
Projection of responsibility	5.45	1.35	75.2
Sensitivity to others' soft spots	4.87	1.01	79.26
Attempts to divide staff	2.34	0.65	72.2
Flattering behavior	3.15	1.37	85.7
MIIS	29.11	6.65	77.15

Note. MIIS = Manic Interpersonal Interaction Scale (Janowsky et al. 1974).

When manic patients were treated with lithium, this style of interpersonal behavior disappeared, and the patients returned almost completely to normal. In this trial, patients were treated with lithium for several weeks. Had they been followed longer after discharge, it is quite possible that further improvement would have been found. These personality differences may therefore not be enduring traits but rather may be a personality style that develops as part of the illness. "Playing the manic game" may be as much a symptom of mania as is euphoric mood or rapid speech, and it is an aspect of symptomatology that is not generally recognized in textbooks. Recognition of the manic game as part of the illness is important so that the staff can prepare to deal with it psychologically.

It is well-known that manic patients can be very difficult to manage on a psychiatric ward. They can play one staff member against another in a divisive way, weakening the self-esteem of staff members by attacking sensitive spots and provoking anger not only at themselves but also among staff members. It is helpful for the ward staff to identify concrete behaviors in these areas as abnormal and part of the manic syndrome. The staff can then develop a unified response to each behavior. If a patient is testing limits, then the staff can agree on just how they will set those limits. When the staff discusses the manic patient's ability to project responsibility on the staff, they can uniformly react to the patient by maintaining a consensus of whose responsibility a given item is. If the staff realizes how the patient is attacking their own soft spots, they can support each other and realize that it is characteristic of the patient's illness, rendering it a less personal attack. If they are aware of how the patient is attempting to divide them, they can stand together rather than split apart. They would also then be less likely to take flattering behavior literally. By being able to deal with the manic patient more effectively, they will be less vulnerable to being infuriated by him or her. Thus, the identification of concrete examples of these behaviors and the attainment of a consensus about how to cope with them can be invaluable in helping the staff to avoid participating in the manic game by the manic patient's rules.

Epidemiology

The risk of developing bipolar illness is roughly one-half to one percent. The incidence of new cases per year is .01 or .015 percent for men and from .01 to .03 percent for women (Weissman and Boyd 1983).

GENETIC STUDIES IN MANIC ILLNESS

Early family studies in affective disorders were nosologically based on Kraepelin's classifications, and probands were not differentiated as bipolar and unipolar. The concept of bipolarity in affective disorders was brought into focus by Leonhard (1957, 1963; Leonhard et al. 1962) and others who demonstrated that bipolar patients had greater genetic loading for affective disorders than unipolar patients. In addition, bipolar probands had a higher frequency of family members showing similar bipolar symptomatology. Indeed, there was a large proportion of bipolar relatives who exhibited only unipolar symptoms. Unipolar probands, however, had relatives with predominantly unipolar symptoms.

Affective Illness

Morbidity risk for relatives of manic patients is estimated to be between 15 and 35 percent and is similar in different types of first-degree relatives, such as parents, siblings, and children (Gershon et al. 1975; Helzer and Winokur 1974; James and Chapman 1975; Smeraldi et al. 1978; Trzebiatowska-Trzeciak 1977; Winokur et al. 1971). This is consistent with a dominant mode of transmission. As shown in Table 3, we analyzed the data from studies of monozygotic and dizygotic twins (see Bertelsen et al. 1977) using the Mantel-Haenszel (1959) test and found a much greater concordance in the monozygotic than the dizogotic pairs ($p < 10^{-22}$).

In our review of twin studies (Bertelsen et al. 1977; Zerbin-Rudin 1969; 1979), we observed that only one-fourth of the identical twins were not concordant for affective disease. Among those with some degree of concordance, it was relatively unusual for one to be bipolar and the other to be unipolar; this occurred in 10 percent of the twins, or roughly one-seventh of the patients with some degree of concordance. Some of the twins presenting with a unipolar illness may not have yet had their first bipolar illness and would change their polarity with the passage of time, resulting in a higher degree of concordance for polarity. The presence of a genetic component to depressive illness was also reported in the adoption study of Mendlewicz and Rainer (1977), who found a greater degree of affective psychopathology among the biologic parents than the adoptive parents.

Early linkage studies supported the role of a major locus for bipolar disorders on the X chromosome as one possible mode of transmission (Goetzl et al. 1974; Mendlewicz and Fleiss 1974; Winokur et al. 1969; Zompo et al. 1984). In investigations using families of unipolar depressive probands, researchers have, however, been unable to link unipolar depressive illness with protanopia or Xg blood groups, making X-linked inheritance in unipolar illness improbable (Mendlewicz and Fleiss 1974). Also, X-linked inheritance has not been demonstrated in all bipolar families (Mendlewicz and Fleiss 1976), and this mode of transmission may be nonspecific in that it has been demonstrated in families of schizoaffective probands as well as in those with other psychoses (Barton 1977; Belmaker and Wyatt 1976).

Table 3. Concordance and Discordance of Affective Illness in Pairs of Twins

Study	Monozygotic		Dizygotic	
Luxenburger (1928)	2	1	0	13
Rosanoff et al. (1934)	16	7	11	56
Essen-Moller (1941)	2	6	0	3
Slater and Shields (1953)	4	4	7	23
Kallmann (1954)	25	2	13	42
Da Fonseca (1959)	15	6	15	24
Kringlen (1967)	2	4	0	20
Allen et al. (1974)	5	10	0	34
Bertelsen et al. (1977)	32	23	9	43

Note. $\chi^2(1) = 98.7$, $p < .10^{-22}$ (Mantel-Haenszel, 1959).

Location of the Bipolar Gene

In a more recent linkage study, using recombinant DNA techniques, researchers attempted to identify a major locus for affective illness, reporting findings obtained from one large, old-order Amish family (Kidd et al. 1984). The family consisted of 51 individuals, of whom 11 had confirmed major affective diagnosis of either unipolar or bipolar disease. The investigators reported that a major locus for affective disorder may be located on the short arm of Chromosome 11. This study needs additional confirmation.

Lithium Ratio

The ratio of red blood cell (RBC) to plasma lithium expresses the relationship between intracellular and extracellular lithium concentrations. In clinical studies of lithium administration, this ratio varies from 0.15 to 0.60, with an average of 0.30. The ratio is constant for each individual and independent of change in symptoms. There is evidence that patients with bipolar illness have a higher mean lithium ratio. In addition, a higher proportion of first-degree relatives of bipolar probands have an elevated lithium ratio. Interestingly, in families of bipolar patients, those relatives who have a history of affective disorder have a significantly higher lithium ratio. This has been demonstrated using statistical models (mixture distributions) and genetic models (Dorus et al. 1983; Gibbons et al. 1984).

Dorus et al. (1975) proposed a genetic determinant of the lithium ratio among individuals. In a study of the in vitro RBC uptake of lithium and the in vivo lithium ratio in monozygotic and dizygotic twins, Dorus et al. noted significantly greater variance for dizygotic twin pairs than for monozygotic twin pairs. This was accepted as evidence for genetic control of these parameters, although more precise estimates of heritability were not concluded (Dorus et al. 1975). An extension of this genetic finding was carried out in a family study of bipolar probands. Once again, using segregation analysis on measurements of lithium ratio in members of 120 normal families and 31 families of bipolar probands, Dorus et al. (1983) obtained support for genetic control. Genetic polymorphism at a major gene locus, in which an allele caused an elevated lithium ratio and also increased susceptibility to some forms of affective disorder, was identified.

Lithium–sodium transport, located in the cell membrane, is the process that controls the lithium ratio. An abnormality in this function of the cell membrane may represent a heritable marker of susceptibility to development of affective disorders (Dorus et al. 1979).

NORADRENERGIC AND SEROTINERGIC THEORIES OF MANIA

In the 1950s and 1960s, the predominant theories of mania and depression were psychoanalytic. The general approach to biological factors was screening schizophrenic patients for abnormal substances in urine or plasma. The rise of biological psychiatry began with serendipitous therapeutic discoveries, starting with the antimanic action of lithium in 1947, the antipsychotic action of chlorpromazine in 1952 and 1953, the antidepressant actions of the monoamine oxidase (MAO) inhibitors and tricyclics in 1957, and the observation that reserpine and alpha-methyldopa produced depression. The more recent discoveries by Japanese workers of the antimanic action of carbamazepine and the discovery of the antimanic properties of physostigmine are also relevant.

Schildkraut (1965) and Bunney and Davis (1965) independently formulated the catecholamine hypothesis of depression, which suggested that depression is caused by low brain norepinephrine and mania by high brain norepinephrine. These workers, however, indicated that the defect could be either a hypo- or hyperadrenergic function in either condition. Through a variety of mechanisms, the same reasoning could be applied to serotonin. This type of thinking introduced into psychiatry a new paradigm that could be used to infer theories of disease from the mechanism by which therapeutic drugs (or drugs which precipitate disease) produced alterations in neurotransmitter substances.

We can sharpen this further by suggesting two basic and separate stages: first, the mechanism by which a drug produces a therapeutic benefit in a given disease and, second, the relationship between this mechanism and the pathogenesis of the disease.

We now return to the norepinephrine and serotonin theory: Let us revisit the norepinephrine theory 20 years later. A number of new drugs that inhibit norepinephrine reuptake have been tested in the clinic and have been found to be efficacious. Because these drugs were screened for an action on norepinephrine, it is not surprising that they inhibit norepinephrine reuptake. If the antidepressant properties of these drugs were produced through a mechanism not involving norepinephrine, we would not expect all these drugs to prove efficacious. The same argument applies to MAO inhibitors. In addition, the fact that thyroid hormone can shorten the time of response to antidepressants and that this might be through a noradrenergic mechanism also is consistent with the norepinephrine theory.

Some novel agents are neither uptake inhibitors nor MAO inhibitors. Iprindole, for example, is an effective antidepressant that is neither a norepinephrine uptake inhibitor nor an MAO inhibitor. Because iprindole downregulates norepinephrine beta-receptor sites, however, it may affect norepinephrine through a different mechanism. In our view, downregulation of norepinephrine beta-receptors is a compensatory effect from an increase in noradrenergic transmission. More recently, alprazolam and buproprion have been found to have antidepressant properties, and in our laboratory, we demonstrated that both these drugs downregulate beta-receptors. Mianserin increases norepinephrine synthesis and, hence, is a fifth type of agent that potentiates norepinephrine and helps depression.

There are two dominant animal models of depression, the learned helplessness model and the separation model. Both models may be mediated by norepinephrine. The norepinephrine theory is a simple, dynamic theory: It posits low norepinephrine in depression and high norepinephrine in mania. Contrary data, however, do exist. Lithium can clearly prevent the recurrence of both the manic and depressed phases and is a good antimanic drug and a fair antidepressant, and electroconvulsive therapy (ECT) can benefit both depression and mania. Because they are efficacious in both depression and mania, these two somatic treatments provide the strongest pharmacological evidence inconsistent with this simple, dynamic (up/down) theory.

There is a substantial body of evidence that antipsychotic drugs also have a beneficial effect on mania. Some antipsychotic agents are both noradrenergic- and dopaminergic-receptor blockers. Others are more specific dopaminergic-receptor blockers. For example, chlorpromazine affects both transmitter substances, but pimozide is a relatively specific dopaminergic-receptor blocker. In a double-blind comparative trial of pimozide and chlorpromazine, both agents were equally effective in producing an antimanic effect (Cookson et al., 1981). This evidence is consistent with the hypothesis that the antipsychotic drugs exert their antimanic effects because they are dopaminergic-receptor blockers. Chlorpenthixol has two isomers, the cis form and the trans form. The cis form possesses antidopaminergic properties, whereas the trans form does not. Three out of five patients who received the cis form experienced an antimanic effect, whereas none of the five administered the trans form received an antimanic effect (Nolen 1983). Although the sample was small, this study also supported an antidopamine mechanism of action.

There is some evidence that antinorepinephrine drugs may help mania. Clonidine, which stimulates presynaptic alpha-2 receptors, can lower central norepinephrine neurotransmission by decreasing norepinephrine synthesis and release. Several small, open studies have suggested that clonidine may be an effective antimanic drug, presumably through its antinorepinephrine mode of action (Zubenko et al. 1984). Yohimbine, a drug with the opposite action to clonidine, can precipitate mania, as reported in a few patients (Price et al. 1984).

There is some limited clinical evidence from a few manic patients that high-dose propranolol may have an antimanic effect. These results were reported in a double-blind, placebo-controlled trial comparing racemic propranolol with d-propranolol, the stereoisomer that has no beta-blocking activity (Zerssen and Emrich

1983). In a small sample, d-propranolol was found to be half as effective as the racemic mixture for mania. This evidence suggests that the antimanic properties of propranolol do not reside entirely in the beta-blocking properties of the drug. There is also a case report demonstrating some effect of verapamil maintenance in affective illness (Gitlin and Weiss 1984).

Serotonin Theory of Mania

According to the serotonin theory, depression is caused by low brain serotonin and, by implication, mania may be caused by high brain serotonin. The so-called permissive theory of Prange suggests that low brain serotonin increases susceptibility to both mania and depression, which are primarily caused by norepinephrine abnormalities, depression by low norepinephrine and mania by high norepinephrine (Prange et al. 1974). This theory of depression has not been supported as well on a pharmacological level. There are many new, effective antidepressants that are not serotonin-uptake inhibitors. Furthermore, many drugs initially thought to be specific serotonin-uptake inhibitors, such as chlorimipramine, amitriptyline, and zimelidine, are metabolized to active metabolites that inhibit the reuptake of norepinephrine and, hence, affect both norepinephrine and serotonin. Fluoxetine is a specific serotonin-uptake inhibitor, but there is some evidence that it may downregulate norepinephrine beta-receptors and, therefore, also have adrenergic effects. Trazodone also downregulates norepinephrine beta-receptors and so may have noradrenergic effects.

Evidence on cerebrospinal fluid 5-hydroxy-indoleacetic acid (CSF 5-HIAA) is critical to one aspect of the serotonin hypothesis and is reported in this volume, so we will not review it. Depending on whether we chose to test the single-transmitter hypothesis or the permissive two-transmitter theory, we would have expected manic individuals to have altered CSF 5-HIAA.

There is some evidence that antiserotonin drugs may have a beneficial effect on mania: Several studies indicate that the antiserotonin agent methysergide has an antimanic effect (Dewhurst 1968), and several other studies show that the antimanic drug cinanserin has an antimanic effect (Kane 1970). Additionally, there are case reports that fenfluramine has an antimanic effect (Pearce 1973). There is also some evidence that tryptophan, a serotonin precursor, may have antimanic properties (Chouinard et al. 1979).

TREATMENT OF MANIA

Cholinergic Compounds

Central cholinergic mechanisms, in reciprocal interaction with the catecholamines, have been implicated in the etiology and regulation of affective disorders. Briefly, mania has been hypothesized to be a syndrome of relatively diminished central acetylcholine activity, compared to normal or increased noradrenergic and/or dopaminergic activity (Janowsky et al. 1972). The proposed interaction model was considered analogous to similar adrenergic–ACh interactions occurring in the control of peripheral autonomic functions such as heart rate or pupillary size. Similar interactions have been well documented with central dopaminergic and cholinergic activity in the modulation of extrapyramidal motor activity. Supporting evidence for this hypothesis is discussed in Chapter 2 of this monograph by Dr. David Janowsky.

Manic patients, supposedly having a decrease in central cholinergic activity, might then be predicted to respond to physostigmine. Indeed, physostigmine has been found to antagonize hypomanic and manic symptoms rapidly. In addition to inducing an inhibitory state, physostigmine reduces flight of ideas, pressure of speech, and euphoria (Davis et al. 1978; Janowsky et al. 1972a, 1972b). Interestingly, the effects of physostigmine on manic symptoms are more demonstrable on behavioral symptoms, as already described, and less so on cognitively related symptoms such as grandiosity and other delusions.

Because physostigmine converts manic patients to depressed patients, it may be hypothesized that any agent that increases brain acetylcholine may improve mania. Cohen et al. (1982) administered lecithin to manic individuals in a double-blind, placebo-controlled trial. They found that five out of six manic subjects showed definite improvement following lecithin, in comparison to the placebo.

Apart from the psychopharmacological evidence already presented, cholinergic interaction with numerous physiological parameters has been reported among affectively disordered subjects, including bipolar and unipolar ones. Cholinergic induction of rapid-eye-movement sleep (REM induction) has been shown to be enhanced in affective patients, suggesting some form of supersensitivity to cholinomimetics (Sitaram et al. 1980). The increased hypothalamic–pituitary–adrenal activity seen in a large percentage of endogeneously depressed patients and reflected by nonsuppression on the dexamethasone suppression test may, in part, be mediated by increased central cholinergic tone. Physostigmine administration can convert a dexamethasone suppression test from suppression to nonsuppression (Carroll et al. 1978).

Lithium in Acute Mania

There have been few controlled trials of lithium alone in acute mania because of the practical difficulties in managing excited manic patients. Lithium is used throughout the world for the treatment of mania. Its antimanic properties are sufficiently dramatic that despite individual biases, lithium's efficacy is generally well accepted. The efficacy of lithium is supported by controlled trials as well, although some discussion on methodological issues is needed. There is no absolute difference between the spectrum of controlled trial and the spectrum of anecdotal information. A good controlled trial should be a double-blind, random-assignment trial, with careful effort going into randomization and blinding. Another critical design element is a concomitant control group. The most important artifact is spontaneous remission consequent to the demand characteristic of other situations—the so-called Hawthorne effect—and the natural history of the disease.

Crossover designs are less useful. If a patient is treated with an effective drug, the disease process is essentially stopped. The natural history of affective disease is such that patients, once effectively treated, relapse at a rate of about 10 percent per month. The half time to relapse is generally four to six months for a patient with frequent recurrences and longer for a patient with very infrequent recurrences. Thus, in a crossover design, during randomization, if the patient were to receive an effective compound initially and achieve a remission, no change would be seen at crossover, especially if the study were of short duration. Crossover designs are most useful when patients relapse within a few days and when clinical improvement is clearly dependent on continued drug administration.

Another design is the naturalistic study, which introduces some degree of control by including a placebo period and using partially blind raters. Of course, any effort to control error bias can be applauded in a naturalistic study, really a variant of the open study. It is important to make a distinction between the crossover trial with patients assigned to an A–B order or B–A order by a table of random numbers and a naturalistic study, which also uses periods of drugs and placebo but without random assignment to controlled conditions of fixed length. If patients are followed on a research ward and given placebos, new drugs, and standard drugs at various times, the introduction of new and standard drugs is usually far from random. It is common practice to give patients placebos either early in their stays or when they are doing relatively well; when a patient is deteriorating disastrously, he or she is often placed on a standard drug. New drugs tend to be administered only when clinical symptoms are present and stable or deteriorating gradually. Therefore, in a naturalistic study, there is clearly a tendency to use placebo early and drug late during the episode. The later in the episode, however, the greater is the chance of spontaneous recovery. Therefore, using placebo early and drug late introduces a systematic bias.

Patients have a tendency to gradually deteriorate until they hit rock bottom and then often improve spontaneously. Unless the study is well controlled, it is not impossible in a naturalistic study for patients to be put on a new drug just before they are about to experience a spontaneous remission.

Another important aspect is blindness of the raters. On a research ward where a patient's condition is discussed from time to time in clinical conferences and where raters are active participants or in situations where raters interact with the ward's staff, professionally and/or socially, it is not uncommon for the rater to unwittingly obtain clinical information regarding the patient. Although it is sometimes possible to have raters who have no contact whatsoever with the research ward, in the more usual situation, raters are only partially blinded. Nonetheless, to have partially blinded raters is useful, and research, like politics, should be considered the art of the possible. It is our view that such naturalistic studies are closer to the open, frankly uncontrolled study than they are to the double-blind, parallel-group design and that the interpretation of the two should not be mixed.

The naturalistic, mirror-image study has certain virtues that the double-blind, controlled study does not. Often, patients who are assigned to a double-blind, random-assignment study are highly selected, but the naturalistic, so-called mirror-image study includes a wider variety of patients and may more closely mimic what happens in actual practice. Therefore, these are important sources of data and complement controlled studies by helping to make broader based generalizations.

The first double-blind, placebo-controlled trial was conducted by Schou et al. (1954) on 30 "typical" and 8 "atypical" manic patients. There was an improvement rate of 90 percent for the typical and 62 percent for the atypical group. Maags (1963) performed a double-blind, crossover study in 28 manic patients randomly assigned to two groups. The first group received lithium (1500 mg) for two weeks, followed by a two-week drug-free period and ending with a two-week placebo period, and the second group received medication in the mirror-image order. Lithium was significantly superior to placebo in the 18 patients completing the study. Stokes et al. (1971) studied the effects of lithium and placebo, administered in four alternate periods of 7 to 10 days each, in a double-blind trial conducted with 38 manic patients and found patients to have greater improvement on lithium than placebo.

In a three-week parallel-group trial, manic patients were randomly assigned to lithium, chlorpromazine, or haloperidol treatment (Shopsin et al. 1975). There was no significant difference in ratings between the lithium and haloperidol groups, and both drugs were superior to chlorpromazine. The substantially higher proportion of patients on lithium who were considered ready for discharge were patients on either neuroleptic. The authors concluded that although antipsychotics may help suppress the manic symptoms in the acute phase, lithium was better able to qualitatively change the underlying manic process, thereby resulting in greater subjective improvement. These results are consistent with other reports demonstrating lithium's superiority to antipsychotics in the treatment of mania (Johnson et al. 1971; Takahashi et al. 1975).

Role of Neuroleptics in Acute Mania

Generally, only mild to moderately severe manic patients are treated with lithium because the period between initiation of treatment and therapeutic response is about 10 days. Antipsychotics produce a more rapid response (Garfinkel et al. 1980). A large Veterans Administration (VA) study actually found chlorpromazine to be superior to lithium in so-called highly active psychotics, but the two drugs were equal in the less active patients (Prien et al. 1972b). There is no doubt that lithium has a slower response time than antipsychotics, but we prefer to use lithium alone for purposes of diagnostic clarity. If a patient responds to lithium alone, this is considered evidence that the patient has a bipolar affective disease. We recognize the circularity in this, but in practical therapeutics, this approach carries diagnostic and prognostic information. Antipsychotics are clearly nonspecific in that they help core schizophrenic individuals as well as manic individuals. If the patient is too disturbed to last the 10-day drug lag period, then neuroleptics plus lithium can be used, and neuroleptics can be discontinued after a period of 4 to 7 days.

Prophylactic Use of Lithium

Cade, in his original 1949 paper, observed that manic patients relapsed when medication was discontinued. Gershon and Trautner (1956) and Noack and Trautner (1951) used lithium to maintain remission in patients who experienced frequent relapses and who had previously required maintenance shock treatment. This notwithstanding, the concept of prophylactic lithium was not clearly stated until the work conducted by Baastrup, Schou, Hartigan, and Gershon.

Gershon and Yuwiler (1960) as well as Hartigan (1963) clearly expounded its prophylactic use. The term *normothymic* was proposed by Schou (1963) to describe drugs that act specifically against affective disease.

Baastrup and Schou (1967) analyzed a naturalistic study (which has become a "psychiatric classic") on 88 patients who had experienced recurrent unipolar or manic–depressive illnesses, comparing the frequency of episodes of illness during a period after lithium treatment with their frequency during an equivalent period before lithium treatment. Before lithium, the patients spent an average of 13 weeks a year in a manic or depressed state; after lithium, they spent less than 2 weeks a year in this state. Relapse occurred on an average of every 8 months before treatment; during maintenance treatment, relapse occurred on an average of every 60 to 85 months.

Lithium prevents the recurrence in bipolar patients of both manic and depressive episodes and the recurrence in unipolar patients of depressive episodes. Patients respond better to lithium after treatment for months or years. A long normothymic period may lead to stabilization of the patient's social and vocational functioning, which may in turn reinforce overall stability.

Studies of Lithium Prophylaxis in Affective Disease

We summarize the efficacy of lithium prophylaxis from placebo-controlled, random-assignment, double-blind studies in Table 4, with results separated for unipolar and bipolar patients. Three groups of researchers did not present their results in such a manner that the data could be separately analyzed for unipolar and bipolars, and these results are listed in Table 5.

Table 4. Lithium Prevention of Relapse

Study	Bipolar patients (I and II)		Unipolar depressions	
	Placebo	Lithium	Placebo	Lithium
Baastrup and Schon (1967)				
n	22	28	17	17
Relapsed	12 (55%)	0	9 (53%)	0
Well	10 (45%)	28 (100%)	8 (47%)	17 (100%)
Prien et al. (1971)				
n	10	14	21	23
Relapsed	9 (90%)	5 (31%)	19 (90%)	13 (57%)
Well	1 (10%)	9 (69%)	2 (10%)	10 (43%)
Prien et al. (1973b)				
n	102	97	—	—
Relapsed	91 (89%)	48 (49%)	—	—
Well	11 (11%)	49 (51%)	—	—
Persson (1972)				
n	12	12	21	21
Relapsed	11 (92%)	5 (42%)	14 (67%)	6 (29%)
Well	1 (8%)	7 (58%)	7 (33%)	15 (71%)
Coppen et al. (1971)				
n	21	17	15	11
Relapsed	21 (100%)	3 (18%)	12 (80%)	1 (9%)
Well	0	14 (82%)	3 (20%)	10 (91%)
Fieve et al. (1968)				
n	11	7	—	—
Relapsed (Bipolar 2)	7 (64%)	1 (14%)	—	—
Well	4 (36%)	6 (86%)	—	—
Fieve et al. (1976)				
n	17	15	14	14
Relapsed (Bipolar 1)	17 (100%)	0	9 (64%)	8 (57%)
Well	0	15 (100%)	5 (36%)	6 (43%)
Kane et al. (1982)				
n	7	4	6	7
Relapsed	5 (71%)	1 (25%)	6 (100%)	2 (29%)
Well	2 (29%)	3 (75%)	0	5 (71%)
Glen et al. (1984)				
n	—	—	9	12
Relapsed	—	—	8 (89%)	5 (42%)
Well	—	—	1 (11%)	7 (58%)
Prien et al. (1980)				
n	—	—	34	37
Relapsed	—	—	24 (71%)	21 (57%)
Well	—	—	10 (29%)	16 (43%)
Fyro et al. (1977)				
n	18	18	—	—
Relapsed	18 (100%)	0	—	—
Well	0	18 (100%)	—	—

In the trial, Baastrup and Schou (1967) placed patients maintained on lithium for at least one year to ensure that patients had the type of illness that would respond to lithium. In a five-month prophylactic trial, none of the patients who received lithium relapsed, but 55 percent of the placebo bipolars and 53 percent of the placebo unipolars relapsed (Table 4).

Coppen et al. (1971), at four separate centers in Great Britain, randomly assigned patients to lithium or placebo for a period of up to two years. Of placebo-treated patients and lithium-treated patients, 92 percent and 14 percent, respectively, relapsed. Mendlewicz and associates (1973) reported a relapse rate of 75 percent among patients on placebo, compared with 33 percent for those on lithium. In studies with a zero or essentially zero relapse rate on lithium, patients selected usually had classical manic disease and/or had been receiving lithium treatment with good results.

Prien and associates (Prien et al. 1971, 1972b, 1973a, 1973b, 1974) followed manic and depressed patients in VA hospitals and public and private hospitals to assess a two-year program of lithium prophylactic maintenance therapy. In these studies, 71 to 90 percent of placebo patients relapsed, in comparison with 49 to 67 percent of lithium-treated patients. In such studies, many patients had not previously received lithium or were atypical manic or schizoaffective. The higher base rate of relapse on lithium reflects the entrance criteria to the study, but an even greater percentage of placebo-patient groups relapsed. In both types of studies, there was a difference between drug and placebo groups of about 40 to 50 percent, although the base rate for relapse differed from study to study. Studies in several countries confirmed the prophylactic

Table 5. Effectiveness of Lithium Versus Placebo in Preventing Relapse

	Lithium group					Placebo group				
		Relapsed		Not relapsed			Relapsed		Not relapsed	
Study	*N*	*n*	%	*n*	%	*N*	*n*	%	*n*	%
Hullen et al. (1972, 1975)	18	1	6	17	94	18	6	33	12	67
Mendlewicz et al. (1973)	36	12	33	24	67	36	27	75	9	25
Cundall et al. (1972)	16	7	44	9	56	16	13	81	3	19

value of lithium. In the studies summarized in Table 4, 66 percent of the patients on lithium did not relapse. This contrasts sharply with the 22 percent of the placebo patients who did not relapse. For the purpose of testing the significance of the lithium prophylactic effects relative to placebo in combined unipolar and bipolar patients, we collapsed the data from Table 4 into a fourfold table giving the number of patients who relapsed or did not relapse on lithium or placebo, regardless of whether they were unipolar or bipolar. We used these data in calculating the Mantel-Haenszel (1959) statistics. The superiority of lithium over placebo was highly significant ($p = 2 \times 10^{-39}$). A detailed discussion of this method is available (Cochran 1954).

Lithium for Prophylaxis of Unipolar Depression

Because there is evidence from natural history, drug response, and genetic data indicating that unipolar affective disease is a separate entity from bipolar depression (Angst et al. 1970; Hullen et al. 1972; Leonhard et al. 1962; Robins and Guze 1972), the lithium prophylactic effect should be examined separately in unipolar and bipolar individuals. Further information from a collaborative longitudinal study conducted in three European countries (Angst et al. 1970; Grof et al. 1970) provides evidence on a larger number of patients and supplements the evidence from placebo-controlled trials.

The International Collaborative Study (Angst et al. 1970; Schou et al. 1970a, 1970b; Grof et al. 1970) compared the effect of lithium treatment on the course of recurrent unipolar or bipolar illness with the course in the same patients before receiving lithium. This design was similar to that used in Baastrup and Schou's (1968) classic naturalistic study. The size effect of the prophylactic properties of lithium, compared with the historical or mirror-image control period, can be measured in the multiple regression analysis. This is not identical to the drug–placebo differences in Table 4 because it represents episodes and not individual patients. It is intended here only as a rough approximation and provides a quantitative comparison of the differential efficacy of lithium in preventing relapse in both unipolar and bipolar individuals. The same design was applied to both unipolar and bipolar groups, so the contrast between groups is a valid comparison. The magnitude of the association of a good response to lithium treatment reveals that in comparison with their course before receiving lithium, unipolar patients had a slightly better prophylactic effect with lithium ($d = .54$) than did bipolar patients ($d = .44$).

We would distinguish statistical significance from the magnitude of correlations. A high correlation involving four or five subjects may just barely be statistically significant, but a low correlation involving thousands of subjects may be highly significant. Because most of these studies had more bipolar than unipolar patients, it is important to distinguish the overall findings from the degree of prophylaxis (size effect) exercised by lithium in each subgroup of patients. This can be expressed as the correlation

Table 6. Lithium Versus Placebo phi Coefficients for Individual Studies and Average Weighted Correlation

	Bipolar		Unipolar	
Study	Phi	*n*	Phi	*n*
Baastrup et al. (1967)	0.63	50	0.60	34
Prien et al. (1971)	0.54	24	0.38	44
Prien et al. (1972)	0.43	199	—	—
Persson et al. (1972)	0.53	24	0.38	42
Coppen et al. (1971)	0.85	38	0.70	26
Fieve et al. (1968)	0.48	18	—	—
Fieve et al. (1976)	1.00	32	0.07	28
Kane et al. (1982)	0.45	11	0.73	13
Glen et al. (1984)	—	—	0.48	21
Prien et al. (1980)	—	—	0.14	71
International Collaborative Study (Angst et al. 1970; Grof et al. 1970; Schou et al. 1970[a]	0.44	450	0.54	196
Average weighted correlation	0.48		0.44	

[a]Regression coefficient.

coefficient between degree of prophylaxis of lithium or placebo when quantitative data are available or as the phi coefficient when categorical data are available. The phi coefficient is the correlation between relapsed versus nonrelapsed states and lithium versus placebo treatment where each category is assigned a numerical score of 1 or 0.

One should, therefore, compare the phi coefficients for the degree of prophylaxis of lithium for the bipolar patients and the unipolar patients. In addition, inspection of the raw numbers given for each study in Table 4 gives the reader an intuitive impression of the magnitude of the prophylactic effect in unipolar versus bipolar patients. Table 6 concludes with an average weighted correlation for each group, including all the studies in the table in addition to the International Collaborative Study.

In Table 7, the overall prophylactic effects of lithium, antidepressants, and thc combination of lithium and antidepressants in

Table 7. Prophylactic Effects of Lithium and Tricyclic Antidepressants in Bipolar and Unipolar Depression

Depression	% Relapse	% Well	*p*	Homogeneity
Bipolar				
Lithium	32	68	2×10^{-28}	*ns*
Placebo	86	14		
Unipolar				
Lithium	39	61	1×10^{-9}	*ns*
Placebo	74	26		
Unipolar				
Antidepressants	29	71	5×10^{-13}	*ns*
Placebo	57	43		
Unipolar				
Lithium	51	49	*ns*	.002
Antidepressants	57	43		
Bipolar				
Lithium	44	56	.002	*ns*
Antidepressants	78	22		
Unipolar				
Lithium and imipramine	29	71	.03	*ns*
Lithium	52	48		
Bipolar				
Lithium and imipramine	40	60	*ns*	*ns*
Lithium	38	62		

both unipolar and bipolar patients are compared. Lithium proves to be clearly efficacious prophylactically in both bipolar and unipolar disease, and antidepressants have a prophylactic action in unipolar disease. Although there appears to be no difference between lithium and antidepressants in the prevention of unipolar disease, there is a clear loss of homogeneity between the individual studies. The combination of lithium and imipramine is no more effective than lithium alone in bipolar disease. The same comparison in unipolar disease demonstrates an interesting trend in that the combination is marginally superior. Further work is needed to establish whether this is consistently the case.

Efficacy of Prophylaxis in Manic Versus Depressive Phases

The conceptual distinction between lithium's effect in preventing depression in unipolar illness and its relative prophylactic action against either the manic phase only or the depressive phase only in bipolar illness should be preserved. Prien et al. (1973b) and Cundall et al. (1972) found that lithium had a larger effect in preventing the manic phase of bipolar illness than it did in preventing the depressive phase of bipolar illness (Kane et al. 1981). In contrast, Baastrup and Schou (1967) and Coppen and associates (1971) found essentially similar prophylactic effects against the manic and the depressive phases of bipolar affective illness. These differences may represent random variation within the small samples used. More data are needed.

Lithium Prophylaxis in Atypical Affective Syndromes

The success of lithium prophylaxis in classical manic illness encourages an extension of the indications for its use. Hanna et al. (1972) demonstrated lithium's effectiveness in patients with a 48-hour periodic psychosis. In a classic study, Baastrup and Schou (1968a) reported that atypical manic patients did not respond to lithium as well as typical manic patients did, but showed a substantial reduction in episodes per year (1.22 without lithium and

0.35 with lithium). The researchers in the International Collaborative Study (Angst et al. 1970; Grof et al. 1970; Schou et al. 1970a, 1970b) found statistically significant lithium prophylaxis in schizoaffective patients, even though the results were less impressive than those found in classic affectively ill patients.

Smulevitch's (1973) and Gardner's (1973) open studies provide clinical evidence of lithium's efficacy in schizoaffective or atypical manic patients. Perris (1974) studied a syndrome referred to as *cycloid*, which resembles schizoaffective psychosis in the standard *DSM–III* nomenclature. Eighteen subjects were administered lithium. There was a mean of 2.06 affective episodes during the pretreatment period, in contrast to .5 episodes after the lithium period ($p < .01$). Patients spent an average of 2.34 months in the hospital during the pretreatment period versus .2 months ($p < .01$) during the lithium period.

Dyson and Barcai (1970), Annell (1969), and Frommer (1968) successfully treated affectively disturbed children with lithium. Gram and Rafaelsen (1962) performed a 12-month randomized, double-blind, crossover study on 18 psychotic children given lithium or placebo; 11 responded better during the lithium period.

Because mental deficiency can coexist with manic–depressive disease, Penrose (1963), Reid (1970), and Naylor et al. (1974) conducted 2-year random-assignment, double-blind, crossover trials of lithium versus placebo in the treatment of mentally defective persons with bipolar disorder. Lithium had a beneficial effect.

Research is needed to establish clinical indications for lithium in atypical cases, but at this time, there is a modest empirical basis for proposing lithium prophylaxis for selected atypical manic or schizoaffective patients. Although definitive data are lacking, a good clinical response during the acute period may suggest that lithium prophylaxis is a better long-term treatment than antipsychotic medication, which carries the risk of tardive dyskinesia.

Clinical Issues

Should prophylactic lithium be recommended in patients who have had only a relatively small number of manic or depressive episodes or both? Most lithium maintenance studies have used patients with documented recurrent illness, with several episodes in the previous two to four years. It is difficult to do research on patients who have had infrequent episodes because a large sample is required for purposes of statistical analysis if relapses are infrequent. There are no data pertinent to the frequency of illness necessary to justify maintenance medication. The clinician needs to generalize to the particular patient from the controlled trials, taking into account the nature of the affective disorder (that is, severity of the illness, degree of suicidal or foolish behavioral problems, polarity, typical or atypical states, and classical affective versus schizoaffective variant). For infrequent episodes, an alternate approach would be to observe the patient closely for early signs of relapse and initiate treatment immediately at the onset of even mild symptoms.

In recommending either, the physician must also consider the patient's reliability: Patients must take their tablets regularly; come for monitoring of plasma level; and understand that conditions such as thiazide diuretics, low-salt diets, or dehydration can increase their lithium levels. For various reasons (such as lack of intelligence, cooperativeness, or conscientiousness), patients may occasionally be unable to cooperate. Enlisting the aid of family members can sometimes help with patient reliability issues. Such issues need to be considered. Lithium does not protect patients against or ameliorate normal feelings of sadness.

Breakthrough Depression

If a patient develops a depressive episode during lithium maintenance, MAO inhibitors, tricyclics, or ECT are indicated and can be added to the lithium regimen. It is not generally necessary, except for ECT administration, to discontinue lithium. Most clinical observations have indicated that tricyclics and MAO inhibitors can be used with lithium without adverse interactions and with good therapeutic effect (Heninger et al. 1983; Jepson and Beaumont 1973; Lingjaerde et al. 1974). Lingjaerde et al. (1974) studied the effect of lithium plus tricyclics versus tricyclics alone in treating depression and found that the combination produced somewhat better results than did tricyclics alone. This difference was significant principally in one hospital out of the network studied, but the general trend was consistent for all facilities. Typically, after the depression has abated, the tricyclics can gradually be tapered off, and maintenance lithium can be continued. In an open study of MAO inhibitors in conjunction with lithium in three treatment-resistant patients, Zall (1971) reported good results. Similarly, Himmelhoch et al. (1972) described a series of patients who had good results with lithium and tranylcypromine in an open design.

Rapid Cyclers

Dunner and Fieve (1974) and Stancer et al. (1970) have described a subtype of manic–depressive patients who undergo a very rapid cycle (four or more affective episodes per year) and respond poorly to lithium, both therapeutically and in terms of side effects of lithium treatment. Whether these rapid cyclers represent a diagnostically different subtype of manic–depressive illness or just a particularly severe form of the disorder is not known.

Effects of Electroconvulsive Therapy

Prior to the discovery of ECT, the outcome of mania could be disastrous. Derby (1933) reported that approximately 23 percent of all admissions to Brooklyn State Hospital for manic–depressive psychosis died. Some had complete recoveries due to spontaneous remissions, a typical feature of the course of bipolar illness. After the discovery of ECT, there were a number of open trials showing ECT to produce a dramatic remission in mania (Langley et al. 1959; Rennie 1943; Thorpe 1947). Controlled trials were not customary during the ECT period of psychiatry; this methodology was developed only recently. Some evidence of efficacy comes from retrospective case-control study comparing three groups of patients—controls, ECT patients, and chlorpromazine patients.

The results in the control group were unsatisfactory and included four patients who died. Relatively good results were seen with both ECT and chlorpromazine, with virtually all patients improved and discharged home. Of the 28 patients treated with chlorpromazine, 10 did not respond satisfactorily, and ECT had to be added. The results are not definitive because we do not know if chlorpromazine was given an adequate trial. Despite these limitations, ECT probably produced a slightly better clinical response than did chlorpromazine, although these results need to be confirmed in controlled clinical trials. More than one-third of the ECT patients relapsed shortly after the ECT period was stopped. This certainly indicates that patients should be started on lithium immediately after an ECT trial has been completed.

Thomas and Reddy (1982) did a case-control study of lithium, chlorpromazine, and ECT, finding all three treatments to be approximately equal in efficacy. Long-term maintenance or prophylactic treatment with lithium and chlorpromazine is widely used, but long-term prophylactic ECT is rare. Despite ECT's being an acute treatment, there was a somewhat better long-term outcome after ECT in the sense that the length of time from discharge to readmission was on average 414 days for patients on lithium, 373 days for those on chlorpromazine, and 1,466 days for patients completing ECT.

All patients in these ECT studies received bilateral ECT. In a study of six patients receiving unilateral ECT, none had a positive therapeutic response. In fact, some became worse during the period of the trial. One of those patients was switched to bilateral ECT and promptly recovered (Small et al. 1985). This observation suggests that unilateral ECT is not clinically effective in mania but that bilateral ECT is. For that reason, these authors performed a retrospective case-control investigation of patients initially started on unilateral ECT who either remained on unilateral ECT or were switched to bilateral ECT (Small et al. 1985). The comparison was between those patients who initially started on unilateral treatment but switched to bilateral treatment and those who remained on unilateral treatment. The authors noted that the characteristics distinguishing the switched patient were, regardless of diagnosis, manic features of unrestrained behavior, hurried speech, elevated mood, superiority, dramatization, and dominating behavior. Despite the patients' diagnosis, the most noteworthy factor that distinguished the switched patients from either age- and sex-matched controls or concurrent controls was the presence of active manic symptoms. It would be theoretically important if bilateral ECT had been required to treat mania, but unilateral ECT was sufficient for virtually all cases of depression. Most researchers have found unilateral ECT as effective as bilateral treatment in treating the depressed phase of either bipolar or unipolar disorders.

ECT is not widely used for mania. In the emergency situation, it should be considered. There is a fair degree of clinical evidence suggesting its efficacy. There are certain theoretical implications to be derived from ECT's efficacy relative to neurochemical theories by which treatments produce their response. If we hypothesize that ECT produces an improvement in depression by increasing brain norepinephrine and that mania is the opposite of depression, how can we explain the beneficial effect of ECT in both of these conditions? The reduction in beta-adrenergic-receptor binding, on consequent potential stabilization of noradrenergic responses, reported in rats after repeated ECT may be related to this.

Other Drugs Used in the Treatment of Mania

One of the most interesting new developments in the treatment of mania is the clinical observation in a partially studied trial that verapamil, a calcium-channel antagonist, may be effective in mania (Dubovsky et al. 1982, 1985; Giannini et al. 1984; Gitlin and Weiss 1984). Another calcium-channel blocker, Nifedipine, was also effective in mania in small, uncontrolled trials (Dubovsky and Franks 1983). Before this can be considered proven, the proper controlled trials must be done. This is an important lead for further investigation.

Because carbamazepine and related drugs, such as valproic acid, are reviewed elsewhere in this volume, they will not be discussed here (see the chapter by Drs. Post, Uhde, Rubinow, and Weiss).

Bacher and Lewis (1979) treated six outpatients who had atypical mania or schizoaffective disorders with small doses of reserpine and lithium and observed a good response, often clearly better than previous treatment with neuroleptics or lithium alone. This is an intriguing suggestion and awaits further investigation.

Several workers have observed a dramatic effect on mania when the minor tranquilizer clonazepam has been used (Freinhar and Alvarez 1985; Greenspan and Levin 1985; Jones and Chouinard 1985; Victor et al. 1984); its efficacy is supported by a small, double-blind study comparing it with lithium (Chouinard et al. 1983). Although this evidence is suggestive and cannot be considered definitive until verified further by double-blind studies, the results are quite interesting. Researchers will have to work out the relative efficacy of various new drugs, such as verapamil, clonazepam, clonidine (Giannini et al. 1983; Jouvent et al. 1980), and carbamazepine, in the treatment of an acute manic episode. It is not unusual for a few promising case reports to appear in psychiatry, only to be followed by evidence that they were blind alleys. Suggestions should therefore not be accepted as fact until confirmatory evidence is available, but we do note these promising leads.

Lithium Response as a Biological Marker

Much previous research on the affective disorders, particularly mania, has included only clinical and phenomenological information for diagnosis. A couple of the variables that have been taken into consideration in attempting to define biologically homogeneous groups are polarity of the disorders, that is, unipolar versus bipolar, and the presence or absence of affected first-degree relatives. Common phenomenology need not be a manifestation of common biology. The need for a biochemical or pharmacological variable, able to consistently differentiate subgroups from the heterogeneity of affective disorders, has become painfully evident.

Lithium has been established as an effective acute or prophylactic treatment for bipolar affective disorders. Response to lithium therapy is not universal, so it differentiates essentially two groups, responders and nonresponders. The presence or absence of lithium response may differentiate biologically different forms of manic illness that may be distinct etiologically and possibly genetically.

Assumptions of biological homogeneity can be tested by genetic models. In a study of 145 probands with primary affective disorders and 864 of their first-degree relatives, probands were categorized according to whether they had responded to prophylactic lithium over a period of three years (Smeraldi et al. 1978). A greater frequency of affective disorder was found among the relatives of lithium-responding probands, and once genetic analysis was carried out, the data from both groups fit both a single, major locus and a multifactorial, polygenic model. The authors concluded that patients who respond to lithium may have a more severe form of the disease from a genetic point of view but a better clinical outcome. Similar experimental data demonstrating increased susceptibility and morbidity for affective disorders among relatives of patients responding to lithium has been reported previously (Mendlewicz et al. 1973; Cazzullo et al. 1979).

Lithium responsivity, like other biological tools (such as the dexamethasone suppression test), may help, in the context of other variables, to identify biologically distinct groups.

References

Abrams R, Taylor MA: Unipolar mania: a preliminary report. Arch Gen Psychiatry 30:441–443, 1974

Abrams R, Taylor MA: Catatonia: a prospective clinical study. Arch Gen Psychiatry 33:579–581, 1976a

Abrams R, Taylor MA: Mania and schizo-affective disorder, manic type: a comparison. Am J Psychiatry 133:1445–1447, 1976b

Abrams R, Taylor MA: Importance of schizophrenic symptoms in the diagnosis of mania. Am J Psychiatry 138:658–661, 1981

Abrams R, Taylor MA, Hayman MA, et al: Unipolar mania revisited. J Affective Disord 1:59–68, 1979

Alexander PE, van Kammen DP, Bunney WE Jr.: Antipsychotic effects of lithium in schizophrenia. Am J Psychiatry 136:283–287, 1979

Allen MG, Cohen S, Pollin W, et al: Affective illness in veteran twins. A diagnostic review. Am J Psychiatry 131:1234–1239, 1974

Altschule MD: The Development of Traditional Psychopathology. New York, Wiley, 1976

American Psychiatric Association: Diagnostic and Statistical Manual of Mental Disorders (Third Edition): Washington, DC, American Psychiatric Association, 1980

Angst T, Weiss P, Grof P, et al: Lithium prophylaxis in recurrent affective disorders. Br J Psychiatry 116:604–614, 1970

Annel A: Lithium in the treatment of children and adolescents. Acta Psychiatr Scand [Supplement] 207: 19–30, 1969

Baastrup PC, Schou M: Lithium as a prophylactic agent against recurrent depressions and manic-depressive psychosis. Arch Gen Psychiatry 16: 162–172, 1967

Baastrup PC, Schou M: Prophylactic lithium. Lancet 1:1419–1422, 1968a

Baastrup PC, Schou M: Prophylactic lithium. Lancet 2:349–350, 1968b

Bacher NM, Lewis HA: Lithium plus reserpine in refractory manic patients. Am J Psychiatry 136:811–814, 1979

Baron M: Linkage between an X-chromosome marker (dentan color blindness) and bipolar affective illness. Arch Gen Psychiatry 34:721-725, 1977

Baron M, Gruen R, Asnis L, et al: Schizoaffective illness, schizophrenia and affective disorders: morbidity risk and genetic transmission. Acta Psychiatr Scand 65:253–262, 1982

Belmaker RH, Wyatt RJ: Possible X-linkage in a family with varied psychosis. Israel Annals of Psychiatry and Related Disciplines 14:345–353, 1976

Bertelsen A, Harvald B, Hauge M: A Danish twin study of manic–depressive disorders. Br J Psychiatry 130:330–351, 1977

Biederman J, Lerner Y, Belmaker RH: Combination of lithium carbonate and haloperidol in schizo-affective disorder: a controlled study. Arch Gen Psychiatry 36:327–333, 1979

Bleuler E: Dementia Praecox oder Gruppe der Schizophrenien. Leipzig, East Germany, and Vienna, Austria, Deuticke, 1911 [English translation by Zinkin R, International Universities Press, New York, 1950]

Brockington IF, Kendell RE, Wainwright S, et al: The distinction between the affective psychoses and schizophrenia. Br J Psychiatry 135:243–248, 1979

Brockington IF, Perris C, Kendell RE, et al: The course and outcome of cycloid psychosis. Psychol Med 12:97–105, 1982

Bunney WE Jr.: Psychopharmacology of the Switch Process in Affective Disorders in Psychopharmacology: A Generation of Progress. Edited by Lipton MA, DiMascio A, Killam KF. New York, Raven Press, 1978

Bunney WE Jr, Davis JM: Norepinephrine in depressive reactions. Arch Gen Psychiatry 13:483–494, 1965

Cade JFJ: Lithium salts in the treatment of psychotic excitement. Med J Aust 2:349–352, 1949

Carlson GA, Goodwin FK: The stages of mania. Arch Gen Psychiatry 28:221–228, 1973

Carroll BJ, Greden JF, Rubin RT: Neurotransmitter mechanism of neuroendocrine disturbance in depression. Acta Endocrinal [Supplement] 220:14, 1978

Cazzullo CL, Smeraldi E, Sachetti E, et al: Psychotropic drugs and their relationship with psychopathology of affective disorders. Progress in Neuro-psychopharmacology and Biological Psychiatry 3:25–28, 1979

Chouinard G, Jones BD, Yound SN: Potentiation of lithium by tryptophan in a patient with bipolar illness. Am J Psychiatry 136:5, 1979

Chouinard G, Yound SN, Annable L: Antimanic effect of clonazepam. Biol Psychiatry 18:451–466, 1983

Cochran WG: Some methods of strengthening the common chi-square tests. Biometrics 10:417–451, 1954

Cohen BM, Lipinski JF, Altesman RI: Lecithin in the treatment of mania: double-blind placebo-controlled trials. Am J Psychiatry 139:1162–1164, 1982

Cookson J, Silverstone T, Wells B: Double-blind comparative clinical trials of pimozide and chlorpromazine in mania: a test of the dopamine hypothesis. Acta Psychiatr Scand 64:381–397, 1981

Coppen A, Noguera R, Bailey J, et al: Prophylactic lithium in affective disorders. Lancet 2:275–279, 1971

Coryell W, Tsuang MT: DSM-III schizophreniform disorder. Arch Gen Psychiatry 39:66–69, 1982

Cundall RL, Brooks PW, Murray LS: A controlled evaluation of lithium prophylaxis in affective disorders. Psychol Med 2:308–311, 1972

Da Fonseca AF: Analise Heredo-Clinica das Pertubacoes Afectivas (Estudo de 60 Pares de Gemeos e Seus Consanguineos). Porto, Portugal: Imprensa Portuguesa, 1959

Davis KL, Berger PA, Hollister LE, et al: Physostigmine in mania. Arch Gen Psychiatry 35:119–122, 1978

Derby IM: Manic–depressive "exhaustion" deaths. Psychiatr Q 7:436, 1933

Dewhurst WG: Methysergide in mania. Nature 219:506–507, 1968

Dorus E, Pandey GN, Davis JM: Genetic determinant of lithium ion distribution. Arch Gen Psychiatry 32:1097, 1975

Dorus E, Pandey GN, Shaughnessy R, et al: Lithium abnormality across red cell membrane: a cell membrane abnormality in manic–depressive illness. Science 205:932-934, 1979

Dorus E, Cox NJ, Gibbons RD, et al: Lithium ion transport and affective disorders within families of bipolar patients. Arch Gen Psychiatry 40:545, 1983

Dubovsky SL, Franks RD: Intracellular calcium ions in affective disorders: a review and hypothesis. Biol Psychiatry 7:781–797, 1983

Dubovsky SL, Franks RD, Lifschitz M, et al: Effectiveness of verapamil in the treatment of a manic patient. Am J Psychiatry 139:502–503, 1982

Dubovsky SL, Franks RD, Schrier D: Phenelzine-induced hypomania: effect of verapamil. Biol Psychiatry 20:1009–1014, 1985

Dunner DL, Fieve RR: Clinical factors in lithium carbonate prophylaxis failure. Arch Gen Psychiatry 30:229–233, 1974

Dunner DL, Dwyer T, Fieve RR: Depressive symptoms in patients with unipolar and bipolar affective disorder. Compr Psychiatry 17:447–451, 1976a

Dunner DL, Gershon GS, Goodwin FK: Heritable factors in the severity of affective illness. Biol Psychiatry 11:31, 42, 1976b

Dunner DL, Vijayalakshmy P, Fieve RR: Rapid cycling in manic depressive patients. Compr Psychiatry 18:561–566, 1977

Dyson WL, Barcai A: Treatment of children of lithium-responding parents. Current Therapeutic Research 12:286–290, 1970

Edelstein P, Schultz J, Hirschowitz J, et al: Physostigmine and lithium response in the schizophrenias. Am J Psychiatry 138:1078–1081, 1981

Essen-Moller E: Psychiatrische untersuchungen an einer serie von zwillingen. Acta Psychiatrica Neurologica Scandinavica (Supplement) 23, 1941

Feighner JP, Robins E, Guze SB, et al: Diagnostic criteria for use in psychiatric research. Arch Gen Psychiatry 26:57–63, 1972

Fieve RR, Platman SR, Plutchik RR: The use of lithium in affective disorders: II. Prophylaxis of depression in chronic recurrent affective disorders. Am J Psychiatry 125:492–498, 1968

Fieve R, Dunner DL, Kumbaraci T, et al: Lithium carbonate prophylaxis of depression in three subtypes of primary affective disorders. Pharmacopsychiatry 9:100–107, 1976

Fogelson DL, Cohen BM, Pope HG: A study of DSM-III schizophreniform disorder. Am J Psychiatry 139:1281–1285, 1982

Fowler RC, Liskow BI, Tanna VL, et al: Schizophrenia-primary affective disorder discrimination. I. Development of a data-based diagnostic index. Arch Gen Psychiatry 27:811–814, 1980a

Fowler RC, Mezzich J, Liskow BI, et al: Schizophrenia-primary affective disorder distinction. II. Where unclassified psychosis stands. Arch Gen Psychiatry 37:815–817, 1980b

Freinhar JP, Alvarez WH: Use of clonazepam in two cases of acute mania. J Clin Psychiatry 46:29–30, 1985

Frommer E: Depressive illness in childhood, in Recent Developments in Affective Disorders [British Journal of Psychiatry Special Publication 2]. Edited by Coppen A, Walk A. London, London Royal Medico-Psychological Association, 1968

Fyro B, Peterson U: A double-blind study of the prophylactic effect of lithium in manic–depressive disease. Acta Psychiatr Scand [Supplement] 269:17–22, 1977

Gardner R: Lithium prophylaxis. Paper presented at the World Psychiatric Association Symposium on Aspects of Schizophrenia, Yerevan-Tibilisi, USSR, October 1973

Garfinkel PE, Stancer HC, Persad E: A comparison of haloperidol, lithium carbonate and their combination in treatment of mania. J Affective Disord 2:279–288, 1980

Garver DL, Zemlan F, Hirschowitz J, et al. Dopamine and non-dopamine psychoses. Psychopharmacology 84:138–140, 1984a

Garver DL, Hitzemann R, Hirschowitz J: Lithium ratio in vitro. Arch Gen Psychiatry 41:497–505, 1984b

Garver DL, Hirschowitz J, Fleishmann R, et al: Lithium response and psychoses: a double-blind, placebo-controlled study. Psychiatry Res 12:57–68, 1984c

Gershon ES, Miron B, Leckman JF: Genetic models of the transmission of affective disorders. J Psychiatr Res 12:301–307, 1975

Gershon S, Trautner EM: Treatment of shock dependency by pharmacological agents. Med J Austr 1:783–787, 1956

Gershon S, Yuwiler A: Lithium ion: a specific psychopharmacological approach to the treatment of mania. Journal of Neuropsychiatry 1:229–241, 1960

Giannini AJ, Extein I, Gold MS, et al. Clonidine in mania. Drug Development Research 3:101–103, 1983

Giannini AJ, Houser WL Jr, Loiselle RH, et al: Antimanic effects of verapamil. Am J Psychiatry 141:1602–1603, 1984

Gibbons RD, Dorus E, Ostrow DG, et al: Mixture distributions in psychiatric research. Biol Psychiatry 19:935, 1984

Gitlin MJ, Weiss J: Verapamil as maintenance treatment in bipolar illness: a case report. J Clin Psychopharmacol 4:341–343, 1984

Glen AIM, Johnson AL, Shepherd M: Continuation therapy with lithium and amitriptyline in unipolar depressive illness: A randomized, double-blind, controlled trial. Psychol Med 14:37–50, 1984

Goetzl U, Green R, Whybrow P, Jackson R: X-linkage revisited (a further family study of manic–depressive illness). Arch Gen Psychiatry 31:665–672, 1974

Gram LF, Rafaelsen OJ: Lithium treatment of psychotic children and adolescents: a controlled clinical trial. Acta Psychiatr Scand 48:253–260, 1962

Greenspan D, Levin D: Use of clonazepam in a patient with schizoaffective disorder. Am J Psychiatry 142:774–775, 1985

Groat RD, MacKenzie TB: The appearance of mania following intravenous calcium replacement. J Nerv Mental Dis 168:562–563, 1980

Grof P, Cakuls P, Dostal T: Lithium drop-outs: a follow-up study of patients who discontinued prophylactic treatment. International Pharmacopsychiatry 5:162–169, 1970

Haier RJ: The diagnosis of schizophrenia: a review of recent developments, in Special Report: Schizophrenia 1980. Edited by Keith SJ, Mosher LR. Washington DC, US Government Printing Office, 1980

Hanna SM, Jenner FA, Pearson IB, et al: The therapeutic effect of lithium carbonate on a patient with a forty-eight hour periodic psychosis. Br J Psychiatry 121:271–280, 1972

Hartigan GP: The use of lithium salts in affective disorders. Br J Psychiatry 109:810–814, 1963

Helzer JE, Winokur G: A family interview study of male manic depressives. Arch Gen Psychiatry 31:73, 1974

Heninger GR, Charney DS, Sternberg DE: Lithium carbonate augmentation of antidepressant treatment. Arch Gen Psychiatry 40:1335, 1983

Himmelhoch JM, Detre T, Jupfer D, et al: Treatment of previously intractable depression with tranylcypromine and lithium. J Nerv Ment Dis 155:216–220, 1972

Himmelhoch JM, Fuchs CZ, May SJ, et al: When a schizoaffective diagnosis has meaning. J Nerv Mental Dis 169:277–282, 1981

Hirschowitz J, Casper R, Garver D, Chang S: Lithium response in good prognosis schizophrenia. Am J Psychiatry 137:916–920, 1980

Hitzemann R, Mark C, Hirschowitz J, et al: Characteristics of phospholipid methylation in human erythrocyte ghosts: relationship(s) to the psychoses and affective disorders. Biol Psychiatry 20:397–407, 1985

Hitzemann RJ, Hirschowitz J, Hitzemann B, et al: The prolactin response in schizophrenic, schizophreniform, and manic disorders. Biol Psychiatry 19:913–918, 1984a

Hitzemann RJ, Sautter F, Hitzemann B, et al: Platelet monoamine oxidase activity in the psychoses: relationship to symptoms and lithium response. Psychiatry Res 11:211–221, 1984b

Hullen RP, McDonald R, Allsopp M: Prophylactic lithium in recurrent affective disorders. Lancet 1:1044–1046, 1972

Hullen RP, McDonald R, Allsopp M: Further report on prophylactic lithium in recurrent affective disorders. Br J Psychiatry 126:281–284, 1975

James NM, Chapman CJ: A genetic study of bipolar affective disorder. Br J Psychiatry 126:449–456, 1975

Jampala VC, Abrams R, Taylor MA: Mania with emotional blunting: affective disorder or schizophrenia? Am J Psychiatry 142:608–612, 1985

Janowsky DS, El-Yousef MK, Davis JM, et al: A cholinergic–adrenergic hypothesis of mania and depression. Lancet 2:6732–6735, 1972a

Janowsky DS, El-Yousef M, Davis JM, et al: Cholinergic antagonism of methylphenidate-induced stereotyped behavior. Psychopharmacology 27:295–303, 1972b

Janowsky DS, El-Yousef M, Davis JM, et al: Interpersonal maneuvers of manic patients. Am J Psychiatry 131:250–254, 1974

Jepson K, Beaumont GA: A comparative trial of opipramol and chlordiazepoxide in the treatment of anxiety. Journal of International Medical Research 1:145–150, 1973

Johnson G, Gershon S, Burdock E, et al: Comparative effects of lithium and chlorpromazine in the treatment of acute manic state. Br J Psychiatry 119:267–276, 1971

Jones BD, Chouinard G: Clonazepam in the treatment of recurrent symptoms of depression and anxiety in a patient with systemic lupus erythematosus. Am J Psychiatry 142:354–355, 1985

Josephson AM, MacKenzie TB: Thyroid-induced mania in hypothyroid patients. Br J Psychiatry 137:222–228, 1980

Jouvent R, Lecrubier Y, Puech AJ, et al: Antimanic effect of clonidine. Am J Psychiatry 137:1275–1276, 1980

Kallman FJ: Genetic principles in manic–depressive psychosis, in Depression. Edited by Hoch P, Zubin J. New York: Grune & Stratton, 1954

Kane FJ: Treatment of mania with cinanserin, an antiserotonin agent. Am J Psychiatry 126:1020–1023, 1970

Kane JM, Quitkin FM, Rifkin A, et al: Prophylactic lithium with and without imipramine for bipolar I patients: a double-blind study. Psychopharmacology Bull 17:144–145, 1981

Kane JM, Quitkin FM, Rifkin A, et al: Lithium carbonate and imipramine in the prophylaxis of unipolar and bipolar II illness. Arch Gen Psychiatry 39:1065–1069, 1982

Kendell RE, Brockington IF: The identification of disease entities and the relationship between schizophrenic and affective psychoses. Br J Psychiatry 137:324–331, 1980

Kendler KS, Davis KL: The genetics and biochemistry of paranoid schizophrenia and other paranoid psychoses. Schizophr Bull 7:698–709, 1981

Kendler KS, Hayes P. Paranoid psychosis (delusional disorder) and schizophrenia. Arch Gen Psychiatry 38:547–551, 1981

Kidd KK, Gerhard DS, Kidd JR, et al: Recombinant DNA methods in genetic studies of affective disorders. Clin Neuropharmacol [Supplement 1] 7:198, 1984

Klein E, Bental E, Lerer B, et al: Carbamazepine and haloperidol vs. placebo and haloperidol in excited psychoses. Arch Gen Psychiatry 41:165–170, 1984

Klerman GL: The spectrum of mania. Compr Psychiatry 22:11–20, 1981

Klerman GL, Cole JO: Clinical pharmacology of imipramine and related compounds. Pharmacology Review 17:101, 1965

Krauthammer C, Klerman GL: Secondary mania: Manic syndromes associated with antecedent physical illness on drugs. Arch Gen Psychiatry 35:1333–1339, 1978

Kringlen E: Heredity and Environment in the Functional Psychoses. Oslo, Norway: Universitetsforlaget, 1967

Langley DG, Enterline JD, Hickerson GX Jr: A comparison of chlorpromazine and EST in treatment of acute schizophrenic and manic reactions. Archives of Neurological Psychiatry 81:384–391, 1959

Laurell B, Ottosson JO: Prophylactic lithium? Lancet 2:1245–1246, 1968

Leonhard K: Aufteilung der Endogenen Psychosen, 1st–4th ed. Berlin, Akademie, 1957

Leonhard K: Die prapsychotische temperamente bei den monopolaren und bipolaren phasischen psychosen. Psychiatric Neurology 146: 105–115, 1963

Leonhard K, Korff I, Schulz H: Temperament in families with unipolar and bipolar phasic psychoses. Psychiatric Neurology 143:416–434, 1962

Lewis NDC, Piotrowski ZA: Clinical diagnosis of manic-depressive psychosis, in Depression. Edited by Hoch P, Zubin J. New York, Grune & Stratton, 1954

Lingjaerde O, Edlung A, Gormsen CA, et al: The effect of lithium carbonate in combination with tricyclic antidepressant in endogenous depression. Acta Psychiatr Scand 50:233–242, 1974

Luxenburger H: Vorlaufiger Bericht uber psychiatrische Serieuntersuchungen an Zwillingen. Zeitschr Neurol Psychiatrie 116:297–326, 1928

Maags R: Treatment of manic illness with lithium carbonate. Br J Psychiatry 109:56–65, 1963

Mantel N, Haenszel W: Statistical aspects of the analysis of data from retrospective studies of disease. Journal of the National Cancer Institute 22:719–748, 1959

Marder SR, van Kammen DP, Docherty JP, et al: Predicting drug-free improvement in schizophrenic psychosis. Arch Gen Psychiatry 36:1080–1085, 1979

Marengo J, Harrow M: Thought disorder. A function of schizophrenia, mania, or psychosis? J Nerv Ment Dis 173:35–41, 1985

Mavroidis ML, Garver DL, Kanter DR, et al: Plasma haloperidol levels and clinical response: confounding variables. Psychopharmacol Bull 21:62–65, 1985

McCabe MS, Norris B: ECT versus chlorpromazine in mania. Biol Psychiatry 12:245–254, 1977

McCabe MS, Fowler RC, Cadoret RJ, et al: Familial differences in schizophrenia with good and poor prognosis. Psychol Med 1:326–332, 1971

McCabe MS, Fowler RC, Cadoret RJ, et al: Symptom differences in schizophrenia with good and poor prognosis. Am J Psychiatry 128:1239–1243, 1972

McGlashan TH, Carpenter WT Jr: Affective symptoms and the diagnosis of schizophrenia. Schizophr Bull 5:547–553, 1979

Mendlewicz J, Fieve RR, Rainer JD, et al: Manic-depressive illness: a comparative study of patients with and without a family history. Br J Psychiatry 120:523–530, 1972

Mendlewicz J, Fieve RR, Stallone F: Relationship between effectiveness of lithium therapy and family history. Am J Psychiatry 130:1011–1013, 1973

Mendlewicz J, Fleiss JL: Linkage studies with X-chromosome markers in bipolar (manic depressive and unipolar (depressive)) illness. Biol Psychiatry 9:261–294, 1974

Mendlewicz J, Linkowski P, Wilmotte J: Relationship between schizoaffective illness and affective disorders or schizophrenia. J Affective Disord 2:289–302, 1980

Mendlewicz J, Rainer JD: Adoption study supporting genetic transmission in manic–depressive illness. Nature 268: 327–329, 1977

Naylor GJ, Donald JM, LePoidevin D, et al: A double-blind trial of long-term lithium therapy in mental defectives. Br J Psychiatry 124:52–57, 1974

Noack CH, Trautner EM: The lithium treatment of maniacal psychosis. Med J Aust 2:219–222, 1951

Nolen WA: Dopamine and mania: the effects of trans- and cis-clopenthixol in a double-blind pilot study. J Affective Disord 5:91–96, 1983

Pearce JB: Fenfluramine in mania. Lancet 24:427, 1973

Penrose L: The Biology of Mental Defect. New York, Grune & Stratton, 1963

Perris C: A study of cycloid psychosis. Acta Psychiatr Scand [Supplement] 50:1–7, 1974

Pope HG, Lipinski JF: Diagnosis in schizophrenia and manic–depressive illness. Arch Gen Psychiatry 35:811–828, 1978

Pope HG, Lipinski JF, Cohen BM, et al: Schizoaffective disorder: an invalid diagnosis? A comparison of schizoaffective disorder, schizophrenia, and affective disorder. Am J Psychiatry 137:921–927, 1980

Potter WZ, Murphy DL, Wehr TA, et al: Clorgyline: a new treatment for patients with rapid-cycling disorder. Arch Gen Psychiatry 39:505–510, 1982

Prange AJ Jr, Wilson IC, Knox A, et al: Enhancement of imipramine by thyroid stimulating hormone. Clinical and theoretical implications. Am J Psychiatry 127:191–199, 1970

Prange AJ Jr, Wilson IC, Lynn CB, et al: L-tryptophan in mania. Contribution to a permissive hypothesis of affective disorders. Arch Gen Psychiatry 30:56, 1974

Price LH, Charney DS, Heninger GR: Three cases of manic symptoms following yohimbine administration. Am J Psychiatry 141:1267–1268, 1984

Prien RF, Caffey EM Jr, Klett CJ: Lithium carbonate. Diseases of the Nervous System 32:521–531, 1971

Prien RF, Caffey EM Jr, Klett CJ: A comparison of lithium carbonate and chlorpromazine in treatment of excited schizo-affectives. Arch Gen Psychiatry 27:182–189, 1972a

Prien RF, Caffey EM Jr, Klett CJ: A comparison of lithium carbonate and chlorpromazine in the treatment of mania. Arch Gen Psychiatry 26:146–153, 1972b

Prien RF, Klett CJ, Caffey EM Jr: Lithium carbonate and imipramine in prevention of affective episodes. Arch Gen Psychiatry 29:420–425, 1973a

Prien RF, Caffey EM Jr, Klett CJ: Prophylactic efficacy of lithium carbonate in manic-depressive illness. Arch Gen Psychiatry 28:337–341, 1973b

Prien RF, Caffey EM Jr, Klett CJ: Factors associated with lithium response in the prophylactic treatment of bipolar manic-depressive illness. Arch Gen Psychiatry 312:189–192, 1974

Prien RF, Kupfer DJ, Mansky PM, et al: Continuation therapy in depression: preliminary findings from the National Institute of Mental Health–Pharmacologic and Somatic Treatments Research Branch Collaborative Study of Long-Term Maintenance Drug Therapy in Affective Illness. Paper presented at the 19th Annual Meeting of the American College of Neuropsychopharmacology, San Juan, Puerto Rico, December 1980

Reid AH: Psychosis in adult mental defectives. I. Manic depressive psychosis. Br J Psychiatry 120:205–212, 1970

Rennie TAC: Manic-depressive disease: prognosis following shock treatment. Psychiatr Q 17:642, 1943

Robins E, Guze SB: Establishment of diagnostic validity in psychiatric illness: its application to schizophrenia. Am J Psychiatry 126:983–987, 1970

Robins E, Guze SB: Classification of affective disorders: the primary–secondary, the endogenous–reactive and the neurotic–psychotic concepts, in Recent Advances in the Psychobiology of the Depressive Illnesses [US Department of Health, Education and Welfare Publication 70–9053]. Edited by Williams TA, Katz MM, Shield JA Jr. Washington, DC, US Government Printing Office, 1972

Roff JD: Long-term outcome for a set of schizophrenia subtypes, in Life History Research in Psychopathology [Volume 4]. Edited by Wirt RD, Winokur G, Roff M. Minneapolis, University of Minnesota Press, 1975

Rosanoff AJ, Handy LM, Plesset IR: The etiology of manic–depressive syndromes with special reference to their occurrence in twins. Am J Psychiatry 91:725–762, 1934

Rosenthal NE, Rosenthal LN, Stallone F, et al: Toward the validation of RDC schizoaffective disorder. Arch Gen Psychiatry 37:804–810, 1980

Ross RJ, Hauger R, Scheinin M, et al: Mechanism of Action of Clorgyline. Paper presented at the annual meeting of the American Psychiatric Association, New York, May 1983

Sautter F, Garver D: Familial differences in lithium responsive versus lithium nonresponsive psychoses. J Psychiatr Res 19:1–8, 1985

Schildkraut JJ: The catecholamine hypothesis of affective disorders (a review of supporting evidence). Am J Psychiatry 122:509, 1965

Schou M: Normythymics "mood normalizers" are lithium and the imipramine drugs specific for affective disorders. Br J Psychiatry 109:803–804, 1963

Schou M: Lithium in psychiatric therapy and prophylaxis. J Psychiat Res 6:67–95, 1968

Schou M, Juel-Neilson N, Strimgren E, et al: The treatment of manic psychosis by the administration of lithium salts. J Neurol Neurosurg Psychiatry 17:250–260, 1954

Schou M, Baastrup PC, Grof P, et al: Pharmacological and clinical problems of lithium prophylaxis. Br J Psychiatry 116:615–619, 1970a

Schou M, Thomsen K, Baastrup PC: Studies on the course of recurrent endogenous affective disorders. International Pharmacopsychiatry 5:100–106, 1970b

Shopsin B, Gershon S, Thompson H: Psychoactive drugs in mania. Arch Gen Psychiatry 32:34–35, 1975

Sitaram N, Nurnberger J, Gershon E, et al: Faster cholinergic REM sleep induction in euthymic patients with primary affective illness. Science 208:200–202, 1980

Slater E, Shields J: Psychotic and neurotic illnesses in twins. Medical Research Council Special Report Series 278. London, Her Majesty's Stationary Office, 1953

Small, JG, Small IF, Milstein V, et al: Manic symptoms: an indication for bilateral ECT. Biol Psychiatry 20:125–134, 1985

Smeraldi E, Negri F, Melica AM: A genetic study of affective disorders. Acta Psychiatr Scand 56:382–398, 1978

Smulevitch A: The treatment and prevention of affective and schizoaffective psychoses. Paper presented at the World Psychiatric Association Symposium on Aspects of Schizophrenia, Yerevan-Tibilisi, USSR, October 1973

Stancer HC, Furling FW, Godse DD: A longitudinal investigation of lithium as a prophylactic agent for recurrent depression. Canadian Psychiatric Association Journal 15:29–40, 1970

Stokes PE, Stohl PM, Shamolan CH, et al: Efficacy of lithium as acute treatment of manic-depressive illness. Lancet 1:1319–1325, 1971

Takahashi R, Sakuma A, Itoh K, et al: Comparison of efficacy of lithium carbonate and chlorpromazine in mania. Arch Gen Psychiatry 32:1310–1318, 1975

Taylor MA, Abrams R: Manic states: a genetic study of early and late onset affective disorders. Arch Gen Psychiatry 28:656–659, 1973a

Taylor MA, Abrams R: The phenomenology of mania. Arch Gen Psychiatry 29:520–522, 1973b

Taylor MA, Abrams R: Acute mania: a clinical and genetic study of responders and nonresponders to treatments. Arch Gen Psychiatry 32:863–865, 1975a

Taylor MA, Abrams R: Manic–depressive illness and good prognosis schizophrenia. Am J Psychiatry 132:741–742, 1975b

Taylor MA, Abrams R: Catatonia: prevalence and importance in the manic phase of manic–depressive illness. Arch Gen Psychiatry 1223–1225, 1977

Taylor MA, Abrams R: Mania and DSM–III schizophreniform disorder: J Affective Disord 6:19–24, 1984

Taylor MA, Gaztanaga P, Abrams R: Manic–depressive illness and acute schizophrenia: a clinical, family history, and treatment–response study. Am J Psychiatry 131:678–682, 1974

Thienhaus OJ, Khosla NL: Meningeal cryptococcus misdiagnosed as a manic episode. Am J Psychiatry 141:1459–1460, 1984

Thomas J, Reddy B: The treatment of mania: a retrospective evaluation of the effects of ECT, chlorpromazine, and lithium. J Affective Disord 4:85–92, 1982

Thorpe FT: Intensive electrical convulsive therapy in acute mania. Journal of Mental Science 93:89–92, 1947

Trzebiatowska-Trzeciak: Genetical analysis of unipolar and bipolar endogenous affective psychoses. Br J Psychiatry 131:478–485, 1977

Tsuang MT, Woolson RF, Fleming JA: Long-term outcome of major psychoses. I. Schizophrenia and affective disorders compared with psychiatrically symptom-free surgical conditions. Arch Gen Psychiatry 36:1205–1301, 1979

Victor BS, Link NA, Binder RL, et al: Use of clonazepam in mania and schizoaffective disorders. Am J Psychiatry 141:1111–1112, 1984

Weissman M, Boyd J: The epidemiology of affective disorders: rate and risk factor. Psychiatric Update 2:406–426, 1983

Winokur G, Clayton P, Reich T: Manic depressive illness. St. Louis, Mo, CV Mosby, 1969

Winokur G, Cadoret R, Dorzab J, et al: Depressive disease: a genetic study. Arch Gen Psychiatry 24:135–144, 1971

Zall H; Lithium carbonate and isocarboxazid: an effective drug approach in severe depression. Am J Psychiatry 127:1400–1403, 1971

Zemlan FP, Hirschowitz J, Garver DL: Mood-incongruent versus mood-congruent psychosis: differential antipsychotic response to lithium therapy. Psychiatry Res 11:317–328, 1984

Zerbin-Rudin E: Zur genetik depressiver erkrankungen, in Das Depressive Syndrome. Edited by Hippius, Selbach. Munich and Berlin, Urban and Schwarzenberg, 1969

Zerbin-Rudin E: Genetics of affective psychoses, in Origin, Prevention and Treatment of Affective Disorders. Edited by Schou M, Stromgren E. London, Academic Press, 1979

Zerrsen DV, Emrich HM: New drugs for mania. Br J Psychiatry 142:532–533, 1983

Zompo MD, Bocchetta A, Goldin LR, et al: Linkage between X-chromosome markers and manic–depressive illness. Acta Psychiatr Scand 70:282–287, 1984

Zubenko GS, Cohen BM, Lipinski JF, et al: Clonidine in the treatment of mania and mixed bipolar disorder. Am J Psychiatry 141:1617–1618, 1984

2

A Role for Acetylcholine in Mania

David S. Janowsky, M.D.

2

A Role for Acetylcholine in Mania

A role for catecholamines in the etiology of the affective disorders has been emphasized since the pioneering work of Schildkraut (1965) and Bunney and Davis (1965). These researchers noted that drugs that improve mood and are effective in the treatment of depression increase noradrenergic neurotransmission and, conversely, that drugs that produce depression and are used in the treatment of manic behavior often antagonize or decrease noradrenergic activity (Schildkraut 1973; Schildkraut and Kety 1967).

In 1972, Janowsky et al. proposed the adrenergic–cholinergic hypothesis of affective disorders. According to this hypothesis, mania is a disorder of adrenergic predominance, relative to decreased acetylcholine activity, and depression is considered to be the converse. In the following pages, we will review evidence that mania is indeed related to an alteration in adrenergic–cholinergic balance.

Animal Studies

A variety of animal studies suggest that adrenergic and cholinergic stimulation produces divergent effects on behavior. Centrally active cholinomimetics usually produce depressant-inhibitory behavioral effects, including lethargy, decreased locomotion, and decreased self-stimulation (Carlton 1963; Domino and Olds 1968; Pradhan and Kavat 1972; Olds 1958); these effects are the opposite of those caused by psychostimulants. That these behaviors are increased and decreased by cholinergic and adrenergic agents, respectively, is consistent with the hypothesis that mood is likewise regulated by a balance between adrenergic and cholinergic factors (Janowsky et al. 1972).

General and Antimanic Effects of Cholinomimetics in Man

Between 1950 and 1970, Rowntree et al. (1950), studying normal, depressive, and manic subjects; Gershon and Shaw (1961), observing insecticide-poisoned normal individuals; and Bowers et al. (1964), observing normal individuals, reported that different cholinesterase inhibitors exerted anergic-inhibitory effects. More recently, Janowsky et al. (1973a, 1974) gave the centrally active cholinesterase inhibitor, physostigmine, and neostigmine, a similar cholinesterase inhibitor that does not cross the blood–brain barrier, to patients so that they could study the behavioral sequelae of central cholinergic stimulation. In contrast to neostigmine or placebo, physostigmine rapidly exerted inhibitory effects in virtually all patients who received it. These effects consisted of lethargy, anergy, feelings of tiredness, psychomotor retardation, feelings of being drained, the perception of having no thoughts or decreased thoughts, social withdrawal, and occasional nausea or vomiting (Janowsky et al. 1974).

Researchers have also demonstrated that cholinergic agonists and cholinesterase inhibitors possess antimanic properties. In the study already mentioned, Rowntree et al. (1950) administered the irreversible cholinesterase inhibitor, diisopropylfluorophosphate (DFP) to 9 manic–depressive subjects and 10 normal subjects. The normal subjects developed irritability, lassitude, depression, apathy, and slowness or poverty of thoughts, which appeared before the onset of peripheral cholinergic symptoms. The 2 manic–depressive patients tested while in remission showed mental changes similar to those in the normal subjects, and 2 hypomanic patients improved with DFP and continued euthymic after its administration. One hypomanic patient became less manic and was minimally depressed after each of the two courses of DFP but relapsed when DFP was withdrawn, and one nearly remitted hypomanic patient became floridly manic when DFP was withdrawn.

In addition, the effects of physostigmine on manic behavior were studied by Janowsky et al. (1973a). In eight manic patients studied following physostigmine administration, the Beigel-Murphy (1971) manic elation–grandiosity scale score was reduced by 78 percent, and the manic intensity scale score was reduced by 48 percent. Thus, physostigmine dramatically reduced manic behavior, and this reduction was both statistically significant and of large magnitude clinically. Physostigmine caused a decrease in specific manic symptoms as defined by Beigel and Murphy (1971). A decrease in "is talking," "is active," "jumps from one subject to another," and "looks happy and cheerful" occurred in every patient. The average changes in the individual Beigel-Murphy Manic Rating Scale items were of considerable magnitude, with "is talking" reduced by 53 percent; "is active," by 62 percent; "jumps from one subject to another," by 51 percent; and "looks happy and cheerful," by 77 percent. Grandiosity was significantly decreased in the three patients in whom it was present during the baseline period. Irritability decreased in three patients and increased in five. The effects of physostigmine lasted from 20 to 90 minutes. In different patients, the total amount of physostigmine necessary to cause a decrease in manic symptoms varied from 0.25 to 3.0 mg. In addition, the average depression score of the patients, as measured using the Bunney-Hamburg scale, more than doubled, and there was a statistically significant increase in the patient group's sadness score. Five of the patients developed a depressed mood, but three experienced no increase in depression after receiving physostigmine (Janowsky et al. 1973a).

In addition to alleviating manic symptoms and causing an increase in depression in some patients, physostigmine caused a psychomotor-retarded, inhibitory state, with a dramatic increase in a number of items from an inhibitory scale. Physostigmine did not produce obtunded behavior, slurred speech, or ataxia or cause the patient to fall asleep, as might be seen with high doses of sedative drugs.

In the six manic patients to whom both neostigmine and physostigmine were administered, neostigmine caused bradycardia but did not cause other peripheral somatic effects such as cramps or vomiting. In some, a minimal, transient behavioral sluggishness occurred as neostigmine was administered. No significant changes in the manic intensity scale score or the manic elation–grandiosity scale score occurred following neostigmine administration.

Report of Cases

The following are examples of the cases studied (Janowsky et al. 1973a):

Case 1. A 28-year-old, white, female bipolar manic–depressive patient demonstrated euphoria, constant rambling speech with marked flight of ideas, hyperactivity, irritability, and lability of affect and behavior. She was extremely demanding and verbally aggressive. She quickly became angry when her demands were denied. Administration of 3.0 mg of physostigmine in 0.5 doses every five minutes caused the patient to appear sad, and she showed depression for the first time during her hospitalization. For the hour following physostigmine administration, the patient remained calmer, less active, lethargic, and somewhat confused. Although she had flights into euphoria and hyperactivity, these were short-lived. She also became more irritable after receiving physostigmine and complained of feeling drained. The patient's behavior subsequently returned to baseline.

Case 2. A 27-year-old, white, male schizoaffective patient demonstrated increased interactions, cheerfulness, manipulative behavior of the staff, and talkativeness in addition to intermittent paranoid ideation throughout the placebo–baseline phase. Administration of 1.5 mg of physostigmine caused the patient to become dysphoric and depressed and to become preoccupied with the pain caused by the needle in his arm. He stated that he felt sad, hopeless, and worthless and that he felt mildly suicidal. Initially, he cried uncontrollably. He then exhibited psychomotor retardation, drained feelings, and decreased thoughts. He sat in his chair with his head in his hands, speaking only when spoken to. Manic symptoms ceased completely, and the patient became irritable as he became depressed and wanted to be left alone. The patient reported nausea five minutes after the onset of depression but did not vomit.

Case 3. A 34-year-old, white, female bipolar manic–depressive patient demonstrated marked flight of ideas, increased talkativeness, rapid fluctuations from cheerfulness and euphoria to anger and argumentativeness, as well as manipulative behavior of staff members, consisting of aggressive and incisive verbal attacks. Administration of placebo injections caused no change in the patient's clinical state. Administration of physostigmine caused the patient to rapidly become more passive, quiet, and reflective, and her anger dissipated. She said that she felt sad and scared but on an "even keel" and that she felt warmth for the staff. She showed decreased talkativeness and decreased flight of ideas. She was not confused, lethargic, or disoriented. After receiving a total of 2.0 mg of physostigmine, about 20 minutes after the onset of the more subdued behavior, the patient became nauseated and vomited; 1 mg of atropine administered intravenously partially reversed the "antimanic" state and the vomiting within five minutes of administration.

Case 4. A 23-year-old, white, male patient with a history of bipolar manic–depressive illness showed signs of hypomania during the baseline–placebo phase of the experiment. He talked continuously, was moderately active and irritable, and was critical of staff members. He showed moderate flight of ideas and distractibility. He sought out others and interacted with them. A total of 2.0 mg of physostigmine caused the patient to report that he felt sedated, drowsy, and heavy. Although he continued to communicate verbally, he talked less and became less hyperactive, and his argumentativeness and anger decreased considerably. He interacted less and showed a decrease in distractibility and flight of ideas. He showed no evidence of depressive affect but was more subdued. He intermittently reported nausea after receiving his last physostigmine injection but did not vomit. The patient had spontaneously returned to his baseline hypomanic state 30 minutes after receiving his last physostigmine injection.

Case 5. A 43-year-old white woman with a history of bipolar manic–depressive illness showed hypomanic symptoms. She showed moderate talkativeness, flight of ideas, grandiosity, and cheerfulness during the placebo–baseline phase. She was energetic and friendly, and showed increased interactions, although she was occasionally hostile. Administration of a total of 1.75 mg of physostigmine caused the patient to show a marked decrease in interactions, talkativeness, grandiosity, cheerfulness, and flight of ideas. She became withdrawn, lethargic, and drained; wanted to be left alone; and exhibited moderate psychomotor retardation. She stated that she lacked thoughts and was somewhat depressed. She complained of nausea five minutes after the onset of the anergic syndrome. Administration of 5.0 mg of methylphenidate reversed the nausea and the anergic syndrome and partially restored the patient's hypomanic behavior.

Case 6. A 19-year-old schizoaffective woman was giddy, hypertalkative, and euphoric during the baseline–placebo phase. While receiving a total of 2.5 mg of physostigmine in 0.5 doses, the patient became progressively more lethargic, sad, and withdrawn. She stated that she wanted to be left alone. After the last injection, she became very withdrawn, psychomotor retarded, and negative and claimed that she had no thoughts. She stated that she was feeling very hostile and ran to her room and hid under her blankets. She appeared sad and depressed and made remarks indicating that she felt hopeless. She spoke only when spoken to and showed no euphoria. The patient had returned to her baseline hypomanic state 1½ hours after the last physostigmine injection.

Case 7. A 40-year-old, married white man with a 10-year history of bipolar manic–depressive illness presented during the baseline–placebo phase with moderate anger and irritability, increased interactions, and increased talkativeness. He showed moderate flight of ideas and was very manipulative of staff members. He was moderately euphoric. After receiving a total of 3.0 mg of physostigmine intravenously, the patient abruptly showed a complete cessation of his manic symptoms. He became depressed, sad, and dysphoric. He stated that he was "no good" and began to cry. He then ceased to be active and did not wish to communicate. He stopped talking except when spoken to and asked to be left alone. He said that he felt moderately drained and sad. He was apathetic, withdrawn, and lethargic and showed psychomotor retardation. Irritability and anger increased as the patient became depressed. A dose of 0.75 mg of atropine caused a partial return of manic symptoms, including talkativeness and increased interactions, and a complete reversal of the patient's dysphoria, lethagy, and drained feelings.

Case 8. A 35-year-old, white, married woman showed increased talkativeness, irritability, extreme flight of ideas, increased interactions, decreased impulse control; distractability, irritability, and anger also occurred. The patient became more lethargic, had slow thoughts, and appeared drained, psychomotor retarded, and less interested in her surroundings. She did not become depressed. The patient vomited 12 minutes after the onset of the more subdued behavior. Physostigmine's antimanic, anergic, and emetic effects were partially reversed by ½ mg of atropine.

After Janowsky et al.'s (1972, 1973a, 1974) reports, Modestin et al. (1973a, 1973b) also noted that physostigmine had antimanic and mood-depressant effects, and Carroll et al. (1973) demonstrated that physostigmine decreased the motor and mood symptoms of cortisol-induced mania, whereas the cognitive aspects of mania were not affected. Davis et al. (1978) also observed that physostigmine had rapid and dramatic antimanic and mood-depressant effects. They observed that these effects occurred predominantly in manic patients who were not hostile.

ANTAGONISTIC EFFECTS OF PHYSOSTIGMINE AND METHYLPHENIDATE

Because methylphenidate generally causes behavioral activating effects that in many ways parallel manic symptoms (that is, increased thoughts, talkativeness, and euphoria), we studied the potential antagonistic effects of methylphenidate and physostigmine in man as a pharmacologic model of naturally occurring adrenergic–cholinergic balance in bipolar disorders (Janowsky et al. 1973b, 1973c).

It is well-known that a balance between cholinergic activity and adrenergic activity regulates such somatic functions as heart rate, gastric motility, and pupillary size (Goodman and Gilman 1970). There is also a great deal of indirect evidence that suggests that antagonistic adrenergic and cholinergic systems exist in the central nervous system and that these systems regulate certain forms of behavior (Brodie et al. 1959; Carlton 1963; David 1970).

In a series of experiments, manic and schizophrenic patients were first given physostigmine and then methylphenidate. Other manic and schizophrenic patients received the converse sequence—methylphenidate followed by physostigmine (Janowsky et al. 1973c). For the patients who were first given methylphenidate, followed by physostigmine, methylphenidate caused significant increase in the activation scale rating, consisting of a composite of interaction, talkativeness, cheerfulness, and friendliness. This increase was rapidly reversed following the administration of physostigmine.

Conversely, physostigmine-induced behavioral inhibition and anergy was antagonized by methylphenidate 30 to 120 seconds after methylphenidate administration. In contrast, patients who received neostigmine, followed by methylphenidate, displayed no initial behavioral inhibition, and neostigmine failed to inhibit the activating effects of methylphenidate.

Thus, methylphenidate, an adrenergic activating agent, and physostigmine, a cholinomimetic agent, produced opposite effects when each was given alone and produced antagonistic effects when they were given sequentially (Janowsky 1973c). The simplest explanation for the antagonistic effects of adrenergic and cholinergic agents is that these effects correspond to a balance between functionally opposite neurobiologic systems, one system being catecholaminergic and the other system being cholinergic.

MANIC-REBOUNDING EFFECTS OF PHYSOSTIGMINE

In addition to antagonism, there is evidence that when either the central adrenergic or cholinergic systems are activated, there may be a later compensatory activation of the other system. Fibiger et al. (1971) demonstrated in rats that the increase in cholinergic activity that is caused by the administration of physostigmine leads first to a decrease in locomotion but subsequently leads to an increase in locomotion as a presumed adrenergic mechanism begins to exert its effect. The effect becomes apparent as the cholinergic predominance induced by physostigmine decreases.

As with the work of Fibiger et al. (1971), there is some evidence that an adrenergic rebound following physostigmine infusion also can occur in humans. A case of rebounding euthymia into mania was reported by Rowntree et al. (1950) in one of his DFP-treated bipolar subjects. Subsequently, Shopsin et al. (1975) demonstrated rebounding into hypomania in two out of three manic patients given physostigmine. Here, toward the end of a physostigmine infusion, patients showed behavioral inhibition and some antimanic effects. Clear-cut rebounding in two manics subsequently took place approximately two hours after the physostigmine infusion had ended. In these patients, a marked exacerbation or intensification of the manic state was observed. For example, in one of these individuals, a psychotomimetic, or activating, effect occurred in the form of primary process behavior, which was not observed either previous to or since that time in that patient. In a third patient, almost total normalization of mood, affect, ideation, and behavior occurred. The observed rebounding was transient in nature, beginning two hours after the last physostigmine injection and lasting three to four hours thereafter. A return to baseline at approximately six hours following the last physostigmine injection was noted.

ACTIVATION OF ADRENERGIC PHENOMENA BY CHOLINOMIMETICS

Apart from the information already described indicating that cholinomimetics may induce what appears to be activation of catecholaminergic mechanisms, leading to rebound hyperactivity and mania, Dilsaver and Greden (1984) reviewed considerable information to support the possibility of cholinergic-induced interaction between adrenergic and cholinergic factors following tricyclic withdrawal. They proposed that this interaction leads to manic symptoms secondary to compensatory adrenergic activation, following unmasking of upregulated muscarinic receptors. Also, Brezenoff and Guiliano (1982) reviewed evidence of adrenergic activation in response to cholinomimetic exposure. Centrally active cholinomimetic drugs, including physostigmine, carbachol, arecoline, and acetylcholine, raise blood pressure in a variety of animal species. These cardiovascular effects in animals appear to be mediated by central muscarinic stimulation of the sympathetic adrenal system (Brezenoff and Guiliano 1982). Furthermore, when cholinomimetics are given centrally to rats, liberation of adrenal catecholamines occurs. In addition, central administration of carbachol increases serum epinephrine and norepinephrine levels (Brezenoff and Guiliano 1982). In humans, minutes after its infusion, physostigmine causes a significant and dramatic increase in plasma epinephrine activity and an increase in mean pulse rate and blood pressure level (Janowsky et al. 1985; Kennedy et al. 1984). The catecholamine-releasing and cardiovascular effects of physostigmine in humans appear to be centrally mediated by muscarinic factors because they can be blocked by centrally acting scopolamine but not by peripherally acting agents, such as methscopolamine or propantheline (Janowsky et al. unpublished data.)

POTENTIAL CLINICAL APPLICATIONS

A number of potential clinical applications exist with respect to the treatment of mania with cholinomimetic drugs. For example, in recent years, oral physostigmine has become available and can be given around the clock and at frequent intervals. Oral physostigmine has been shown to be effective in the treatment of hereditary ataxias and related syndromes when given in 1.0- to 2.0-mg doses every two hours during wakefulness (Kark et al. 1979).

Also, this form of physostigmine has been used for patients with Alzheimer's disease in similar doses and with equivocal results (Bajada 1982). Some success for oral physostigmine, used as a treatment for mania, has been reported (Cohen et al., personal communication 1985). Circumvention of the need to use parenteral physostigmine would make physostigmine therapy for manic patients a practical possibility.

Acetylcholine precursors may also have potential therapeutic value in the treatment of mania. Depressed mood has been observed in subjects receiving acetylcholine precursors such as deanol, choline, and lecithin. Thus, Davis et al. (1979) and Tamminga et al. (1976) found an increase in depressive symptoms in schizophrenic individuals with tardive dyskinesia and treated with choline, and others have noted that depression is a side effect of choline and lecithin treatments, used in an attempt to reverse the memory deficits of Alzheimer's disease (Smith et al. 1982). Thus, acetylcholine precursors generally induce depressive symptoms, a finding consistent with the hypothesis of adrenergic–cholinergic balance. In an open and uncontrolled study, Cohen et al. (1980) reported that lecithin exerted at least partial antimanic effects. In a subsequent double-blind, placebo–controlled crossover study in the same group, pure oral lecithin, given three times a day for one to two weeks, caused a decrease in manic symptoms, compared to placebo, in five of six manic patients (Cohen et al. 1982). A limitation of this study, however, was that it did not use formal mania rating scales, and the subjects were concurrently being treated with a variety of psychotropic agents, including antipsychotic drugs and lithium.

It is also possible that directly acting muscarinic agonists, such as oxotremorine and arecoline, may have clinically usable antimanic properties. To this point, Risch et al. (unpublished data) and Nurnberger et al. (1982a, 1982b) showed that arecoline, like physostigmine, exerts inhibitory–anergic–depressant effects when given to affective disorder patients as well as to normal individuals. It is, thus, possible that these directly acting muscarinic, cholinergic agonists may also be potentially useful as antimanic agents.

Recently, a number of techniques have been developed by gerontologists and other investigators to enhance the effectiveness of such acetylcholine precursors as choline, lecithin, and possibly deanol. These techniques may have potential in the treatment of affective disorders. A combination of physostigmine and lecithin appears to exert synergistic effects on cholinergic function, as manifested by effects on memory (Peters and Levin 1982). The combined use of an acetylcholine precursor such as lecithin and a centrally acting cholinesterase inhibitor such as physostigmine might also be expected to have augmented antimanic effects. Similarly, reserpine, in doses of 1.0 to 2.0 mg a day, and possibly propranolol have been found to have antimanic properties. Both of these agents not only block and/or decrease central adrenergic activity but also increase absolute and relative central and peripheral cholinergic activity (Janowsky et al. 1972). Indeed, in rats, an increase in physostigmine-induced lethality and toxicity following reserpine pretreatment has been shown (Janowsky et al. 1974). Thus, it is possible that a combination of a cholinergic agonist or a cholinesterase inhibitor and a centrally acting antiadrenergic agent, such as alpha-methyldopa, reserpine, or propranolol, would be especially effective as an antimanic treatment because such a treatment would shift adrenergic–cholinergic balance toward a cholinergic predominance.

Along the same line, another potential treatment for mania involves the coadministration of marijuana or tetrahydrocannabinol (THC) and physostigmine or other centrally active cholinesterase inhibitors, acetylcholine precursors, or cholinergic agonists. The rationale for this possibility is the observation of El-Yousef et al. (1973) that normal volunteers, intoxicated on recreational doses of marijuana and given low doses of physostigmine, developed profound anergia and depression. Later, Davis et al. (1976) reported a similar finding in a woman who received physostigmine and who had not revealed concomitant use of marijuana. Thus, a combination of THC and physostigmine or another cholinomimetic may be a powerful antimanic preparation. Of course, side effects of cholinomimetic administration exist. These include depression, anergia, and nausea-emesis. It's possible that using a cholinomimetic to rapidly antagonize mania and then partially antagonizing adverse effects with titration using scopolamine or methylphenidate would be a useful therapeutic strategy.

As already reviewed, it is likely that a cholinomimetic drug, such as physostigmine, given chronically, would be followed by tolerance development. This possibility is, in part, predicted from the work of Fibiger et al. (1971), who showed that a compensatory increase in locomotor activity in rats, presumably due to increased central adrenergic activity, occurred after physostigmine administration, and the work of Shopsin et al. (1975), who showed a hypermanic rebound in manic patients treated with physostigmine.

There is considerable evidence that lithium may exert its effects, in part, via a cholinergic mechanism. Several studies suggest that lithium, given chronically, causes an increase in cholinergic activity. Jope and his collaborators (Jope et al. 1979) demonstrated that a trial of Li_2Co_3, given chronically in doses producing "clinical" blood levels in rats, increased central acetylcholine availability. Consistent with these observations are the results of Samples et al. (1977), who found that chronic lithium treatment caused an increase in physostigmine-induced lethality in rats that was preventable with antimuscarinic agents, and the observation that this result has also been noted when DFP and lithium have been given concurrently (Roger Russell, personal communication, 1985). Some clinical evidence also supports the possibility that lithium exerts cholinergic effects. Lithium, at least in normals, exerts effects parallel to those of centrally acting cholinergic agents, including induction of feelings of anergia, being drained, lethargy, weakness, depression, and tiredness (Judd et al. 1977). Thus, information supports the possibility that an increase in acetylcholine availability occurs after exposure to chronic lithium treatment.

These lithium studies suggest some therapeutic possibilities. It is conceivable that giving acetylcholine precursors, such as choline or lecithin, or a cholinesterase inhibitor, such as physostigmine, along with lithium could increase lithium's effectiveness as an antimanic agent.

Cautionary Statements

In considering the potential use of cholinergic precursors and agonists and cholinesterase inhibitors, alone or with other facilitatory agents such as lithium, lecithin, reserpine, or THC, it is important to emphasize that these agents are not benign compounds. Specifically, cholinesterase inhibitors and cholinergic agonists have profound peripheral effects, such as bradycardia, bronchoconstriction, hypersalivation, and gastrointestinal hypermotility, which can be disabling and, at the extreme, lethal. For this reason, pretreatment and protection of the periphery with an antimuscarinic agent that does not cross the blood–brain barrier, such as propantheline, glycopyrrolate, or methscopolamine, is probably indicated, although some researchers have not used an anticholinergic before giving a cholinomimetic drug. Furthermore, to antagonize the depressive, dysphoric, and anergic effects of the cholinomimetic drugs, it may be necessary to balance or titrate such negative effects with a centrally acting antimuscarinic agent, such as tropine or scopolamine, or with a psychostimulant.

SUMMARY

In conclusion, we have reviewed the possibility that cholinomimetic compounds, alone and in combination with antiadrenergic drugs, may exert antimanic effects and may have potential in the rapid treatment of mania. Obviously, the possibilities presented in the preceding pages have not stood the test of time nor, in most cases, even been tried. For the most part, they are highly speculative. Nevertheless, it is possible that some or all will prove clinically useful. Trials along the lines described, using the described precautions, will ultimately demonstrate whether these speculations are viable and, at the same time, will be useful in supporting or contradicting the theoretical assumptions of the adrenergic–cholinergic balance hypothesis of affective disorders.

References

Bajada S: A trial of choline chloride and physostigmine in Alzheimer's dementia, in Alzheimer's Disease: A Report of Progress [Aging, Volume 19]. Edited by Corkin S, Davis K, Growdon J, et al. New York, Raven Press, 1982

Beigel A, Murphy DL: Assessing clinical characteristics of the manic state. Am J Psychiatry 128:688–694, 1971

Bowers MG, Goodman E, Sim BM: Some behavioral changes in man following anticholinesterase administration. J Nerv Ment Dis 138:383, 1964

Brezenoff HE, Guiliano R: Cardiovascular control by cholinergic mechanisms in the central nervous system. Ann Rev Pharmacol Toxicol 22:341–381, 1982

Brodie BB, Spector S, Shore PA: Interaction of drugs with norepinephrine in the brain. Pharmacol Rev 11:548–564, 1959

Bunney WE, Davis JM: Norepinephrine in depressive reactions. Arch Gen Psychiatry 13:483–494, 1965

Carlton PL: Cholinergic mechanisms in the control of behavior by the brain. Psychol Rev 70:16–39, 1963

Carroll BJ, Frazer A, Schless A, et al: Cholinergic reversal of manic symptoms. Lancet i:427, 1973

Cohen BM, Lipinsky JF, Altesmar RF: Lecithin in the treatment of mania. Am J Psychiatry 139:1162–1164, 1973

Cohen BM, Miller AL, Lipinsky JF, et al: Lecithin in mania: a preliminary report. Am J Psychiatry 137:242–243, 1980

Davis JM: Theories in the biological etiology of affective disorders. Int Rev Neurobiol 12:145–175, 1970

Davis KL, Berger PA, Hollister LE, et al: Physostigmine in man. Arch Gen Psychiatry 35:119–122, 1978

Davis KL, Hollister LE, Berger PA: Choline chloride in schizophrenia. Am J Psychiatry 136:1581–1584, 1979

Davis KL, Hollister LE, Overall J: Physostigmine effects on cognition and affect in normal subjects. Psychopharmacology 51:23–27, 1976

Dilsaver SC, Greden JF: Antidepressant withdrawal-induced activation (hypomania and mania): mechanism and theoretical significance. Brain Research Reviews 7:29–48, 1984

Domino EF, Olds ME: Cholinergic inhibition of self-stimulation behavior. J Pharm Exp Ther 164:202–211, 1968

El-Yousef M, Janowsky DS, Davis JM, et al: Induction of severe depression by physostigmine in marijuana intoxicated individuals. Br J Addict 68:321–325, 1973

Fibiger HD, Lynch GS, Cooper HP: A biphasic action of central cholinergic stimulation on behavioral arousal in the rat. Psychopharmacologia 20:366–382, 1971

Gershon S, Shaw FH: Psychiatric sequelae of chronic exposure to organophosphorus insecticides. Lancet i:1371–1374, 1961

Goodman LS, Gilman A (Eds.): The Pharmacological Basis of Therapeutics (4th Ed.). Toronto, Canada, Collier-MacMillian, 1970

Janowsky DS, Davis JM, El-Yousef MK, et al: Acetylcholine and depression. Psychosom Med 36:248–257, 1974

Janowsky DS, El-Yousef MK, Davis JM, et al: A cholinergic–adrenergic hypothesis of mania and depression. Lancet ii:6732–6735, 1972

Janowsky DS, El-Yousef MK, Davis JM, et al: Parasympathetic suppression of manic symptoms by physostigmine. Arch Gen Psychiatry 28:542–547, 1973a

Janowsky DS, El-Yousef MK, Davis JM, et al: Provocation of schizophrenic symptoms by intravenous administration of methylphenidate. Arch Gen Psychiatry 28:185–190, 1973b

Janowsky DS, El-Yousef MK, Davis JM, et al: Antagonistic effects of physostigmine and methylphenidate in man. Am J Psychiatry 130:1370–1376, 1973c

Janowsky DS, Risch SC, Huey LY: Central cardiovascular effects of physostigmine in humans. Hypertension 7:140–145, 1985

Jope RS: Effects of lithium treatment in vivo and in vitro on acetylcholine metabolism in rat brain. J Neurochem 33:487–495, 1979

Judd LL, Hubbard B, Janowsky DS, et al: The effect of lithium carbonate on affect, mood and personality of normal subjects. Arch Gen Psychiatry 34:346–351, 1977

Kark RAP, Rodriguez-Budelli M, Blass JP, et al: Oral physostigmine and inherited ataxias, in Brain Acetylcholine and Neuropsychiatric Disease. Edited by Davis K, Berger P. New York, Plenum, 1979

Kennedy B, Janowsky DS, Risch SC, et al: Central cholinergic stimulation causes adrenal epinephrine release. J. Clin Investigation 74:972–975, 1984

Modestin JJ, Hunger J, Schwartz RB: Uber die depressogene workung von physostigmine. Arch Psychatri Nervenkr 218:67, 1973a

Modestin JJ, Schwartz RB, Hunger J: Zur frage der beeinflussung schizophrener symptome physostigmine. Pharmakopsychiatrie 9:300–304, 1973b

Nurnberger J, Gershon ES, Sitaram, et al: Dextroamphetamine and arecoline as pharmacogenetic probes in normals and remitted bipolar patients. Psychopharmacol Bull 17:80–82, 1982a

Nurnberger J, Jimerson DC, Simmons S, et al: Responses to arecoline in normal twin and "well state" patients with affective disorders. Paper presented at the 13th Annual Convention of the Biological Society, Toronto, Canada, 1982b

Olds J: Self-stimulation of the brain. Science 127:315–324, 1958

Peters BH, Levin HS: Chronic oral physostigmine and lecithin administration in memory disorders of aging, in Alzheimer's Disease: A Report of Progress [Aging, Volume 19]. Edited by Corkin S, Davis K, Growdon J, et al. New York, Raven Press, 1982

Pradhan SN, Kavat KA: Action and interaction of cholinergic agonists and antagonists on self-stimulation. Arch Int Pharmacodyn Ther 196:321–329, 1972

Rowntree DW, Neven S, Wilson A: The effects of diisopropylfluorophosphonate in schizophrenia and manic depressive psychosis. J. Neurol Neurosurg Psychiatry 13:47–62, 1950

Samples J, Janowsky DS, Pechnick R, et al: Lethal effects of physostigmine plus lithium in rats. Psychopharmacology 52:307–309, 1977

Schildkraut JJ: The catecholamine hypothesis of affective disorders: a review of the supporting evidence. Am J Psychiatry 122:509–522, 1965

Schildkraut JJ: Norepinephrine metabolism in the pathophysiology and classification of depressive and manic disorders, in Psychopathology and Pharmacology. Edited by Cole J, Freeman A, Friedhoff A. Baltimore, Md, Johns Hopkins University Press, 1973

Schildkraut JJ, Kety SS: Biogenic amines and emotion. Science 156:21–30, 1967

Shopsin B, Janowsky DS, Davis JM, et al: Rebound phenomena in manic patients following physostigmine. Neuropsychobiology 1:180–187, 1975

Smith CM, Semple SA, Swash M: Effects of physostigmine on responses in memory tests in patients with Alzheimer's disease, in Alzheimer's Disease: A Report of Progress [Aging, Volume 19]. Edited by Corkin S, Davis K, Growdon J, et al. New York, Raven Press, 1982

Tamminga C, Smith RC, Change S, et al: Depression associated with oral choline. Lancet ii:905, 1976

3

Mixed Mania: Diagnosis and Treatment

Steven K. Secunda, M.D.
Martin M. Katz, Ph.D.
Alan C. Swann, M.D.
Stephen H. Koslow, Ph.D.

3

Mixed Mania: Diagnosis and Treatment

Though the new designation for manic-depressive illness—bipolar disorder—implies polar opposites, the observation that both mania and depression can exist in the same patient has long been recognized (Kotin and Goodwin 1972). Murphy and Beigel (1974), reporting on a study of 30 mania inpatients, noted that 28 of them had some depressive symptoms. Himmelhoch et al. (1976) studied the incidence of mixed affective states in a population of bipolar outpatients. They reported that 31 percent of 84 newly admitted bipolar outpatients showed mixed features.

In this chapter, we detail the construction of an appropriate rating method for the diagnosis of pure and mixed manic states. Mixed mania describes those patients showing significant concomitant depressive symptomatology in the context of classic manic features. Finally, we constructed a test for determining whether the classification is predictive of clinical response to lithium treatment.

Sample and Method

Procedure

As part of the National Institute of Mental Health (NIMH) Clinical Research Branch Collaborative Program on the Psychobiology of Depression, a cohort of manic patients was intensively studied. The background, rationale, and methodology of the overall study have been described in previous publications (Maas et al. 1980; Secunda et al. 1980).

After a 15-day period of placebo washout, active treatment began on Day 16 with 900 mg of lithium carbonate being given at 0800 hours for a lithium kinetic study. On the second and third treatment days, the patients received 1500 mg in three divided doses and from the fourth day of treatment on, 1800 mg. The drug dosage was titrated to maintain a level between 1.0 and 1.5 mEq/L and was then adjusted subject to clinical response and side effects. The total treatment period lasted 24 days. Two weeks after initiating lithium treatment, the mean level of plasma lithium for the total population was 1.14 mEq/L (range-0.74 to 1.90 mEq/L). A comparison between those subjects having a favorable response to lithium treatment and the nonresponder group revealed no significant differences between their levels of plasma lithium on any of the treatment days.

Sample

The sample included 19 manic patients who were admitted over a 4½-year period, 12 men, with a mean age of 44.8 years (range = 23 to 62), and 7 women, with a mean age of 43.9 years (range = 26 to 74). The female patients were better educated, came from higher income families, and were more likely to be married.

In defining the severity of illness of the manic population, history and the present episode were examined. In Table 1, the

Table 1. History of the Present Sample

Variable	Manic		Bipolar depressed	
	M	*SD*	*M*	*SD*
Previous hospitalizations	4.53	5.70	2.91	2.65
Age at first hospitalization	31.47	15.00	32.92	13.02
Previous manic episodes	3.88	2.64	4.70	4.44
Previous depressive episodes	4.94	4.82	7.88	15.85

history of the manic population is contrasted with that of the bipolar depressed population. This reveals that the average manic patient had been sick for at least 10 years (as defined by the first hospitalization), had been hospitalized four and one-half times for an affective illness prior to the present one, and had previously suffered approximately four manic episodes and five depressive episodes. For 2 of the 19 patients, this was the first manic episode. In terms of history, this manic population constituted a severely ill group.

For the present episode, the average manic patient was ill for 7 weeks prior to admission and entered the hospital at or close to the peak of manic symptoms (Table 2). In contrast, the average depressed bipolar patient was ill for approximately 23 weeks before entering the hospital. The Global Assessment Scale (GAS), from the Schedule of Affective Disorders and Schizophrenia (SADS; Endicott et al. 1976), is an overall measure of ability to function, detailing both limitations and positive coping mechanisms. The mean GAS rating of the manic patients (37.7) reflected a severely ill population who could not function outside of a hospital setting. The mean GAS rating for the bipolar depressed patients was 36.5.

Assessing State and Change

No single scale or rating situation can hope to encompass the multifaceted phenomena that a clinical entity represents. A "multivantaged" approach to measuring manic phenomenology, which combined several observational scales from interview,

Table 2. Characteristics of the Present Episode

Variable	Manic		Bipolar Depressed	
	M	Range	*M*	Range
Duration (in weeks)	7.21	1–26	22.8	1–101
Global severity (GAS)				
Worst	35.5	15–51	33.3	11–67
Week prior to admission	37.7	20–55	36.5	20–67
Past week	37.6	15–55	38.5	24–67

Note. GAS = Global Assessment Scale (Endicott and Spitzer 1978).

video, and ward situations, was used. A new measuring instrument, the Mania Diagnostic and Severity Scale (MADS), was constructed to integrate the various subscales used. Construction of this instrument was described in detail by Secunda et al. (1985). Briefly, to measure the symptoms characteristic of mania as judged by the clinician, the SADS-C-17 Scale (Spitzer and Endicott 1978) and the Video Interview Behavior Evaluation Scale (VIBES) Factor B-2 Scale (Katz and Itil 1974) were used.

From the nurse-rated Affective Disorder Rating Scale (ADRS; Murphy et al. 1980), used to characterize symptoms and social behavior on the ward, two separate factors were derived. Factor 1 (nine items) described a core manic syndrome, and Factor 2 (three items) described a euphoric subtype. These four factors were combined, creating the MADS, and it was assessed on Days 3, 10, 15, 22, 26, 33, and 40 to correspond to other major behavioral and biochemical measures performed in the study. The MADS, therefore, represents a combination of previously validated tests, yielding greater breadth and sensitivity in diagnosis and in assessment of severity and change.

Assessing Mixed Mania

Using the multivantaged approach, we used the nurse-rated ADRS (Murphy et al. 1980) Depression factor as our initial screen. Subjects were initially selected on the basis of having a Depression factor score equal to the average of the depressed patient group on at least one of the three pretreatment days (Day 3, 10, or 15). Confirmation of depression was verified using the physician-rated Hamilton Depression Scale (Hamilton 1960). A Hamilton score greater than 15 was required during the pretreatment period. The mean Hamilton score for this group on Day 10 was 20.0, compared to a Hamilton score of 7.5 for the pure manic patients.

Assessing Categorical Outcome

In much earlier research involving prediction of response for manic states, a particular cutting score on a symptom rating scale was used to arbitrarily define a patient as "recovered." To test hypotheses requiring recovery or nonrecovery criteria, we derived a procedure for classification based on the multivantaged concept and making use of both doctors' and nurses' overall judgments of outcome in a set of four quantifiable indexes.

Recovery was defined as a remission to the "well" state, that is, the state prior to the onset of the manic disorder or to being essentially symptom free. Two of the scales (SADS-C-17 and Global Mania) were used to judge the overall severity of the specific manic state, and two scales (VIBES- and SADS-GAS) represented the best global measures of severity.

RESULTS

Manic Diagnostic and Severity Scale: Discriminant Validity and Sensitivity to Change

Table 3 demonstrates the ability of the MADS to differentiate among the various diagnostic groups, compared to the standard diagnostic instrument (SADS). Both measures adequately separated the manic population from the other experimental and control groups. The increase in specificity of the MADS instru-

Table 3. Discriminative Ability of the MADS Compared to the Standard Diagnostic Instrument

	SADS RDC manic syndrome				MADS			
Diagnostic group	*n*	*M*	*SD*	Range	*n*	*M*	*SD*	Range
Unipolar	85	10.2	0.7	10–14	84	1.14	0.45	0.53–2.69
Bipolar	47	21.4	13.9	10–52	47	1.20	0.57	0.47–2.64
Manic	19	39.6	6.8	27–51	18	4.53	1.71	2.55–8.73
Schizophrenic	15	13.3	3.9	10–20	15	1.94	0.80	1.00–3.49
Hospitalized normal	33	10.1	0.3	10–12	33	0.54	0.31	0.00–1.22

Note. SADS RDC = Schedule of Affective Disorders and Schizophrenia Research Diagnostic Criteria (Endicott and Spitzer 1978); MADS = Mania Diagnostic and Severity Scale.

ment was partially achieved through incorporating the SADS-C-17 Scale into a broader measuring vehicle for assessing mania. This was highlighted by the virtual absence of overlap between the range of the manic population and all other diagnostic groups. (One schizophrenic patient's score extended into the bottom range of the manic group.)

The MADS score accurately reflected the clinical course of the manic patients (Table 4). The Categorical Outcome is a discontinuous measure defining response and nonresponse categories (Secunda et al. 1985). Using the criteria described, we found that 5 patients showed no response and 11 patients "recovered," that is, showed minimal or no symptoms after four weeks of treatment. We did not include 3 patients in this analysis: Two patients had an indeterminate response, and 1 spontaneously recovered before treatment.

The Day 10 mean severity scores of the responder and noresponder groups were not significantly different; that is, initial severity did not predict response. There was, moreover, no overlap between the range of the responders' posttreatment MADS scores and the range of the nonresponders' scores. The responders' severity scores were significantly decreased ($p < .01$) following treatment.

Table 4. Comparison of the Pre- and Posttreatment MADS Scores by Response Categories

Response category	*n*	*M* ± *SD*	Range
Pretreatment			
Nonresponders	5	5.00 ± 2.16	2.52–8.24
Responders	11	4.49 ± 1.50	2.01–7.72
Treatment			
Nonresponders	5	4.67 ± 0.61	3.82–5.75
Responders	11	1.06 ± 0.23[a]	0.72–1.46
Hospitalized normal patients	33	0.54 ± 0.31[b]	0.00–1.22

Note. MADS = Mania Diagnostic and Severity Scale.

[a] Treatment responders different from nonresponders ($p < .001$).

[b] Hospitalized normal patients different from pretreatment responders or nonresponders ($p < .01$).

Mixed Versus Pure Mania: Response to Treatment

Using the selection criteria detailed in the Method section, we judged 8 patients to be mixed manic and 10 patients to be pure manic for the present episode (44 percent). The 1 patient who was judged as spontaneously recovered by Day 15 was not included in this analysis. We found no significant difference between the mixed and pure manic groups on the pretreatment MADS severity score (Day 10), using a nonparametric analysis (Wilcoxon two-sample test, $p < .4$). Employing the categorical outcome critieria for response versus nonresponse, we found that 10 out of 11 pure manics responded to lithium therapy by Day 40 of the study and that only 2 out of 7 of the mixed manic subgroup responded by Day 40 (Fisher's exact test, $p = .01$). (See Table 5.) Though more women than men fell into the mixed group, this did not quite reach significance (Fisher's exact test, $p = .07$). Furthermore, being female did not by itself predict a poorer response to lithium therapy (Fisher's exact test, $p = .1$).

TRANSMITTERS AND LITHIUM EFFECTS IN MIXED MANIA

The presence of mixed mania raises the following questions: a) Does mixed mania represent part of a continuum between depression and mania (Court 1972), or does it represent a condition in which full depressed and manic states are simultaneously present (Bunney et al. 1972; Kraepelin 1968)? b) How can mixed mania be reconciled with hypotheses holding that depression and mania

Table 5. Response Outcome by Type

Type	Response	Nonresponse
Pure manic	10	1
Mixed manic	2	5

Note. Fisher's exact test ($p = .01$).

represent opposing abnormalities in neurotransmitter function? c) Is the relative lack of effect on the nonmanic symptoms present in mixed mania?

Mixed Mania: Continuum or Switch?

In Table 6 mixed and pure manic patients are compared with respect to the MADS and to ratings for behavioral constructs derived by Katz et al. (1984). Clearly, the ratings for the core manic syndrome were at least as high in the mixed as in the pure manic patients. In addition, the mixed manic patients had symptoms consistent with a major depressive episode—high ratings for psychomotor retardation or agitation, sleep disturbance, anxiety, and somatization, with an average Hamilton score of about 18. These data suggest that rather than being intermediate between depression and mania, the mixed manic syndrome consists of superimposed depressed and manic episodes, consistent with the view of Bunney et al. (1972) and Kraepelin (1968) that mixed mania is a particularly severe form of affective disorder.

Table 6. Pretreatment Behavioral Measures in Mixed and Pure Manic Patients

Measure	Mixed	Pure
MADS	5.27 ± 2.07	3.93 ± 1.12
Depressed mood	3.54 ± 1.07	1.10 ± 0.61***
Anxiety	3.78 ± 0.58	1.94 ± 0.96**
Agitation	2.13 ± 0.34	1.66 ± 0.25*
Retardation	4.65 ± 1.52	3.21 ± 1.04*
Hostility	3.17 ± 0.80	1.99 ± 1.34
Somatization	2.56 ± 1.09	1.44 ± 0.67*
Sleep disorder	5.22 ± 3.45	2.83 ± 2.78
Hamilton score	18.4 ± 6.2	7.1 ± 2.1***

Note. The table shows the mean and standard deviation of each average score from Days 10 and 15 (pretreatment). The symptom constructs other than the MADS were obtained from composites of physician, nurse, and patient ratings, as described by Katz et al. (1984). MADS = Mania Diagnostic and Severity Scale.

* $p < .05$. ** $p < .005$. *** $p < .0002$.

Mixed Mania and Neurotransmitters

Most attempts to explain affective disorders in terms of neurotransmitters hold that norepinephrine, acetylcholine, or both may vary in opposite directions in depression and mania and that serotonin may be reduced in both. In addition, dopaminergic function may be increased in bipolar manic, compared to bipolar depressed, patients (Koslow et al. 1983). Except for a trend toward increased cerebrospinal fluid homovanillic acid (HVA) in mixed manic patients ($p = 0.06$), there were no differences between mixed and pure manic patients with respect to monoamine measures. This possible difference in HVA was in the opposite direction to that previously reported between bipolar depressed and manic patients (Koslow et al. 1983; Swann et al. 1983).

Specificity of Lithium Effects in Mixed Manics

In Table 7 changes during lithium treatment in behavioral measures for mixed and pure manic patients are compared. These data show that although lithium was relatively ineffective in treating the manic syndrome in mixed manic patients, depression

Table 7. Significant Changes in Behavioral Ratings During Lithium Treatment in Mixed and Pure Mania

Pure	Mixed	Change in mixed > change in pure
Agitation	Depressed mood (0.07)	Depressed mood
Hostility	Agitation	Retardation
Interpersonal sensitivity	Hostility	Positive adaptation
Cognitive impairment	Interpersonal sensitivity	Hamilton score
Hamilton score	Cognitive impairment	
	Hamilton score	

Note. This table lists the behavioral measures, as derived by Katz et al. (1984), that changed significantly during lithium treatment in each group and that changed significantly more in mixed than in pure manic patients. No measures changed more in pure than in mixed manic patients.

improved in some of the patients. The categorical outcome for depression (derived as described by Katz et al. 1984) was recovery in three patients, partial recovery in two, and nonresponse in two. This was comparable to effects of tricyclic drugs in depressed patients without mania (Maas et al. 1982). Lithium, therefore, appeared to be at least as effective in treating depressive as manic symptoms in mixed manic patients.

COMMENT

As part of the NIMH Clinical Research Branch Collaborative Program on the Psychobiology of Depression, a group of manic patients (N = 19) participated in a protocol similar to that for the depressed subjects. The purpose was twofold, a) to study manic phenomenology in its own right and b) to provide a suitable control group for the larger depression study. In the present chapter, we focus on the mixed manic state and its diagnosis and treatment.

In 1971, Beigel and Murphy reported on a ward behavior rating scale for mania consisting of 26 items scored on a frequency and intensity continuum by nursing personnel trained in research. Of the items rated, two concerned observed and verbalized depression. In a follow-up study of 30 manic patients, they noted that 28 had ratable depression and that of these, 17 had moderate to severe depressive symptoms (57 percent). Himmelhoch et al. (1976) reported that 31 percent of 84 newly admitted bipolar outpatients showed mixed features. Unfortunately, they did not report the exact composition of their nonmixed group, which was comprised of both manic and depressed patients. It is likely, therefore, that if the depressed patients were removed from their base population, the percentage of mixed manics in the total manic population would rise considerably. In the present study, using more stringent criteria for depression, we still found that 44 percent of our manic patients showed significant depressive pathology at some point during the pretreatment phase of the study.

In a factor analytic study of their data, Murphy and Beigel (1974) found a dichotomous grouping consisting of elated–grandiose (E–G) and paranoid–destructive (P–D) patients. Though they found a significant correlation between their depressive and P–D indexes ($p < .01$), only the P–D index predicted a poor response to lithium treatment. In the present study, we used the ADRS created by Murphy et al. (1980), which has E–G and P–D clusters. Examining the means of the three baseline days' scores (Days 3, 10, and 15) and using a score of 2 as a cutoff point (on a scale of 1 to 6), we judged 12 manic patients to be E–G; 4 met criteria for both E–G and P–D, and 2 patients fitted into neither category. In all 18 cases, the E–G cluster score was higher than the P–D cluster score. No correlations were found between these indexes and response or between these indexes and type of mania, that is, pure or mixed.

Taylor and Abrams (1981), in a large-scale, retrospective study of 111 manic inpatients, found no correlation between any clinical descriptors and lithium outcome. On the other hand, Himmelhoch et al. (1976) reported that patients with mixed states had a significantly poorer treatment response than did patients with nonmixed states ($p < .001$). Again, their nonmixed group included both manic and depressed patients.

In the present study, we found that the presence of a mixed manic state predicted a poor response to lithium therapy. One caveat is that our total treatment period was only 24 days. It is possible, therefore, that our mixed manic patients were not nonresponders but were slow responders. The finding that the nonresponders' MADS scores did not change at all over the study period argues against this conclusion. Other positive predictors in the literature include the occurrence of less than four episodes of mania and depression within one year, that is, non-rapid cycling; a family history of bipolar illness; and a positive response of affected blood relatives to lithium therapy (Rosen 1981).

We found that female manic patients were significantly more likely to have depressive symptoms than their male counterparts. Himmelhoch et al. (1976) also found that 37.0 percent of their female patients, as compared to only 23.7 percent of their male patients, were diagnosed as mixed manic–depressive. Krishnan et al. (1983), studying abnormal cortisol suppression, reported that 9 out of 10 consecutive admissions who met the criteria for a mixed bipolar state were female. Other than the finding that the female patients in our study differed demographically from the male patients, no clinical observation differentiated them.

Of manic patients, 10 to 20 percent are reported to be lithium resistant (Rosen, 1981), and investigators have sought to find alternative treatments. Okuma et al. (1973) first reported that the anticonvulsant drug carbamazepine has both antimanic and prophylactic effects on bipolar illness. More recently, Post et al. (1983) reported on the successful treatment of lithium nonresponders with carbamazepine in both the acute and maintenance phases. Other alternatives for lithium treatment include other anticonvulsant medications, such as dipropylacetamide and sodium valproate as well as the benzodiazepine clonazepam (Ayd 1984). Although some of the studies cited took into account the presence or absence of rapid cycling, none made note of whether a mixed manic state was found. One recent anecdotal report (Zubenko et al. 1984) noted a favorable response to clonidine in one mixed bipolar patient.

In conclusion, our present study demonstrates that those mixed manic patients who showed significant depressive pathology at baseline were significantly and clearly less likely to respond to lithium therapy than those patients who were pure manic ($p < .01$). The lack of response to lithium by this group was independent of the initial severity of manic symptoms. There was no significant difference between the steady-state plasma-lithium levels obtained by the mixed manic versus the pure manic group. No other historical or baseline clinical finding could account for this treatment response. The results of this study suggest that future work on the treatment of lithium-resistant patients should delineate the mixed state as one subgroup, similar to the case for the subgroup of rapid cyclers.

References

Ayd FJ Jr: Alternatives for lithium. Psychiatric Annals 14:7, 1984

Beigel A, Murphy DL: Assessing clinical characteristics of the manic state. Am J Psychiatry 128:688–694, 1971

Bunney WE Jr, Murphy DL, Goodwin FK: The "switch process" in manic depressive illness. I. A systematic study of sequential behavioral change. Arch Gen Psychiatry 27:295–302, 1972

Court J: The continuum model as a resolution of the paradoxes in manic–depressive psychoses. Br. J. Psychiatry 120:133–141, 1972

Endicott J, Spitzer RL: A diagnostic interview: the Schedule for Affective Disorders and Schizophrenia. Arch Gen Psychiatry 35:837–844, 1978

Endicott J, Spitzer RL, Fleiss JL, et al: The Global Assessment Scale, a procedure for measuring overall severity of psychiatric disturbance. Arch Gen Psychiatry 33:766-771, 1976

Hamilton M: A rating scale for depression. J Neurol Neurosurg Psychiatry 23:56–62, 1960

Himmelhoch JM, Mulla D, Neil JF, et al: Incidence and significance of mixed affective states in a bipolar population. Psychiatry, 33: 1062–1066, 1976

Katz M, Koslow S, Berman N, et al: A multivantaged approach to the measurement of behavioral and affect state for clinical and psychobiological research. Psychol Rep 55:619–671, 1984

Katz MM, Itil TM: Video methodology for research in psychopathology and psychopharmacology. Arch Gen Psychiatry 31:204–210, 1974

Koslow S, Maas J, Bowden C, et al: Cerebrospinal fluid and urinary biogenic amines and metabolites in depression, mania, and healthy controls: a controlled, univariate analysis. Arch Gen Psychiatry 40:999–1010, 1983

Kotin J, Goodwin FK: Depression during mania: clinical observations and theoretical implications. Am J Psychiatry 129:55–61, 1972

Kraepelin E: Lectures on Clinical Psychiatry, facsimile. New York, Hafner, 1968

Krishnan RR, Maltbie AA, Davidson JRT: Abnormal cortisol suppression in bipolar patients with simultaneous manic and depressive symptoms. Am J Psychiatry 140:203–205, 1983

Maas J, Koslow S, Davis J, et al: Biological component of the NIMH Clinical Research Branch Collaborative Program on the Psychobiology of Depression. I. Background and theoretical considerations. Psychol Med 10: 759–776, 1980

Maas JW, Kocsis JH, Bowden CL, et al: Pretreatment neurotransmitter metabolites and response to imipramine and amitriptyline treatment. Psychol Med 12:37–44, 1982

Murphy DL, Beigel A: Depression, elation, and lithium carbonate responses in manic patient subgroups. Arch Gen Psychiatry 31:643–649, 1974

Murphy DL, Pickar D, Alterman IS: Methods for the quantitative assessment of depressive and manic behavior, in Quantitive Techniques for the Evaluation for the Behavior of Psychiatric Patients. Edited by Burdoch I, Sudilovsky A, Gershon S. New York, Marcel Dekker, 1980

Okuma T, Kishimota A, Inoue D, et al: Anti-manic and prophylactic effects of carbamazepine on manic–depressive psychosis. Folia Psychiatr Neurol Jpn 27:282–297, 1973

Post RM, Uhde TW, Ballenger JC, et al: Prophylactic efficacy of carbamazepine in manic–depressive illness. AM J Psychiatry 140:1602–1604, 1983

Rosen H.: A Clinician's Guide to Affective Disorders [Second Edition]. Mnemosyne, Miami, Fla, 1981

Secunda S, Koslow S, Redmond DE Jr, et al: Biological component of the NIMH Clinical Research Branch Collaborative Program on the Psychobiology of Depression. II. Methodology and data analysis. Psychol Med 10:773–793, 1980

Secunda SK, Katz MM, Swann A, et al: Mania: diagnosis, state measurement and prediction of treatment response. J. Affective Disord 8:113–121, 1985

Spitzer RL, Endicott J: Schedule of Affective Disorders and Schizophrenia—Change Version [Third Edition]. New York, Biometrics Research, New York State Psychiatric Institute, 1978

Swann A. Secunda S, Davis J, et al: Cerebrospinal fluid monoamine metabolites in mania. Am J Psychiatry 140:396–400, 1983

Taylor MA, Abrams R: Prediction of treatment response in mania. Arch Gen Psychiatry 38:800–803, 1981

Zubenko GS, Cohen BM, Lipinski JF Jr, et al: Clonidine in treatment of mania and mixed bipolar affective disorder. Am J Psychiatry 141:1618–1718, 1984

4

Antimanic Effects of Carbamazepine: Mechanisms of Action and Implications for the Biochemistry of Manic-Depressive Illness

Robert M. Post, M.D.
Thomas W. Uhde, M.D.
David R. Rubinow, M.D.
Susan R. B. Weiss, Ph.D.

4

Antimanic Effects of Carbamazepine: Mechanisms of Action and Implications for the Biochemistry of Manic-Depressive Illness

Lithium carbonate, a drug useful in the treatment of manic–depressive illness, perhaps equivalent to any other "wonder drug" in medicine for the alleviation of the acute and long-term symptoms of an illness, does not work in every patient. About 20 to 30 percent of manic–depressive patients and a higher percentage of rapid-cycling manic–depressive patients do not respond adequately to lithium (Prien 1984; Tondo and Kukopulos, personal communication). Moreover, lithium has a range of side effects that makes it difficult for some patients to tolerate. Therefore, there is considerable need for alternative treatments for bipolar affective disorders.

Carbamazepine and some related anticonvulsants are emerging as useful treatment options for mania as well as the longer term prophylaxis of bipolar disorders. We will review this evidence and present some of our ongoing clinical experience with the drug. In turn, this clinical evidence for the efficacy of carbamazepine in the treatment of acute mania has important implications for the understanding of the mechanisms underlying the manic syndrome. Thus, we will also review the potential mechanisms of action of carbamazepine because they may provide important leads for understanding the underlying biochemistry of the mood disorders.

It was initially hoped that understanding the mechanisms of action of lithium would rapidly help uncover the biochemistry of mania. After several decades of investigation, this has not proven to be as easy as first expected. With the advent of carbamazepine as an additional treatment for mania, new leverage is gained in comparing and contrasting its mechanisms with those of lithium and the neuroleptics. We wonder, however, whether this new leverage will rapidly be translated to a direct understanding of manic illness because, like lithium, carbamazepine appears to affect a panoply of biochemical systems and physiological mechanisms in the brain. Therefore, there is a surfeit of neurotransmitter, modulator, and neuropeptide candidates for the mechanism of action of both lithium and carbamazepine, with no single mechanism clearly identified as important to their pharmacological effects in this syndrome.

Considerable progress might be expected, however, in that carbamazepine is also a potent anticonvulsant; this provides a readily identifiable behavioral and physiological end point with which to study its biochemistry and pharmacology. Of course, in this instance, it must be hoped that the mechanisms underlying the anticonvulsant effects of carbamazepine are also related to its important psychotropic properties, a proposition that remains to be directly demonstrated.

In this chapter, we will review both the new treatment perspectives that carbamazepine offers and the new conceptual approaches to understanding affective disorders that its clinical efficacy suggests. We became interested in the use of carbamazepine in manic-depressive illness for a number of reasons, for example, its distinctive profile as an excellent agent for dampening limbic system seizures produced experimentally and its clear-cut efficacy as a clinically used anticonvulsant for patients with temporal lobe seizures (Penry and Daly 1975). Limbic system structures have long been postulated as important to affective dysregulation, and we hoped that use of a drug that dampened the excitability of limbic structures might be useful in the treatment of nonconvulsive disorders of mood and behavior (Ballenger and Post 1978; Post et al. 1978a). We were also heartened by the repeated observations that carbamazepine did, in fact, appear to have useful effects on mood and behavior when used in the treatment of epileptic subjects, at times independently of its ability to produce complete anticonvulsant effects (Dalby 1971, 1975). Carbamazepine also suppresses amygdala-kindled seizures, and we had postulated that behavioral sensitization and electrophysiological kindling might underlie some of the longitudinal and progressive components of the course of manic–depressive illness. In addition, the uncontrolled studies of Okuma and associates (1973) and Takezaki and Hanaoka (1971) in Japan suggested the utility of carbamazepine in the treatment of mania.

It remains to be demonstrated whether the initial theoretical rationales for the use of carbamazepine in manic–depressive illness will prove valid. We have discussed whether the psychotropic effects of carbamazepine are related to its ability to dampen limbic system excitability elsewhere (Post in press; Post and Uhde in press-b, in press-c; Post et al. 1982a, 1984c, 1985a). In this chapter, we focus on the biochemical effects of carbamazepine and the implication for its pharmacological effects in manic–depressive illness and epilepsy.

CLINICAL STUDIES

Carbamazepine in Acute Mania

Open and controlled clinical trials of carbamazepine in the treatment of acute mania are summarized in Table 1. Although many of the researchers used open observations of carbamazepine in conjunction with other agents, the results appear to parallel those of more systematic and double-blind clinical studies. In three studies comparing carbamazepine as a single agent to a variety of neuroleptics, carbamazepine or its keto derivative oxcarbazepine was equally effective as the traditionally used neuroleptics, including chlorpromazine and haloperidol. We obtained similar results (Post et al. 1978, 1984; see Figure 1). In each of these studies, the magnitude of clinical effects and rapidity of onset of efficacy compared favorably with the neuroleptics. In several of these studies, side effects were less severe on carbamazepine, compared with the neuroleptics. In our study, the degree of improvement on carbamazepine closely paralleled that of the traditional neuroleptics chlorpromazine or thioridazine as well as the more atypical and relatively more specific blocker of the dopamine receptor pimozide (Post et al. 1980b). For carbamazepine, phenothiazine, and pimozide, 63 percent (12 of 18), 78 percent (7 of 9), and 87 percent (7 of 8) of patients, respectively, showed marked improve-

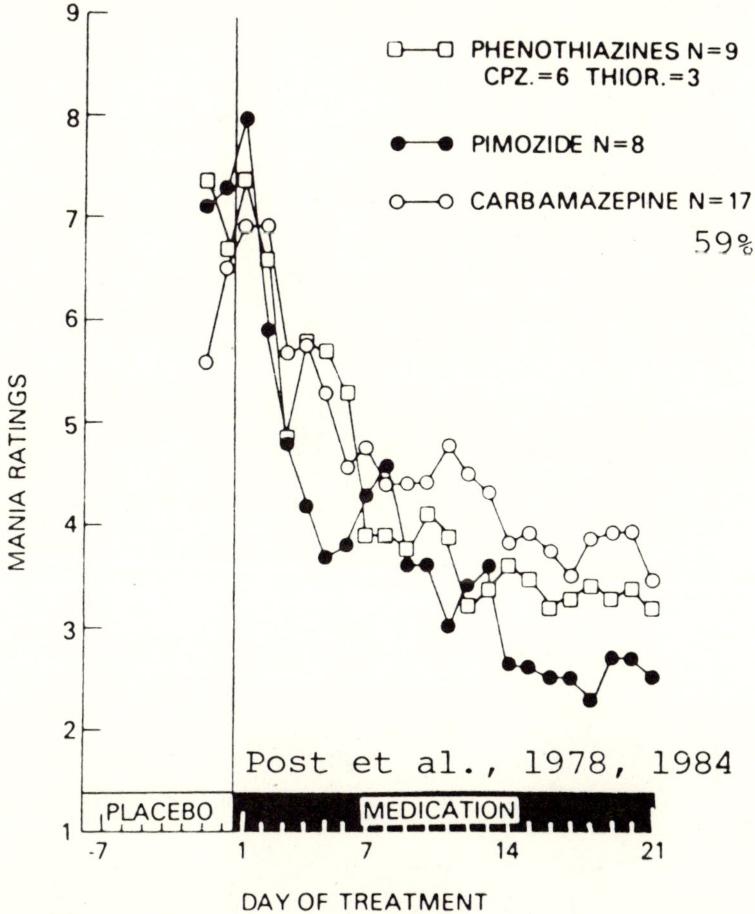

Figure 1. Controlled comparisons of carbamazepine and neuroleptics in mania.

Table 1. Studies of Carbamazepine (CBZ) in Acute Mania

Study	N	Diagnosis	Design	mg/day CBZ (μg/mL blood level)	Other drugs	Duration	Results
Takezaki and Hanaoka (1971)	10	M–D	Open	200–600	Neuroleptics, tricyclics in some cases	1–11 months	6/10 improved
Okuma et al. (1973, 1975)	64	M–D	Open	400–1,200	Neuroleptics	Variable	22/64 improved
Ballenger and Post (1978); Post et al. (1984)	19	M–D	Double blind (B-A-B-A)	600–2,000 (7–15.5)	None	11–56 days	12/19 improved—time course similar to neuroleptics
Okuma et al. (1979)	32 CBZ; 28 CPZ	M–D	Double blind comparison with CPZ 150–450 mg	300–900 (2.7–11.7; M = 7.2 ± 3.4)	Bedtime hypnotics	3–5 weeks	21/32 improved on CBZ; 15/28 improved on CPZ
Inoue et al. (1981)	5	BP	Open	400–800	Li, neuroleptics, tricyclics	Variable	3/5 improved
Folks et al. (1982)	10	4 BP; 1 SA; 3 OA	Open	600–1,600	Other drugs in 6/10	—	8/10 improved—CBZ may be especially effective for affective cases with central nervous system disorder

Table 1. Studies of Carbamazepine (CBZ) in Acute Mania *(continued)*

Study	*N*	Diagnosis	Design	mg/day CBZ (μg/mL blood level)	Other drugs	Duration	Results
Lipinski and Pope (1982)	3	2 BP manic; 1 other	Open; Li discontinuation	Not specified (8.5–9.5)	Li and neuroleptics	Variable	3/3 improved, but all relapsed after Li discontinuation, suggesting combination needed
Moss and James (1982)	1	Major affective disorder; manic	Open	600–800 (4.5–5.7)	Li	—	Partial improvement of patient; relapse after combination of CBZ & Li
Yassa (1982)	1	M–D	Open	600 (8.0)	OXCBZ	26 months	1/1 improved
Emrich et al. (1983)	6	Maniform psychoses	Double blind	1,800–2,100 OXCBZ	Not stated	Variable	5/6 (>25% improvement on IMPS)
Keisling (1983)	3	1 SA; 1 BP; 1 manic	Open	600–1,400	Li (all), tricyclics in one case	2–3 months	3/3 improved in combination with Li
Klein et al. (1984)	11	Excited mania (3 excited SA)	Blind	600–1,600 (6.0–18.0)	15–45 mg/day haloperidol	5 weeks	10/14 improved on CBZ & haloperidol (7/13 improved on placebo & haloperidol)

Table 1. Studies of Carbamazepine (CBZ) in Acute Mania *(continued)*

Study	*N*	Diagnosis	Design	mg/day CBZ (μg/mL blood level)	Other drugs	Duration	Results
Muller and Stoll (1984)	48	M–D	Open	2.1–3.06 m/day OXCBZ	Li and neuroleptics (7); hypnotics (28)	10–86 days (39 days)	40/48 CBZ > placebo, blind (12) OXCBZ = haloperidol (20)
Sethi and Tiwari (1984)	5	M–D	Open randomized vs. CPZ	600–1,600	Not specified	28 days	5/5; CBZ better than CPZ
Grossi et al. (1984)	15	M–D	Blind vs. CPZ randomized	200–1,200	—	21 days	10/15; CBZ had fewer side effects than CPZ
Lerer et al. (1985)	29	M–D	Blind vs. Li randomized	600–1,600	—	28 days	5/14 improved on CBZ
Kwamie et al. (1984)	8	BP manic	Open	300–1,600	Others	23–82 days	5/8 improved; one not confirmed on retest

Note. M–D = manic depressive; BP = bipolar; SA = schizoaffective; OA = organic affective; CPZ = chlorpromazine; OXCBZ = oxcarbazepine; Li = lithium; IMPS = Inpatient Multidimensional Psychiatric Scale. Total number of improved patients from all 17 studies was 159 out of 258.

ment. Grossi et al. (1984) found that 10 out of 15 patients improved during carbamazepine treatment, compared with 13 out of 17 on chlorpromazine; those treated with carbamazepine had fewer side effects.

In several of our patients, we had the opportunity to document clinical responsivity to carbamazepine during repeated clinical evaluations using a double-blind, off–on–off–on design. One such example is illustrated in Figures 2 and 3.

Case Study 1

A 35-year-old female patient had a history of seven manic episodes in the five years prior to National Institute of Mental Health (NIMH) admission, each requiring hospitalization. These severe manias occurred in spite of adequate lithium prophylaxis, although at times there were questions of lithium compliance. Shortly after admission to the NIMH, while she was treated with placebo, a manic episode emerged, and active treatment with carbamazepine was initiated on a blind basis. This led to rapid improvement in manic symptomatology (Figure 2). carbamazepine was discontinued, with placebo substitution; the patient remained well for 24 hours, but on the second day following carbamazepine discontinuation, manic symptoms, identical to those previously observed, began to emerge rapidly. This progressed to a severity approximately equal to that originally noted, such that the patient was again treated with active carbamazepine. Her dosage was more rapidly increased than on the first occasion, and her improvement in mania occurred in a more rapid fashion. Lithium was administered conjointly during the last phase of the carbamazepine

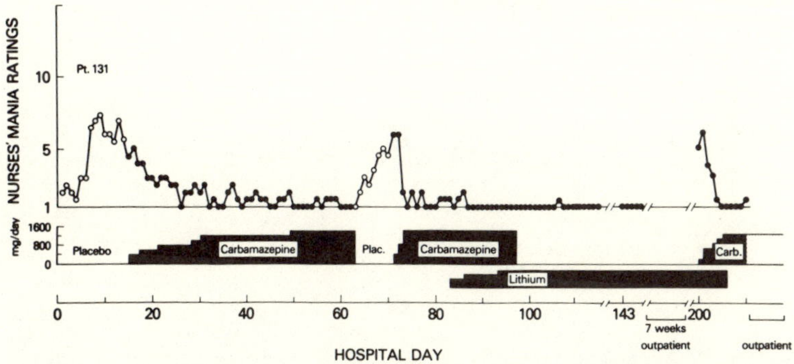

Figure 2. Unequivocal antimanic response to carbamazepine.

trial, and this appeared sufficient to block the reemergence of mania observed previously during placebo substitution alone. In light of this apparent response to lithium and because of prior questions about lithium noncompliance, the patient was treated with lithium alone and carefully monitored in an NIMH outpatient clinic. In spite of lithium levels in the therapeutic range, another manic episode occurred, requiring readmission to the 3-West Clinical Research Unit, and this third episode rapidly responded to carbamazepine treatment, also (Figure 2). Subsequently, the patient was maintained on a combination of lithium and carbamazepine in conjunction, at different times, with other psychotropic agents, including tricyclic antidepressants, monoamine oxidase inhibitors, and neuroleptics given by her treating physician. On this regimen, with the addition of carbamazepine (Figure 3), she experienced no manic episodes requiring hospitalization during five years of follow-up, in contrast to the previous five years, during which seven hospitalizations were necessary. Moreover, when carbamazepine was discontinued on one occasion, approximately three years following treatment, a severe manic episode reemerged.

There have been few systematic comparisons of carbamazepine to lithium carbonate in unselected clinical populations. In our own studies, carbamazepine appeared to show antimanic effects comparable with those of lithium carbonate when both drugs

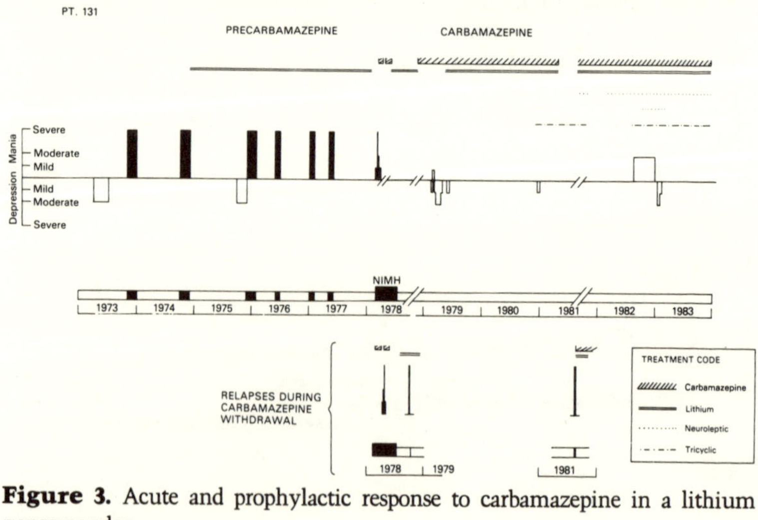

Figure 3. Acute and prophylactic response to carbamazepine in a lithium nonresponder.

were employed in sequentially studied patient populations, using similar diagnostic criteria, rating scales, and nurses who were unaware of which treatment was being employed. Lerer et al. (1985) and Zohar et al. (1982) reported that lithium was significantly better in the treatment of unselected manic patients than carbamazepine, although their completed trials with further patients added suggest that the two have roughly parallel efficacy. carbamazepine and lithium did not differ on a number of outcome measures, although lithium was superior in their studies on several of the rating scales.

These new data are now more parallel with those of Placidi et al. (1984), who found a good response to carbamazepine in 11 of 15 patients; 7 of 14 patients improved on lithium at an assessment after two months. Using a relapse criterion, they found that 10 of 15 patients treated with carbamazepine improved and that 9 of 14 patients treated with lithium improved.

Because Okuma et al. (1973) found some lack of overlap in patients' responsivity to lithium versus carbamazepine, the literature remains to be clarified as to whether lithium and carbamazepine responses are going to occur in separate subgroups of manic patients. Use of double-blind crossover designs, in addition to randomized entry trials, should help clarify this issue of considerable practical and theoretical import. Our initial data reviewed here suggest that many variables associated with poorer response to lithium, such as manic severity, dysphoria, and rapid cycling, are associated with better antimanic response to carbamazepine.

Carbamazepine in the Prophylaxis of Recurrent Mania

As summarized in Table 2, a number of studies indicate that carbamazepine, when used alone or in combination with previously ineffective treatment regimens, may lead to a reduction in the frequency and severity of manic-depressive episodes. Although the majority of these reports are uncontrolled clinical trials or case presentations, double-blind clinical trials show parallel findings. For example, Okuma et al. (1981) reported that carbamaz-

Table 2. Prophylaxis in Manic–Depressive Illness

Study	*N*	Diagnosis	Design	mg/day CBZ (μg/mL blood level)	Other drugs	Duration	Results
Takezaki and Hanaoka (1971)	10	M–D	Open	200–600	Neuroleptics, tricyclics in some cases	1–11 months	9/10 improved
Okuma et al. (1973, 1975)	51	M–D	Open	400–1200	Neuroleptics, lithium, tricyclics	Approximately 25 weeks	34/51 improved
Ballenger and Post (1978; Post et al. (1984[c])	7	6 M–D; 1 conf psychosis	4 blind; 3 open	800–2000 (11.3)	None for 3 patients	6–51 months	6/7 improved, especially Li nonresponsive cyclers
Okuma et al. (1981)	12 CBZ; 10 placebo	M–D	CBZ vs. placebo; blind; random assignment	400–600 (5.6 ± 2.0)	Acute treatments added during episode breakthroughs	12 months either Rx	6/10 improved on CBZ; 2/9 improved on placebo
Inoue et al. (1981)	3	M–D	Open	400–600	Li	18–32 months	2/3 improved
Kwamie et al. (1984)	12	M–D	Open	—	Others	—	5/8 improved (Li resistant)

Table 2. Prophylaxis in Manic–Depressive Illness *(continued)*

Study	*N*	Diagnosis	Design	mg/day CBZ (μg/mL blood level)	Other drugs	Duration	Results
Lipinski and Pope (1982)	3	2 M–D; 1 other	Open	Not specified (8.5–9.5)	Li neuroleptics in one case	3–8 months	3/3 improved, but relapsed on Li discontinuation—combination necessary?
Yassa (1982)	1	M–D	Open	600 (8)	CPZ decreasing doses from 1,700 mg/day	26 months	1/1 improved
Keisling (1983)	3	1 SA; 1 BP; 1 manic	Open	600–1400 (8.0–9.0)	Li (all); 1 tricyclic	2–8 months	3/3 improved on Li combination
Kishimoto et al. (1983); Kishimoto (1984)	87	M–D	Open	100–1200 (6.0–10.0)	Li and others	2–11 years; *M* = 48.8 months	24/32 improved, especially early onset; 43/55 and continuous cyclers
Nolen (1984)	8	M–D	Open	400 (6.0–12.0)	Li, neuroleptics, antidepressants	6–36 months	4/8 improved (all Li resistant)
Fawcett and Kravitz (1985)	34	M–D	Open	*M* = 800 (7.4 ± 2.5)	Li, antidepressants	4 months–10 years 54 months average	22/34 improved—17 CBZ alone

Table 2. Prophylaxis in Manic–Depressive Illness *(continued)*

Study	*N*	Diagnosis	Design	mg/day CBZ (μg/mL blood level)	Other drugs	Duration	Results
Gastpar and Kielholz (1984)	13	8 M–D; 4 SA; 1 UP	Open	200–1000, *M* = 520	Li, neuroleptics, antidepressants	14 months	6/13 (3SAs) relapsed on DC; 9/13 Li resistant
Greil et al. (1984)	13	M–D	Open	600–1200 (5.5–22.0)	Li	11–15 months	3/13 (1 of 9 on OXCBZ responded)
Placidi et al. (1984)	15	7 M–D; 8 SA	Blind vs. Li random	800–1600 (7.0–12.0)	None	2–92 months	11/15 vs. 7/14 on Li at 2 months.; 10/15 vs. 9/14 improved by relapse criteria
Nelson (1984)	1	M–D	Open	400 (6.8–8.0)	None	21 months	1/1 improved

Note. M–D = manic depressive; SA = schizoaffective; BP = bipolar; UP = unipolar; CBZ = carbamazepine; CPZ = chlorpromazine; OXCBZ = oxycarbamazepine; Li = lithium; DC = discontinuation. Total number of improved subjects from all 16 studies was 160 out of 276.

epine was significantly more effective than placebo in preventing affective recurrences. The data of Placidi et al. (1984), using a two-month follow-up as already reported, were also positive.

In our own series, we have followed nine patients for an average of 5.4 years, including 2.7 years on carbamazepine, compared with

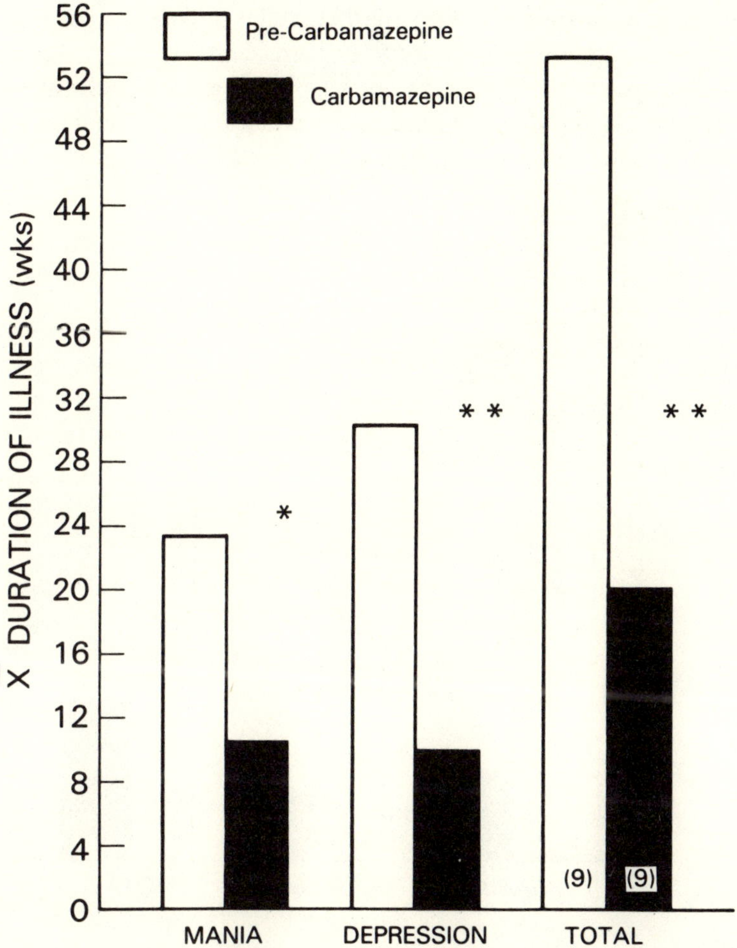

paired t, *p<.05, **p<.01

Figure 4. Decreased time ill during 2.7 years on carbamazepine compared with 2.7 years baseline.

an equal time off this drug in a mirror-image design. There was a significant reduction in the frequency (Figure 4) and duration (Figure 5) of episodes on carbamazepine, compared with an equal time prior to initiation of this drug. In this study, carbamazepine was used either alone under double-blind conditions or as a supplement to previously ineffective treatment regimens, as illustrated in Figure 3. In these patients, the frequency of episodes per year decreased from 8.4 ± 3.3 prior to carbamazepine to 2.8 ± 1.3 on the drug ($p < .05$). Clear-cut evidence of long-term improvement in the illness was demonstrated under double-blind conditions in patients such as the one illustrated in Figures 6–8.

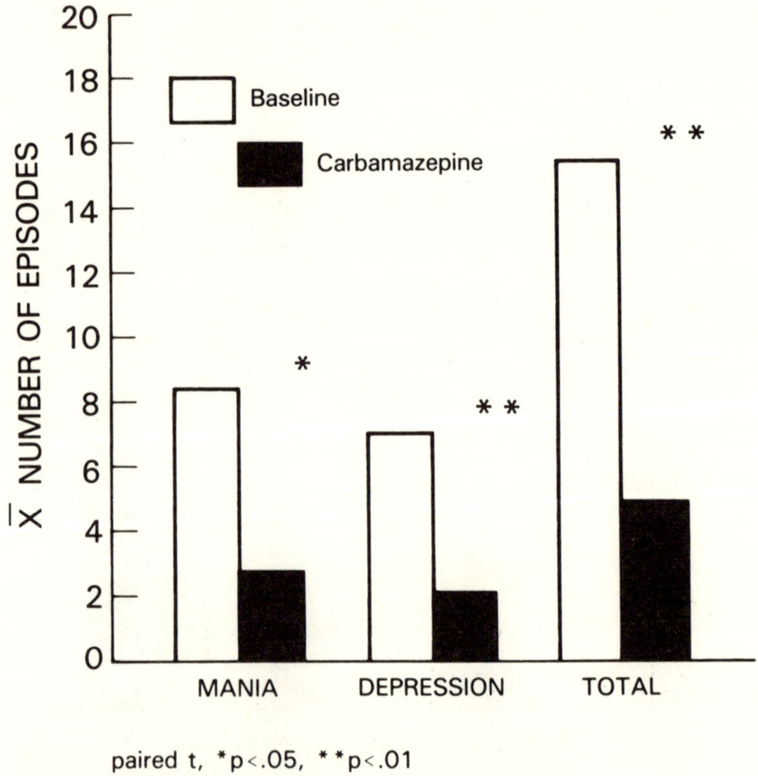

Figure 5. Reductions in manic and depressive episodes in nine patients followed on carbamazepine for an average of 2.7 years compared with 2.7 years baseline.

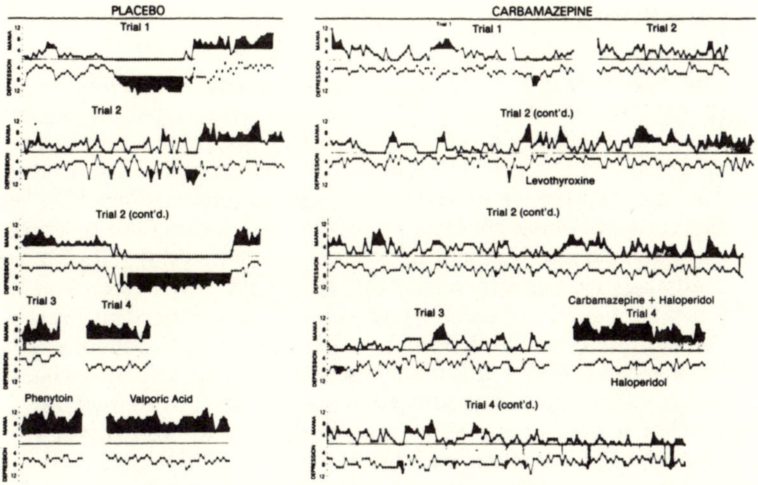

Figure 6. Decreased severity of affective episodes during carbamazepine treatment in a rapidly cycling manic–depressive episode.

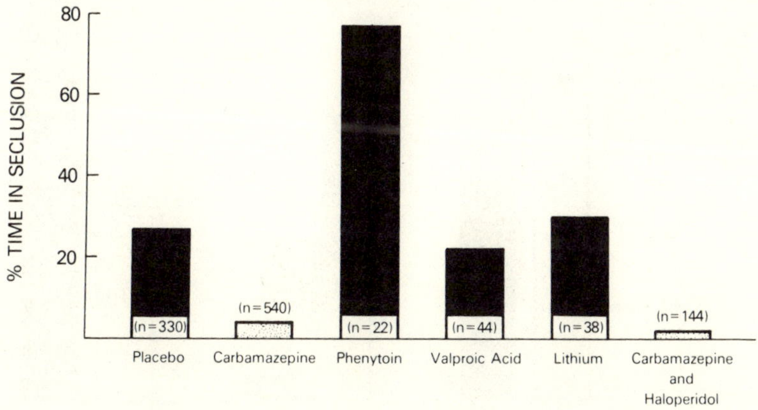

Figure 7. Carbamazepine decreases time required in seclusion for a manic–depressive patient.

Case Study 2

This was a 56-year-old bipolar depressed patient with a history of almost 20 years of continuous hospitalization for rapid cycling between incapacitating depressions and severe manias that required seclusion much of the time (Figure 6). The patient did not respond to lithium, tricyclics, or neuroleptics in various combinations. This severe course of illness continued to be observed during various periods on placebo at the National Institute of Mental Health (NIMH), as illustrated in Figure 7, indicating that the patient required seclusion 26 percent of the time of each 24-hour day while maintained on placebo. During the almost 1½ years on carbamazepine treatment at doses over 800 mg/day, however, this need for seclusion (assessed by nurses blind to medication status) was reduced to just 4 percent. In contrast, other anticonvulsant agents, phenytoin and valproic acid, were ineffective, as was a double-blind trial with lithium carbonate. Moreover, repeated interruption of carbamazepine treatment with dose reduction or placebo substitution again increased the need for seclusion, further documenting the unequivocal nature of the carbamazepine response. When carbamazepine was combined with neuroleptic treatment (haloperidol at 16 mg/day), the need for seclusion was further reduced to 1.6 percent. As summarized in Figure 8, there was a substantial blunt-

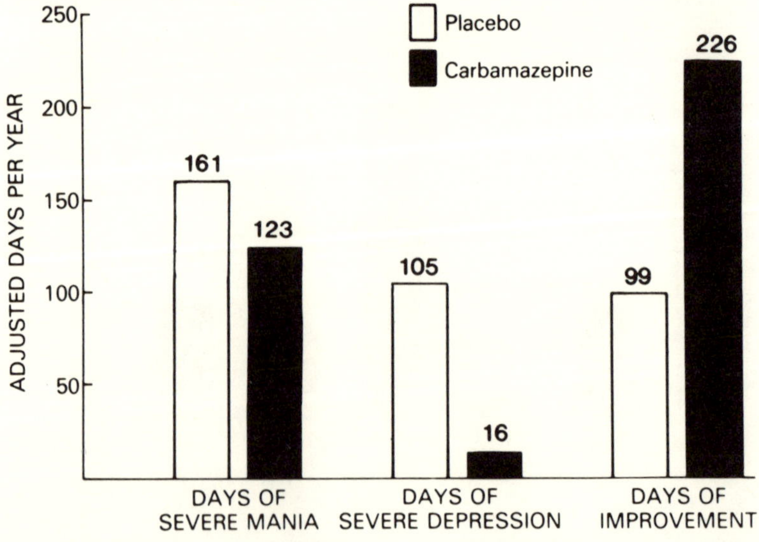

Figure 8. Improvement in manic and depressive phases during carbamazepine prophylaxis.

ing in the incidence of manic and depressive episodes on carbamazepine, compared to other periods of treatment in this double-blind design.

The use of carbamazepine in combination with neuroleptics in this patient and in combination with lithium, as illustrated in Figures 3 and 9, suggests the need for further systematic evaluation of the utility of combination of anticonvulsants with more traditional psychotropic agents in the long-term management of bipolar affective disorder. The case in Figure 9 is particularly suggestive that the combination may be clinically effective when either agent is itself ineffective when used alone. As illustrated, this patient continued to have severe rapid-cycling illness when treated with lithium carbonate in both in- and outpatient trials that were carefully monitored. When this patient was admitted to the NIMH, carbamazepine was used for acute treatment of a manic episode but without much success. When the patient was maintained on the combination, however, no further episodes were observed for a period of 15 months, in contrast to the prior two years, during which he exhibited continuous psychopathology. A relapse did occur when lithium dose was reduced, further supporting the need for the combination of carbamazepine and lithium in this patient. These data parallel those of Kishimoto (1984), who reported a series of 17 patients who were inadequately responsive to either lithium or carbamazepine when administered alone but who showed marked improvement when both agents were used in combination. Parallel results were reported by Fujiwara et al. (1984), Omura et al. (1984), Lipinski and Pope (1982), and Keisling (1983).

Blood Levels and Side Effects

Tomson (1984) documented the wide individual variability in the dose and blood level of carbamazepine at which individual patients show side effects. Some patients are unable to tolerate carbamazepine levels much beyond 4 μg/mL without severe side effects, but other patients tolerate 9- or even 12-μg/mL-carbamazepine blood levels without substantial side effects. We have not seen robust correlations with blood levels of carbamazepine and degree of clinical response (Post et al. 1983 and Figure 10). These data parallel those in the epilepsy literature, where there is little or no relationship between blood levels of carbamazepine and degree of efficacy. In individual patients, however, there appear to be dose-related degrees of clinical improvement. For example, as illustrated in Figure 11, degree of improvement in mania and psychosis ratings clearly increased in a dose-related fashion, particularly as doses over 800 mg/per day were reached.

Taken together, these data suggest the clinical importance of individually titrating dose against clinical efficacy and side effects rather than aiming at any specific dose or blood-level range for a given individual. We have found clinical responses within a dose range of 400 to 2,000 mg per day, with an average dose of approximately 1,000 mg per day, in our series. Blood levels have ranged from 4 to 12 μg/mL, but again, with this range, there is wide individual variability in both degree of clinical response (Figure 10) and side effects. If side effects do occur at a given dose or blood level, particularly those that are typical of the anticonvulsants, such as dizziness, ataxia, and diplopia, we would suggest minor dose reductions until these symptoms clear. In this fashion, pa-

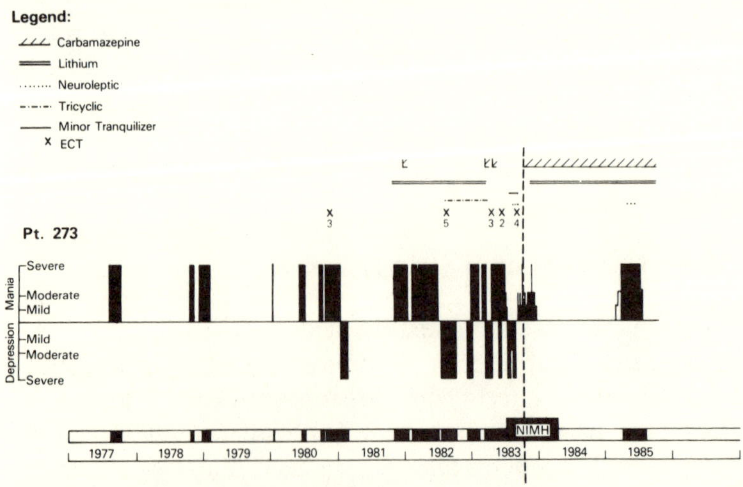

Figure 9. Carbamazepine and lithium in refractory mania.

tients tolerate carbamazepine quite well and are often unable to discern when they are on this drug and when they are on placebo.

At appropriate doses, sedation does not appear to be an important side effect, even though sleep is substantially improved during the course of the clinical trial with carbamazepine, as illustrated in Figure 12. Manic patients who responded showed significant improvement in nurses' assessments of total sleep based

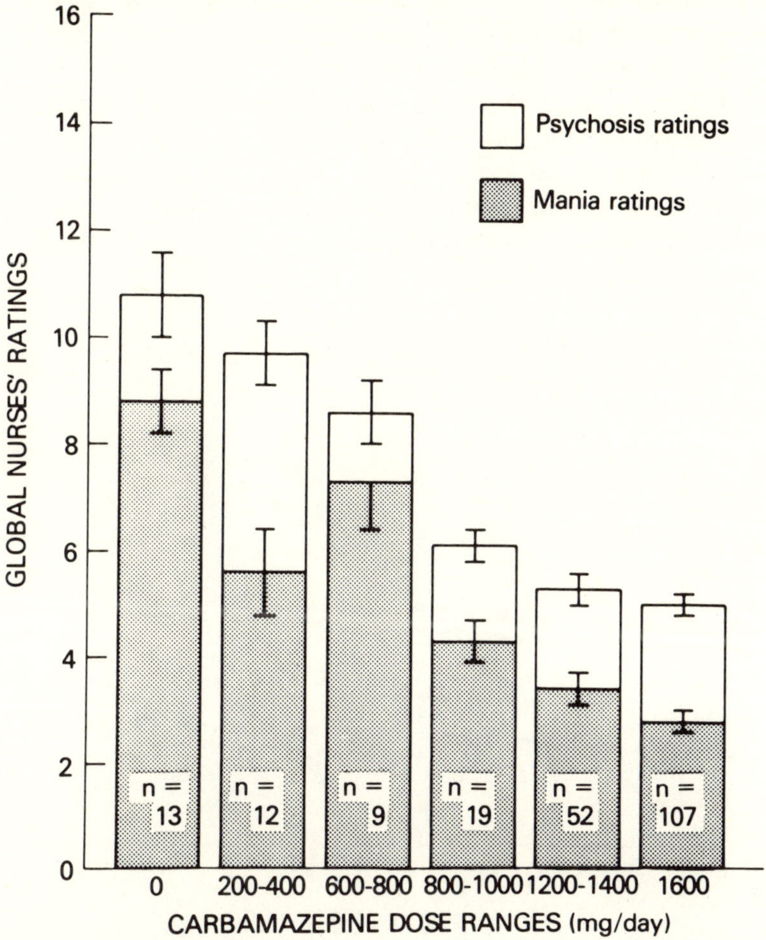

Figure 10. Dose-dependent therapeutic effects of carbamazepine during prolonged manic episode.

on half-hourly sleep checks, and those with poorer response showed nonsignificant increases in sleep during carbamazepine treatment.

To date, 12 of 81, or approximately 15 percent, of the depressed, manic, or euthymic patients treated with carbamazepine have developed a rash that led to discontinuation of the clinical trial. In no patient have we had to discontinue the clinical trial because of a persistent white count less than 3,000/cm (Joffe et al. 1985, in press). Minor liver enzymes have been noted in several patients, leading to discontinuation of the trial. carbamazepine was restarted in one of these patients without subsequent elevations in liver enzymes. One patient experienced benign atrial fibrillation and one, a syncopal episode while treated with carbamazepine. Other side effects relevant to individual neurotransmitter or peptide systems will be discussed in the sections concerning mechanism of action.

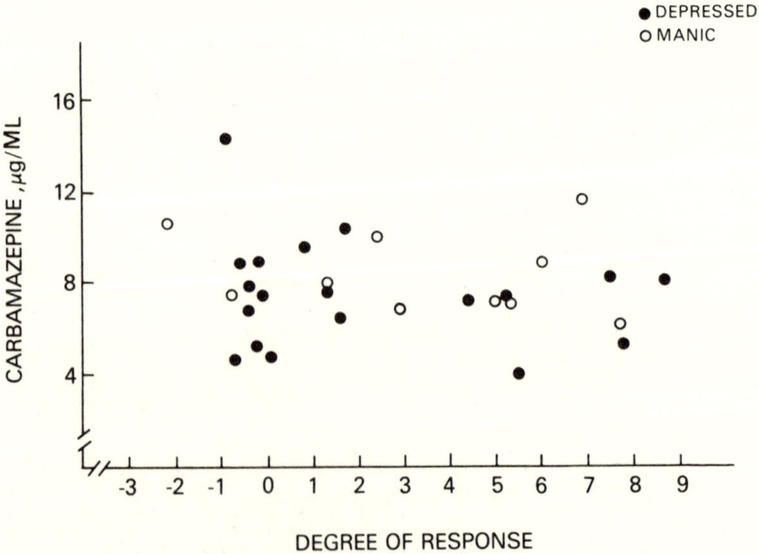

Figure 11. Lack of relationship between carbamazepine level and degree of clinical response.

Possible Clinical Predictors of Carbamazepine Response

Figure 13 illustrates the time course of rapid improvement in the responders to carbamazepine. Those who show a robust antimanic response to the drug were significantly more manic as assessed by nurses' blind global mania ratings prior to initiation of the carbamazepine trial, compared with nonresponders. Thus, it appears that severity of mania is a possible predictor of carbamazepine response.

As noted in the introduction, patients with rapid- or continuous-cycling manic–depressive illness are particularly resistant to the therapeutic effects of lithium carbonate. As such, we were

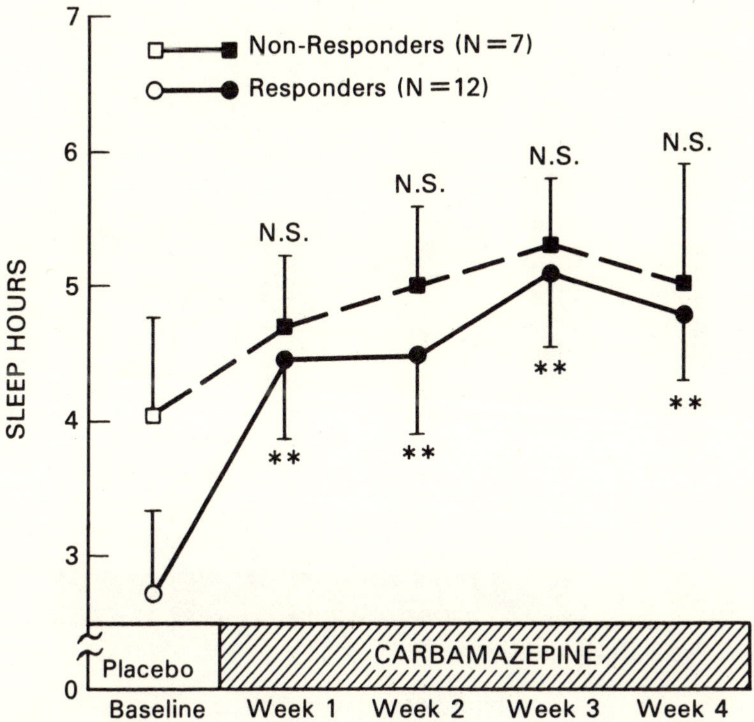

Figure 12. Improvement in sleep following carbamazepine treatment of mania.

interested in assessing whether this group of patients would be responsive to carbamazepine, as was suggested by the relatively high incidence of positive response (Tables 1 and 2) when many of these patients had previously been tried on lithium carbonate. Moreover, our experience particularly included lithium-resistant,

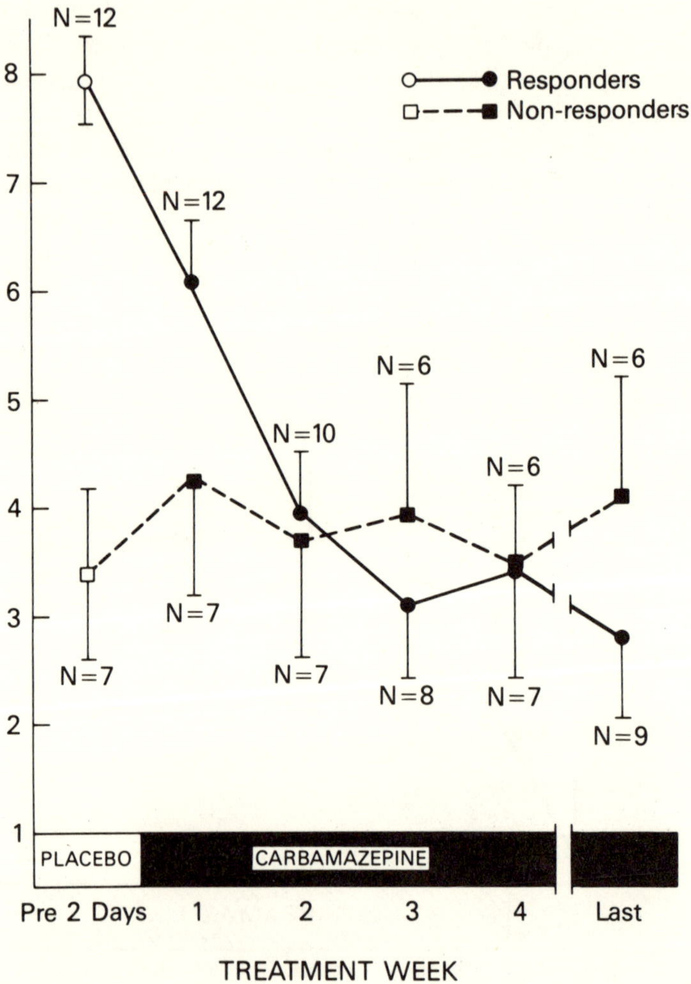

Figure 13. Time course of antimanic response to carbamazepine in marked responders.

rapid-cycling patients, because the NIMH is a tertiary referral center and deals predominantly with treatment-resistant patients.

When we assessed the life-course-of-illness variables in the 12 acute manic responders to carbamazepine, compared to the 7 nonresponders, we found that several variables indicating rapidity of cycling appeared to be directly associated with positive response to carbamazepine. As illustrated in Table 3, the number of episodes in the year prior to NIMH hospitalization significantly differentiated responders from nonresponders. Responders had an average of 7 ± 1.6 episodes in the year prior to NIMH admission, and nonresponders had an average of 2.7 ± .9 episodes in the year prior to NIMH admission. A greater degree of manic dysphoria, which is associated with poor response to lithium (Secunda et al. 1985), tended to be associated with better response to carbamazepine. Age of onset and duration of illness were not associated with antimanic response to carbamazepine in this small sample.

As discussed elsewhere, an increased severity of prior depression appeared to predict acute antidepressant response to carbamazepine (Post and Uhde in press-c). Thus, it appears that both an increased

Table 3. Predictors of Antimanic Response to Carbamazepine

Predictor	Nonresponders (n = 7) $M \pm SEM$	Responders (n = 12) $M \pm SEM$	t
Severity of mania			
Baseline mania ratings	3.4 ± 0.8	8.0 ± 0.4	5.8**
Severity of Manic Dysphoria			
Baseline depression ratings (during manic episode)	4.5 ± 0.8	6.2 ± 0.5	1.9
Rapid Cycling			
Episodes/years ill	1.2 ± 0.3	4.4 ± 1.7	1.4
Episodes in year prior to NIMH admission	2.7 ± 0.9	7.0 ± 1.6	2*
Not associated			
Age of onset (first treatment)	21.0 ± 1.9	21.0 ± 1.7	0
Duration of illness (years)	15.0 ± 4.6	18.0 ± 3.3	0.5

Note. NIMH = National Institute of Mental Health.
*$p < .0001$. **$p < .05$.

severity of acute episodes and a rapidly or continuously cycling pattern are not only not inconsistent with a carbamazepine response but may actually predict it. These data are also consistent with those of Kishimoto et al. (1983) and Okuma et al. (1985), who noted that continuous cycling was associated with carbamazepine response. We did not, however, find that age of onset was associated with response, as they had suggested.

Other pertinent demographic and medical variables that did not appear to predict carbamazepine response in our various series of affectively ill patients include even minor abnormalities on the EEG, a history of para-epileptoid or psychosensory symptoms often reported by patients with complex partial seizures (Bierer et al. 1985; Silberman et al. 1985), and a family history of bipolar illness. Because carbamazepine is an anticonvulsant, one might have predicted that minor EEG aberrations, even those within the normal range, might predict carbamazepine response. This did not appear to be the case in our series of patients and does not appear to be a predictor in relation to other indexes of therapeutic response to this agent. For example, Luchins et al. (1983, 1984) found that carbamazepine was as effective in inhibiting aggressive episodes in patients with and without EEG abnormalities. Similarly, improvement in schizophrenic symptoms with carbamazepine supplementation of neuroleptics may occur in patients with and without EEG abnormalities (Ballenger and Post 1984; Hakola and Laulumaa 1982; Klein et al. 1984; Neppe 1982).

Silberman et al. (1985) rated affectively ill patients for signs and symptoms often reported in patients with temporal lobe epilepsy. These psychosensory and psychomotor symptoms, such as déjà vu, cognitive distortions, illusions, and hallucinatory phenomena, were, in fact, reported by a surprisingly high incidence of our affectively ill patients. In contrast to what we had predicted, however, the incidence of these symptoms appears to be associated with degree of lithium response; our current unpublished data suggest that they are not associated with degree of antidepressant response to carbamazepine (Bierer et al. 1985). A larger series of patients, including manic ones, remains to be studied. P. Grof (personal communication) reported that patients with a family history of primary affective disorder in first-degree relatives are responsive to lithium carbonate and that those without such a history tend to respond to carbamazepine. In our series, we did not find such an association.

The local anesthetic procaine appears to produce some selective activation of limbic system structures in animals, and preliminary evidence from our laboratory (Coppola et al. 1983; Kellner et al. 1985) suggests that it produces selective activation of fast EEG frequencies (26 to 45 Hz) over the temporal lobe. As such, we were interested in assessing whether degree of EEG activation in the temporal lobe might be associated with subsequent response to carbamazepine. Too few affectively ill patients have so far been studied to complete this assessment.

In a series of borderline personality disorder patients studied in collaboration with Cowdry, Gardner, and de Jong (1984), there was no evidence that degree of EEG activation to procaine predicted degree of carbamazepine response; if anything, the trend was in the opposite direction. Thus, taken together, there appear to be few data to support the suggestion that clinical history, EEG, or procaine activation data suggestive of temporal lobe dysfunction predict degree of carbamazepine response.

RELATIONSHIP TO ANTICONVULSANT EFFECTS

Although carbamazepine has useful anticonvulsant effects in temporal lobe seizures (Dalessio 1985; Penry and Daly 1975; Porter and Penry 1978; Ramsay 1983) and in experimental models of limbic epilepsy (Post and Uhde, in press-a, in press-b), it also has a broad spectrum of anticonvulsant effects on seizures in other areas of brain, as summarized in Table 4. Thus, it remains to be determined whether its relatively greater efficacy on limbic system seizures, compared to other anticonvulsants (Albright 1983; Albright and Burnham 1983), is related to its clinical profile. Clearly, carbamazepine prevents seizures in other areas of brain, just as it works in nonictal disorders such as trigeminal neuralgia and some cardiac arrhythmias (Post et al. 1984c). Therefore, it is important not to jump to the conclusion that the efficacy of carbamazepine and related anticonvulsants in mania implies an under-

Table 4. Physiological Effects of Carbamazepine

Dose	Level	Type of Effect	Investigators
0.1 mg/kg, p.o.		decreased Amnesia of elecroconvulsive shock (rat)	Maitre et al. (1984)
0.5 mg/kg, p.o.		picrotoxin (3 mg/kg) low-dose seizures ED_{50}	Koella et al. (1976)
1.0 mg/kg, i.v.		hippocampal ADs; complete block (3 mg/kg i.v.)	Koella et al. (1976)
2.5–5 mg/kg, i.v.	4–9 μg/mL	↓↓ penicillin-focus (rat)	Julien and Hollister (1975)
3 mg/kg, i.p.		↑ firing of locus coeruleus (rat)	Maitre et al. (1984)
5 mg/kg, i.v.		↓ visual cortex focal seizure (cat)	Ito et al. (1977)
5 mg/kg, i.v.		terminates digitalis-induced arrhythmias	Steiner et al. (1970)
6 mg/kg, i.v.		↓ spinal trigeminal nucleus (cat and dog)	Fromm and Killian (1967)
7 mg/kg, i.p.		ED_{50} electroshock (mouse)	Julien and Hollister (1975)
10 mg/kg, p.o.		ED_{50} electroshock (rat)	Koella et al. (1976)
10 mg/kg, i.v.		facilitate segmental inhibition trigeminal n. (cat)	Fromm et al. (1981)
10 mg/kg, i.v.		↓, then ↑ PTP	Theobald et al. (1970)
10 mg/kg, i.v.	6–14 μg/mL	↓ cortical AD duration, threshold (cat)	Julien and Hollister (1975)
10–20 mg/kg, i.p.	3.5–10 μg/mL	No effect PTP (cat)	Julien and Hollister (1975)
15 mg/kg, i.p.		↓ amygdala-kindled seizures > ADs (rat)	Post et al. (1982)
15 mg/kg, i.p.		↓ n. centrum medianum of the thalamus	Hernandez-Peon (1965)
16 mg/kg, i.p.		pentylene tetrazol (metrazol) ED_{50}	Julien and Hollister (1975)
20 mg/kg, i/p.	6–9 μg/mL	↓↓ n. ventralis anterior of the thalamus and lesser effect n.c.m. thal.	Holm et al. (1970)
20 mg/kg, i.m.	4–8 μg/mL	↓ aluminum-oxide (4%) seizures p. central gyrus (rhesus monkeys)	Julien and Hollister (1975)
300 mg/kg, i/p.	12–20 μg/mL	↓ PTP neuromuscular junction (cat) pentylene tetrazol (metrazol) ED_{50}	Koella et al. (1976)
30 mg/kg, i/p.	>15 μg/mL	↓ estrogen-induced spike-wave discharge (cat)	Julien and Hollister (1975)
30–40 mg/kg, i.p.	>15–20 μg/mL	↓ PTP lumbar roots, spinal (cats)	Julien and Hollister (1975)
50–100 mg/kg, p.o.		sedation; ataxia	Koella et al. (1976)
>10 mg/kg, i.v.		No effect cerebellar Purkinje discharges	Julien and Hollister (1975)
>15 mg/kg, i.p.		No prophylaxis of amygdala kindling	Post et al. (1984)
150 mg/kg, p.o.		Strychnine (death) ED_{50}	Koella et al. (1976)
>200 mg/kg, p.o.		High-dose picrotoxin (12 mg/kg) seizures ED_{50}	Koella et al. (1976)
200 mg/kg, p.o.		No Amygdala-kindling prophylaxis (rat)	Baltzer et al. (1981)

Note. AD = after discharge; PTP = posttetanic potentiation.

lying seizure disorder. It may be, however, that similar pharmacological mechanisms mediate its anticonvulsant and psychotropic properties. It is also possible that the anticonvulsant effects of carbamazepine are entirely unrelated to its psychotropic effects. Not only does this suggestion lack parsimony, but as more anticonvulsants with different mechanisms of action are shown to be useful in the treatment of affective disorders (see reviews of Post and Uhde, in press-a; Post et al. 1985a), it becomes increasingly unlikely.

As shown by the work of Albright and Burnham (1983) and Albright (1983), carbamazepine has a relatively strong effect on the ability to suppress both local afterdischarges and elevate the threshold for afterdischarges in limbic areas of the brain (amygdala), compared with similar measures derived from the neocortex. Its profile in this regard is as good as or better than other anticonvulsant treatments in these studies of Albright and associates. The local amygdala afterdischarge is relatively resistant to complete suppression, even with carbamazepine.

The difficulty in suppressing local afterdischarges also extends to the anticonvulsant effects of electroconvulsive shock (ECS) in the rat (Post et al. 1984d, in press-c). ECS in man is an effective antimanic treatment (Small et al. 1982). Paradoxically, the major motor seizures of ECS produce potent anticonvulsant effects. This is discernible in the rat model of amygdala kindling. If rats are kindled once daily with the same stimulation for one second, afterdischarges with increasing duration emerge and spread throughout the brain. Eventually, over a period of several weeks, animals develop full-blown seizures in response to the previously subthreshold stimulation. This classical kindling effect, as originally described by Goddard and associates (1969), is inhibited by pretreatment with ECS in the rat (Post et al. 1984d, in press-c). Again, although ECS potently inhibits the development of the amygdala-kindled seizure, it has only marginal effects on the afterdischarge (Figure 14).

Thus, ECS and other anticonvulsant modalities appear better able to inhibit mechanisms involved in the generalization and spread of seizures than do those that are intimately involved in the

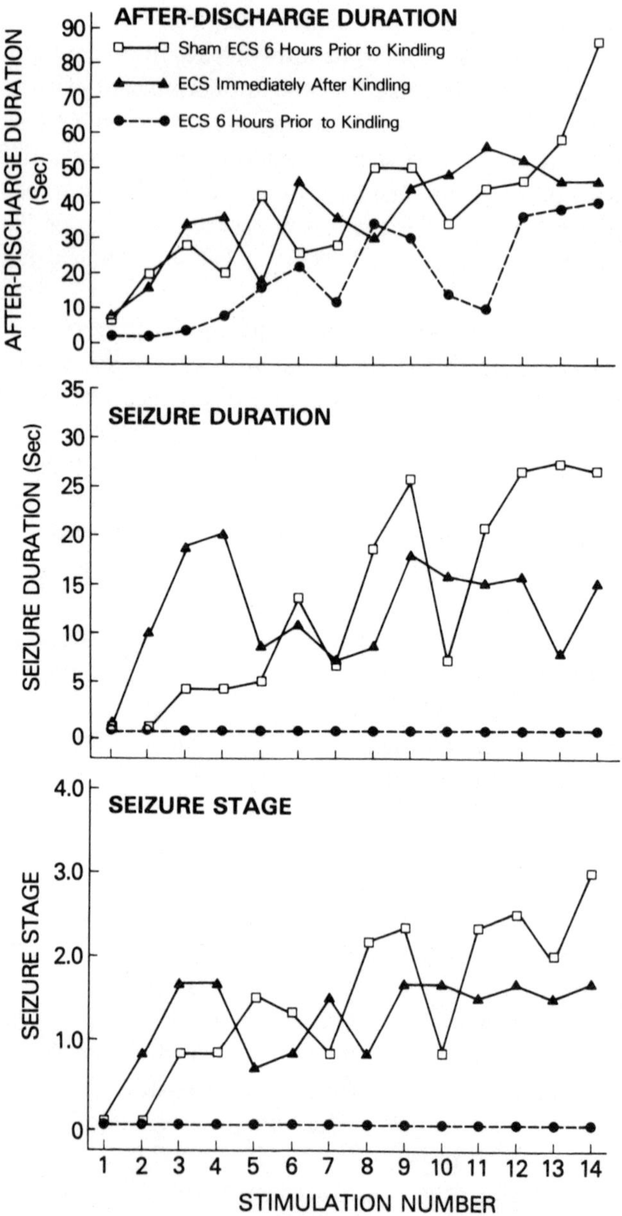

Figure 14. Electroconvulsive seizures inhibit the development of amygdala kindling.

generation of local afterdischarges. We also demonstrated that if animals are fully kindled, a time course of clinically relevant ECS administration to the rat (that is, once daily for seven days) leads to prolonged suppression of amygdala-kindled seizures for up to five days (Post et al. 1984d). These data suggest that a clinical course of ECS may produce anticonvulsant effects in man, a hypothesis that has received direct clinical support in the early observations of a number of workers in the 1930s and 1940s as well as more recently in more controlled observations of Sackeim and associates (1983) in New York. In Figure 12, the potent effects of ECS against the development of amygdala-kindled seizures actually represent an effect of ECS that makes it a more potent anticonvulsant modality than carbamazepine in the rat.

Although carbamazepine inhibits the development of kindling in the cat and nonhuman primates (Wada 1977; Wada et al. 1976), it does not appear to be effective on electrically induced kindling in the rat (Post et al. 1984b). Weiss and Post (unpublished, 1985) recently observed that carbamazepine does, however, markedly inhibit the development of lidocaine-kindled seizures. It is a curiosity (with some potential clinical relevance) that carbamazepine inhibits the development of lidocaine-kindled seizures but is not effective as an anticonvulsant once these seizures become fully manifest. In a parallel and reciprocal fashion, carbamazepine is not effective on the development of electrically kindled seizures in the rat but is an excellent acute anticonvulsant for fully kindled seizures from the amygdala. Pinel (1981) further showed that spontaneous seizures that develop very late after many repeated kindled seizures also respond to different anticonvulsants. For example, phenytoin blocks spontaneous seizures but not kindled seizures, and diazepam shows the opposite effect. Thus, it is apparent that different phases of electrically and chemically kindled seizures respond differentially to anticonvulsants (Figure 15). Similarly, we suggest that different phases in the longitudinal course of affective illness respond differentially to treatment.

These data with carbamazepine also stand in contrast to lithium carbonate, which is not at all effective as an anticonvulsant for amygdala-kindled seizures; that is, it does not inhibit either developing or fully manifested amygdala-kindled seizures (Post et al. 1984b). In contrast, there is some evidence that lithium may alter either acute psychomotor stimulant-induced mood or behavioral activation in animals and humans, and we have preliminary evidence that lithium inhibits the process of behavioral sensitization to repeated doses of cocaine (Post et al. in press-a). That is, lithium may inhibit the process in which repeated administration of low doses of cocaine come to evoke increasingly more profound degrees of psychomotor activation. carbamazepine is not effective in inhibiting this psychomotor stimulant-induced behavioral sensitization. This differential effect on kindling versus sensitization may be of some interest in relation to potential differential responsivity to lithium and carbamazepine in some patients in different phases of manic–depressive illness.

As schematized in Figure 16 there is some evidence over the course of manic–depressive illness that a differential pharmacol-

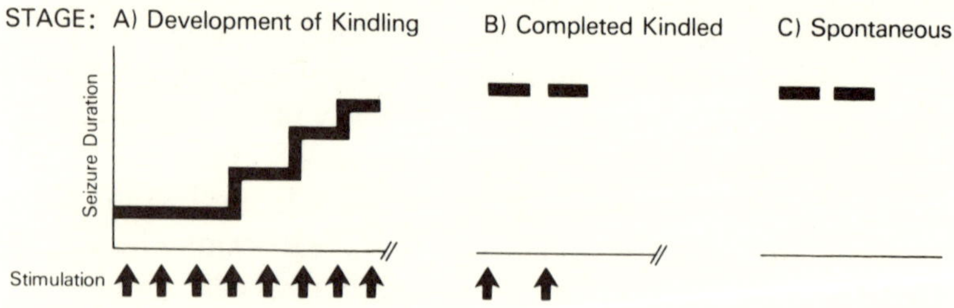

	A) Development of Kindling	B) Completed Kindled	C) Spontaneous
Amygdala Kindling (Electrical)			
Drug	Effectiveness (Rat)		
Diazepam	+++	++	0
Phenytoin	0	+	+++
Carbamazepine	0	+++	?
Lidocaine Kindling (Pharmacological)			
Carbamazepine	+++	0	?
Diazepam	+++	+++	?

Figure 15. Pharmacology of kindling as a function of stimulus type and stage of development.

ogy may be required for effective treatment. Such is readily apparent in the treatment of Parkinson's disease. For example, early in the course of Parkinson's syndrome, levodopa alone is an adequate treatment. But with progression of the underlying neuropathology, changing response to levodopa treatment, or both, breakthrough phenomena need additional treatment with a direct dopamine-receptor agonist such as bromocryptine. In the very late stages of the illness, however, the "on–off" manifestations that occur in treatment with a dopamine agonist are not effectively managed by either levodopa or direct dopamine agonists, and in the latest stages, as dopamine receptors are lost, even combined treatment with direct and indirect agonists is insufficient to manage the illness.

In a parallel fashion (Figure 16), we suggest that lithium alone may be a sufficient treatment for the majority of patients earlier in the course of manic–depressive illness, but with particularly severe cases, as manifested by initial rapid or continuous cycling, or

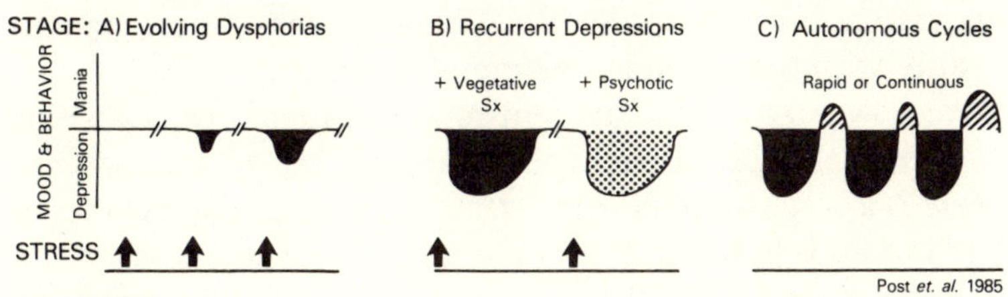

TREATMENT	A) Evolving Dysphorias	B) Recurrent Depressions + Vegetative Sx	B) Recurrent Depressions + Psychotic Sx	C) Autonomous Cycles
Psychotherapy	+++	++		(+)
Benzodiazepines	++	(++)	(+)	
Tricyclics	±	+++	+	– –
MAOI's	±	+++	(+)	– –
ECT		+++	+++	(+)
Tricyclics plus Neuroleptics			+++	
Lithium	±	++	++	(++)
Carbamazepine		(++)	(++)	+++
Lithium plus Carbamazepine				+++

Figure 16. Psychopharmacotherapy of affective illness as a function of type and stage of development.

with progression of the illness and the later emergence of more rapid cycling, some patients may become less responsive to lithium carbonate and require supplemental medications. In these instances, carbamazepine alone or in combination with lithium, or valproic acid in combination with lithium may help attenuate the rapid- or continuous-cycling phase of the illness. In the most severe, recalcitrant forms of the illness, even these two agents in combination may be inadequate, and further supplemental pharmacological manipulations may be indicated.

We have detailed elsewhere the various aspects of manic–depressive illness that appear to evolve progressively over time in a fashion similar to that observed in behavioral sensitization or electrophysiological kindling (Post et al. 1984a, in press-b). We have discussed how the sensitization and kindling perspective may be useful in conceptualizing the apparently dichotomous views of manic–depressive illness as either psychologically or neurobiologically based. In our formulation, we suggest that early in the course of the illness, episodes may occur with psychological precipitants, but later in the illness, episodes may emerge spontaneously with their own autonomous rhythmicity.

We now suggest that different phases of manic–depressive illness may also be differentially pharmacologically responsive. There is a wide range of acute treatments for mania and depression, but until now, there has been little choice among agents for long-term prophylaxis of the illness. The sensitization and kindling paradigms and their differential responsivity to lithium and carbamazepine (and related anticonvulsants) may help provide a theoretical rationale and practical psychopharmacology suggesting that patients in different phases of the evolution of their affective syndromes may need differential pharmacoprophylaxis.

Effects of Carbamazepine on Classical Neurotransmitter and Modulator Substances

Conceptual Background

We will discuss the effects of carbamazepine on each of a series of neurotransmitter and modulator substances thought to be involved in its anticonvulsant, antinociceptive, or psychotropic properties. Whenever possible, we will compare and contrast the effects of carbamazepine to other psychotropic drugs to provide clues to important common mechanisms of action and underlying neurobiochemical substrates of affective dysregulation. In a parallel fashion, one can compare and contrast the effects of carbamazepine with those of other anticonvulsant drugs that do not have the same spectrum of psychotropic effects as carbamazepine.

In beginning this exercise, several caveats are in order, however. The first caveat pertains to whether one is looking for similarities or differences in the biochemical effects of carbamazepine, compared to lithium carbonate. The critical clinical data to clarify this question are not yet available. There is some suggestion of a differential subgroup of responders to carbamazepine and lithium, based either on different populations or on different temporal aspects of their course of illness. If this proves to be the case, then one might actually be looking for differential biochemical actions of these agents rather than a common effect that accounts for their clinical efficacy based on a hypothesized unitary neurotransmitter alteration. We await further clinical data to ascertain whether there is considerable overlap or differentiation in an individual who responds to either drug alone.

Similarly, we must await clarification for the range of anticonvulsants efficacious in affective syndromes. We have preliminary evidence, reviewed elsewhere (Post and Uhde 1983, in press-a; Post et al. 1985a), that anticonvulsants such as valproic acid and clonazepam, if not phenytoin, may be useful in the treatment of some manic–depressive patients. There are no data of which we are aware reporting clinical trials of the petit mal anticonvulsants such as ethosuximide in manic–depressive illness, and this drug has been prominent in inducing alternative psychoses of "forced normalization" (that is, increasing behavioral pathology with better EEG control) in epileptics (Wolf et al. 1984). Thus, we do not have a clinically well-documented rank order of anticonvulsants that are or are not effective in manic–depressive illness with which to compare carbamazepine's biochemical effects. Nonetheless, it is hoped that by comparison of carbamazepine with both other psychotropic agents and other anticonvulsants, with and without efficacy in affective syndromes, that a converging map of the important characteristics for psychotropic effects may be derived.

Effects of Carbamazepine on Noradrenergic Mechanisms

A study of the effects of carbamazepine on noradrenergic metabolism is of particular importance because this system has been implicated in both the underlying dysregulation of manic–depressive illness and in the epilepsies. In addition, there are now several lines of evidence suggesting that the anticonvulsant effects of carbamazepine are importantly linked to noradrenergic effects. Therefore, it remains a likely possibility that these may also be related to its psychotropic properties.

Depletion of norepinephrine with 6-hydroxydopamine substantially reduces the anticonvulsant effects of carbamazepine (Quattrone and Samanin 1977). In a subsequent report, Quattrone et al. (1978) reported that selective depletion of dopamine did not reverse the anticonvulsant effects of carbamazepine, further implicating noradrenergic mechanisms as relevant to the anticonvulsant effects of carbamazepine. Crunelli et al. (1981) found that clonidine, an alpha-2-adrenergic agonist that decreases the firing of the locus coeruleus, reversed the anticonvulsant effects of carbamazepine on maximum electroshock seizures. Moreover, yohimbine, an alpha-2 antagonist that increases the firing of the locus coeruleus, had anticonvulsant effects in this model system. carbamazepine also increases the firing of the locus coeruleus acutely (Olpe and Jones 1983).

We observed opposite effects of clonidine and yohimbine on a different model, that of amygdala-kindled seizures. We found that the anticonvulsant effects of carbamazepine were partially inhibited by yohimbine (10 mg/kg intraperitoneally, or i.p.). These data suggest the possibility that carbamazepine may influence alpha-2-noradrenergic mechanisms that are important, at least, to its anticonvulsant profile and that are possibly related to its psychotropic effects.

Purdy et al. (1977) reported that carbamazepine, which has a tricyclic structure similar to that of imipramine, is a weaker blocker of norepinephrine reuptake than imipramine. These effects appear to occur largely at levels above the therapeutic range of carbamazepine. In support of this notion, Quattrone et al. (1981) found that a 10 mg/kg dose of carbamazepine (which is clinically relevant) was not sufficient to block in vivo reuptake of norepinephrine in rats, as assessed by its inability to protect the noradrenergic system from depletion with 6-hydroxydopamine. In contrast, pretreatment with desmethylimipramine was highly effective in protecting animals from 6-hydroxydopamine.

In addition to carbamazepine's relatively weak effects on blockade of norepinephrine reuptake, Purdy et al. (1977) reported that it blocked stimulated–induced release of norepinephrine in synaptosomal preparations as well as in a rabbit ear artery preparation. Again, there is some question about the potency of carbamazepine for this effect and whether it could occur at clinically relevant concentrations in brain. There is some preliminary evidence that carbamazepine decreases cerebrospinal fluid (CSF) norepinephrine in mania (see Figure 17). In four manic patients, carbamazepine decreased probenecid-induced accumulation of this norepinephrine, compared with pretreatment placebo levels. At the same time, carbamazepine did not significantly alter CSF norepinephrine in depressed patients (Post et al. 1985b), suggesting that it may manifest its ability to decrease norepinephrine only under conditions of high output or release, such as those observed in the manic syndrome (Post et al. 1980a, 1985c). Obviously, this speculation is very preliminary and remains to be confirmed in direct experimental and further clinical observations.

The reported effects of carbamazepine on norepinephrine metabolites and turnover in animal studies are mixed. Only very high levels of carbamazepine increased a 3-methoxy-4-hydroxyphenylglycol (MHPG) sulfate in rat brains (Maitre et al. 1984; Morselli et al. 1977b). This effect, observed at 50 and 100 mg/kg, is not likely to be clinically relevant. carbamazepine (but not valproate, phenobarbitone, phenytoin, or ethosuximide) increases the firing of the locus coeruleus (Olpe and Jones, 1983); this effect was dose related and occurred weakly at 3 mg/kg and was highly significant at 30 mg/kg i.p. Maitre et al. (1984) reported that carbamazepine (100 mg/kg i.p. but not 30 mg/kg) decreased several measures of norepinephrine turnover.

In our patients (Post et al. 1985b), we have observed no signifi-

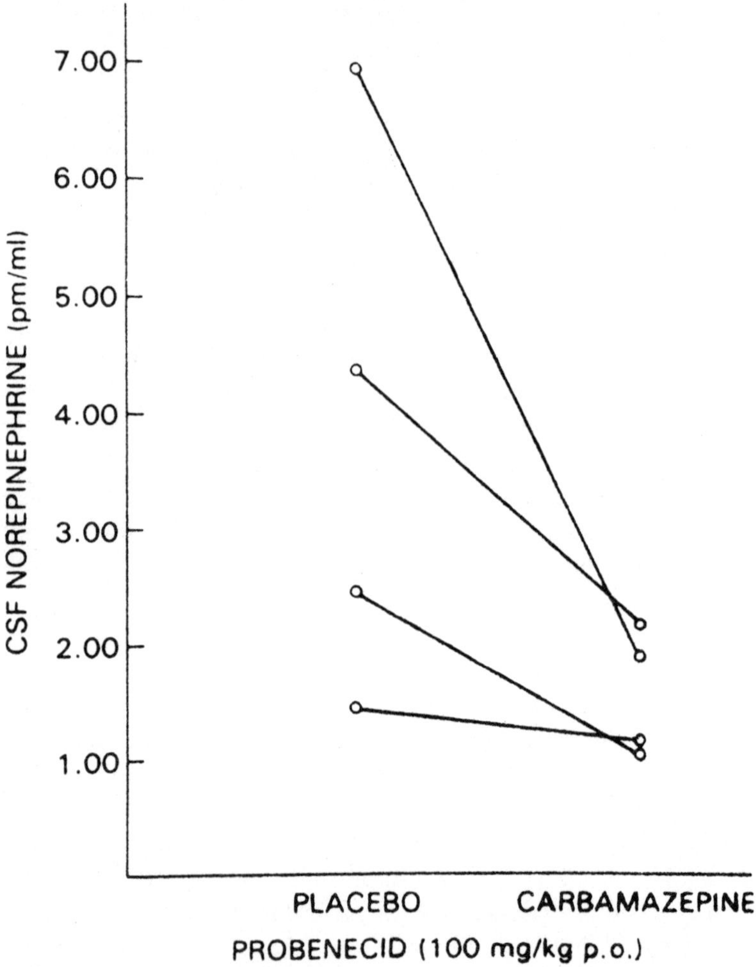

Figure 17. Carbamazepine-induced reduction of cerebrospinal fluid norepinephrine in mania.

cant effect of carbamazepine on CSF MHPG. These data contrast with those seen with a variety of other tricyclic compounds that significantly decrease CSF MHPG (Insel et al. 1985). DeLorenzo (1983) reported that carbamazepine decreased calcium/calmodulin-induced norepinephrine secretion but not basal release of norepinephrine (Kowalik et al. 1984). Palmer et al. (1979) and Lewin and Bleck (1977) also reported that carbamazepine inhibited noradrenergic-stimulated cyclic adenosine monophosphate (AMP) production. Thus, it is possible that this drug may affect noradrenergic mechanisms at a subreceptor level that may be functionally important. carbamazepine does not interact with alpha-2 or beta-receptor mechanisms directly (Marangos et al. 1983). In addition, Marangos et al. (in press) and Joffe, Sulzer, and Post (unpublished, 1985) indicated that chronic treatment with carbamazepine in the rat is not sufficient to decrease beta-adrenergic-receptor density, as has been reported to be characteristic of many other but not all antidepressant compounds.

In summary, carbamazepine appears to have a complex effect on a variety of noradrenergic mechanisms, including weak blockade of reuptake, blockade of release, and stimulation of firing of the locus coeruleus, yet there is evidence of its decreasing norepinephrine turnover in high doses. Alpha-2-noradrenergic mechanisms may be important to its anticonvulsant effects, but beta-adrenergic effects appear to be less important. Thus, the noradrenergic system remains a very active candidate for potential psychotropic effects of this drug.

Carbamazepine's Effects on Serotonergic Mechanisms

Although considerable evidence is still supportive of a serotonergic hypothesis of depression, the data are relatively more scant regarding the role of this neurotransmitter system in the treatment of mania. There is some suggestion that pretreatment with tryptophan or other serotonergic precursors, such as 5-hydroxytryptophan (5HTP), may be useful in the management of acute mania or longer term prophylaxis in manic and depressive illness (van Praag 1984). In this regard, carbamazepine has been reported to be the only anticonvulsant of the series tested to increase plasma tryptophan in epileptic patients (Pratt et al. 1984). It does not, however, increase brain tryptophan levels in the rat or brain levels of serotonin or its metabolite, 5-hydroxyindoleacetic acid (5-HIAA) (Elhwuegi 1978; Morselli et al. 1977b; Pratt et al. 1985), except for increases in 5-HIAA at one isolated point after high doses (50 mg/kg). These data are consistent with our own observations (Post et al. 1978a, 1984c) that carbamazepine does not significantly affect baseline levels or probenecid-induced accumulations of 5-HIAA in the CSF of affectively ill patients. Nonetheless, because of the effects of carbamazepine on plasma tryptophan, the serotonergic system cannot be ruled out as a potential mediator of carbamazepine's psychotrophic properties, Serotonergic lesions, depletions, or both do not appear to affect carbamazepine's anticonvulsant profile, however (Crunelli et al. 1979; Quattrone et al. 1978).

Effects on Dopaminergic Metabolism

The effects of carbamazepine on dopaminergic mechanisms are of considerable clinical and theoretical import. As previously noted, carbamazepine has a time course of acute antimanic efficacy parallel to that of neuroleptics. In contrast to these agents, however, the evidence that carbamazepine does not block dopamine receptors and, consequently, does not produce many of the associated biochemical and behavioral changes characteristic of this class of compounds is now substantial. It does not increase rat brain homovanillic acid (HVA) or other measures of dopamine turnover (see reviews in Post et al. 1984c, in press-e). It does not markedly increase plasma prolactin. Consistent with these observations, we found that carbamazepine did not alter baseline levels of HVA in the CSF of our affectively ill patients. In fact, probenecid-induced accumulations of HVA (which may provide a better measure of dopamine turnover) were significantly decreased on carbamazepine (Post et al. in press-e).

As a consequence of this lack of effect of carbamazepine on

dopamine receptors and the associated biochemical changes typically produced by neuroleptics, carbamazepine does not share the neuroleptics' liability of producing acute parkinsonian side effects or the longer term problem of tardive dyskinesia. Thus, one might consider use of carbamazepine for the supplemental treatment of acute mania when lithium is not sufficient to control profound manic excitement, agitation, or aggressiveness, or all three.

If carbamazepine does demonstrate an acute antimanic response, it may then also pave the way for longer term prophylaxis. If neuroleptic supplementation of lithium is used for the treatment of acute mania, it may, nevertheless, be worth considering substituting carbamazepine for longer term treatment to avoid the potential for tardive dyskinesia. We are not aware of reports of tardive dyskinesia produced with carbamazepine, despite the experience with this drug for several decades in the treatment of trigeminal neuralgia and epilepsy.

Carbamazepine has been reported to decrease dopamine turnover in some animal studies (Waldmeier et al. 1984), consistent with our indirect CSF measure of turnover in affectively ill patients. This might indicate that carbamazepine has effects more parallel to those of dopamine agonists, such as piribedil or bromocryptine, that appear to decrease HVA (Post et al. 1978b). Although the literature is not robust in this regard, there is some indication that dopamine agonists, perhaps particularly in low doses, may be effective in the treatment of some manic syndromes (Jimerson and Post 1984). Thus, it will be of particular interest to elucidate further the mechanisms of carbamazepine's effects on dopamine turnover and to assess more specifically whether it has any agonist properties.

Irrespective of its precise effects on this system, we did find that pretreatment levels of HVA in CSF were associated with the degree of subsequent antidepressant response to carbamazepine (Post et al. in press-e). Those with lower initial levels responded best to carbamazepine. This relationship was dependent, however, on several patients with the lowest HVA levels who showed the best response; we have similarly observed this relationship with other treatments of depression, including the dopamine agonist piribedil (Post et al. 1978b), and the acute antidepressant effects of one night of sleep deprivation (Gerner et al. 1979). Similarly, van Praag and Korf (1975), van Scheyen et al. (1977), and M. Asberg (personal communication, September 1985) have found the relationship between low HVA and subsequent antidepressant response. Thus, the reliability and specificity of the finding that low HVA predicts response to carbamazepine remains to be studied further.

Blockade of dopamine receptors clearly does not appear to be the mode of action of carbamazepine in the treatment of acute mania. What other systems remain candidates? In addition to norepinephrine and serotonin, which we have already reviewed, other possibilities will be discussed.

Effects of Carbamazepine on γ-Aminobutyric Acid Mechanisms

One of the potential candidates for carbamazepine's antimanic effects is its ability to decrease dopamine turnover, presumably as a result of γ-aminobutyric-acid-agonist properties. Bernasconi (1982) reported that carbamazepine as well as valproic acid, propranolol, and lithium decreased GABA turnover. The effects of carbamazepine are more prominent in the hippocampus than the cortex; significant effects, however, appear to occur only with doses of carbamazepine that are beyond those that are clinically relevant; that is, the ED_{50} value was 75 mg/kg oral carbamazepine for the decrease in γ-aminobutyric acid (GABA) synthesis in the hippocampus and 90 mg/kg in the cortex. As summarized in Table 5, different effects of carbamazepine on brain levels of GABA have been reported. In our affectively ill patients, we found no effect of carbamazepine on GABA levels in CSF. Carbamazepine does not appear to affect binding at the GABA receptor (Marangos et al. 1983), does not affect the release of GABA (Skerritt and Johntson 1983), and does not alter GABA responses electrophysiologically (MacDonald et al. 1985).

Potential interactions of carbamazepine with $GABA_b$ mechanisms were suggested by the close structural similarity and parallel

Table 5. Effects of Carbamazepine on GABA Mechanisms

Measure	Effect	Tissue	Species	Dose	Investigators
GABA levels	no change	brain slices	mouse	15 mg/kg	Minchin and Iverson (1976)[a]
GABA levels	no change	brain slices	mouse	N.I.	Varotto et al. (1981)
GABA levels	no change	mesc. PAG	rat	5 mg/kg × 3 days	Hitchcock and Teixiera (1982)
GABA levels	no change	cerebrospinal fluid	human	800 mg/day	Post et al. (1980)
GABA uptake	no change	slices or glial	rat	N.I.	Minchin and Iverson (1976)[a]
GABA-T	slight	cortex	rat	N.I.	Minchin and Iverson (1976)[a]
GABA-T	slight	whole brain homogenates	mouse	0.1–2/mM	Sawaya et al. (1975)
SSAD	slight	whole brain homogenates	mouse	0.1–2.5/mM	Sawaya et al. (1975)
SSAD	slight	mesc. PAG	rat	5 mg/kg × 3 days	Hitchcock and Teixeira (1982)
Glutamate dehydrogenase	slight	mesc. PAG	rat	5 mg/kg × 3 days ED_{50}	Hitchcock and Teixeira (1982)
GABA turnover	slight	hippocampus	rat	75 mg/kg p.o.	Bernasconi (1982)
^{3}H-muscimol binding	no change	forebrain homogenates	rat	$K_I > 200\mu M$	Marangos et al. (1983)

[a]Cited in Koella et al. (1976).

Note. GABA = Gamma-aminobutyric acid; GABA–T = GABA transaminase; mesc. PAG = mesencephalic periacqueductal gray; SSAD = Succinic semialdehyde dehydrogenase; N.I. = not indicated.

effects of carbamazepine and the prototypic $GABA_b$ ligand baclofen on activity of the trigeminal nucleus. In addition to these similarities, Terrence et al. (1983) reported that the inactive d-isomer of baclofen reverses the effects of both l-baclofen and carbamazepine on this trigeminal nucleus preparation thought to be a good model for trigeminal neuralgia. On the basis of these data, Terrence et al. postulated that the therapeutic effects of carbamazepine and baclofen in trigeminal neuralgia might be mediated through $GABA_b$ mechanisms.

We conducted similar studies of the interaction of d-baclofen with carbamazepine on amygdala-kindled seizures. In contrast to the trigeminal nucleus model, we did not find l-baclofen (10 mg/kg) an effective anticonvulsant against amygdala kindling, nor was d-baclofen (10 mg/kg) able to block the anticonvulsant effects of carbamazepine. Therefore, there is little evidence for direct involvement of $GABA_b$ mechanisms in the anticonvulsant properties of carbamazepine, as elucidated by the amygdala-kindling model. The effects of chronic carbamazepine on $GABA_b$ receptors in the frontal cortex remain to be studied, particularly in light of the report of Lloyd (in press) that a variety of antidepressant modalities, including tricyclic antidepressants, monoamine oxidase inhibitors, and ECS, significantly increase $GABA_b$ receptor binding in the frontal cortex of rats. Thus, it remains a possibility that $GABA_b$ receptor mechanisms might be associated with the psychotropic properties of carbamazepine, even though this is unlikely to account for its anticonvulsant effects.

Effects of Carbamazepine on Benzodiazepine Receptor Mechanisms

Carbamazepine is quite weak in its interactions with the classical benzodiazepine receptor site, as marked by ^{3}H-diazepam or ^{3}H-beta-carboline binding. It is more potent in its interactions with the so-called peripheral-type (P-type) benzodiazepine binding sites in the brain, as marked by the binding of ^{3}H-Ro5-4864 (Marangos et al. 1983). Consistent with these biochemical data on relative potencies for receptor binding, we obtained evidence across a variety of studies that suggest that carbamazepine may have physiologically relevant interactions with the P-type binding site in the brain (Weiss et al. 1985b, in press). Because this binding site no longer appears to be an inactive "acceptor" site but has been linked to convulsant and anxiogenic mechanisms in animals (Mizoule et al. in press), the potent interaction of carbamazepine with this site may be of considerable interest in relation to carbamazepine's profile as an anticonvulsant and mood stabilizer with potential antianxiety effects.

We have dissected the differential anticonvulsant mechanisms of action of carbamazepine and diazepam using ligands that have relatively selective effects on the "central-type" (C-type) and P-type benzodiazepine receptor sites. Ro-15-1788 antagonizes benzodiazepine effects at the central site. In low doses, Ro5-4864 has selective effects for the P-type benzodiazepine binding site, and in higher doses, it also affects a picrotoxinin binding site thought to be closely associated with the chloride channel in the benzodiazepine–GABA receptor complex. Its actions at this picrotoxinin site are thought to mediate the convulsant effects of Ro5-4864, and its physiological effects at lower doses are thought to be exclusively involved at the P-type binding site. Another compound, PK-11195, has effects opposite to those of Ro5-4864 at the P-type binding site, so reversal of Ro5-4864's effects by PK-11195 would implicate the P-type benzodiazepine receptor mechanisms rather than those at the picrotoxinin binding site because PK-11195 is inactive at the picrotoxinin site.

As iilustrated in Figure 18, Ro-15-1788 reverses the anticonvulsant effects of diazepam, but Ro5-4864 is without significant effect. In contrast, Ro-15-1788 does not reverse the anticonvulsant effects of carbamazepine, suggesting that this drug does not have physiologically important actions at the classical C-type benzodiazepine site. Ro5-4864 does, however, reverse the anticonvulsant effects of carbamazepine, and this inhibition is itself reversible by PK-11195 (Figure 19); both findings strongly suggest that carbamazepine has important actions involving this P-type binding site. The carbamazepine metabolite carbamazepine-10,11-epoxide, which possesses anticonvulsant effects and was found to be clinically

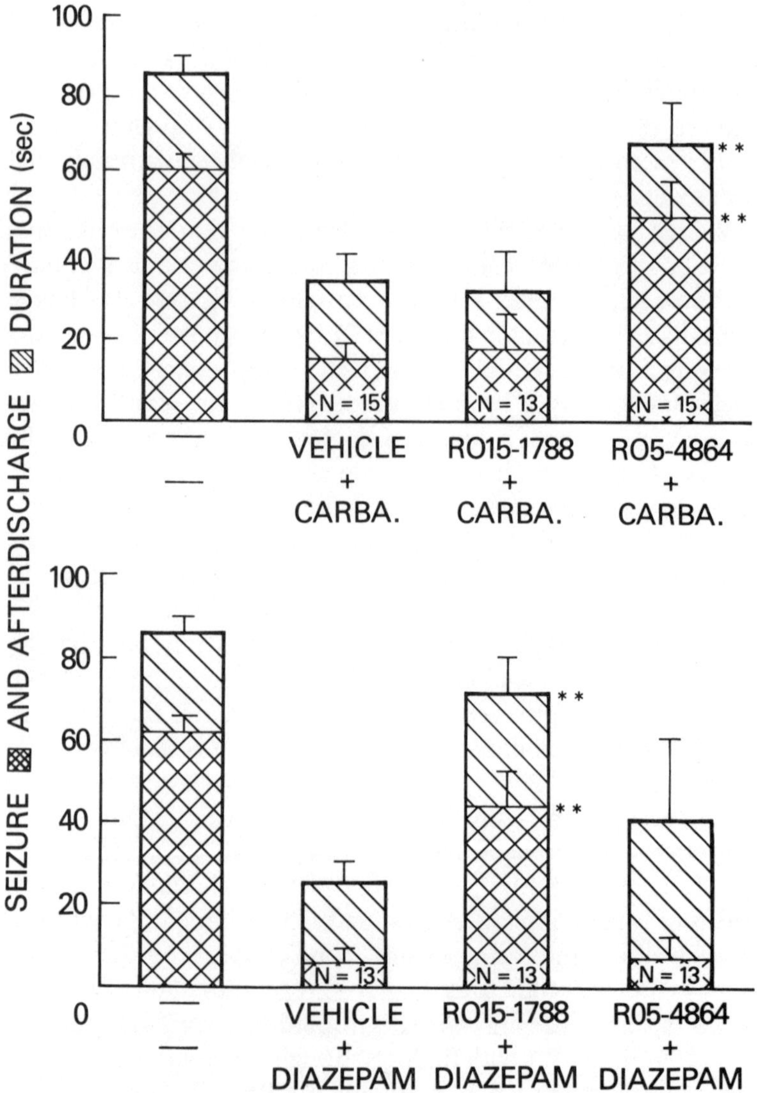

Figure 18. Effects of Ro15-1788 and Ro5-4864 on anticonvulsant activity of carbamazepine and diazepam.

useful in the treatment of trigeminal neuralgia (Tomson and Bertilsson 1984), also has effects on amygdala-kindled seizures that are reversed by Ro5-4864 (Figure 20).

The reversal by Ro5-4864 of the anticonvulsant effects of carbamazepine and its 10,11-epoxide metabolite are not due to a differential potency of these compounds, compared with diazepam. This is documented by the fact that another proconvulsant compound, the beta-carboline derivative B-CCM, not having actions through the P-type benzodiazepine receptor system but having actions with the C-type system, does not reverse the anticonvulsant effects of carbamazepine but does reverse the anticonvulsant effects of diazepam. These and related arguments, discussed in detail elsewhere (Weiss et al. 1985b, in press), suggest that the effects of Ro5-4864 in reversing the anticonvulsant effects of carbamazepine are not due to nonspecific, proconvulsant effects of Ro5-4864. Instead, they suggest that carbamazepine may be exerting physiologically important effects through this system. In summary, these studies provide evidence that at least the anticonvulsant effects of carbamazepine may be mediated through P-type benzodiazepine receptor mechanisms.

Carbamazepine's Interaction With Adenosine Receptors

Carbamazepine has been reported to potently inhibit binding of tritiated adenosine agonists and antagonists to adenosine receptors (Marangos et al. 1983; Skerritt et al. 1982, 1983a, 1983b; Weir et al. 1984). Carbamazepine at clinically relevant concentrations (25 μm) significantly inhibited ^{3}H-phenylisopropyl adenosine binding by 20 percent, but phenytoin, phenobarbital, ethosuximide, trimethodiadone, and sodium valproate were without significant effect. Marangos et al. (1983) found that carbamazepine inhibited binding of agonists and antagonists at the adenosine receptor but that there was no significant relationship between the ability of structural analogues of carbamazepine to inhibit maximum electroshock seizures in mice and the ability to displace adenosine binding in rat brain membranes. These data indirectly suggest that

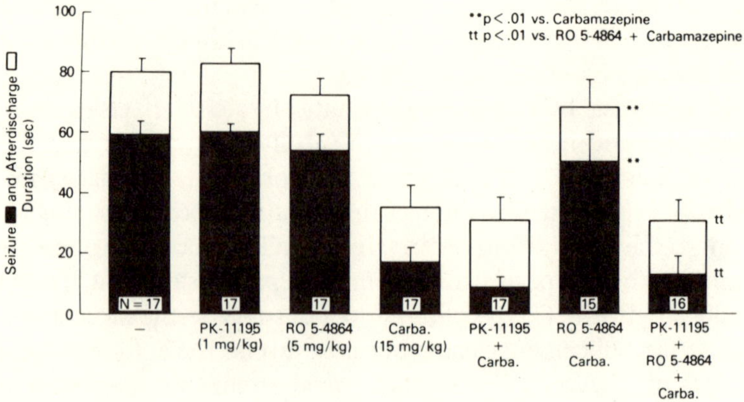

Figure 19. Peripheral benzodiazepine ligands reverse and reinstate the anticonvulsant effect of carbamazepine.

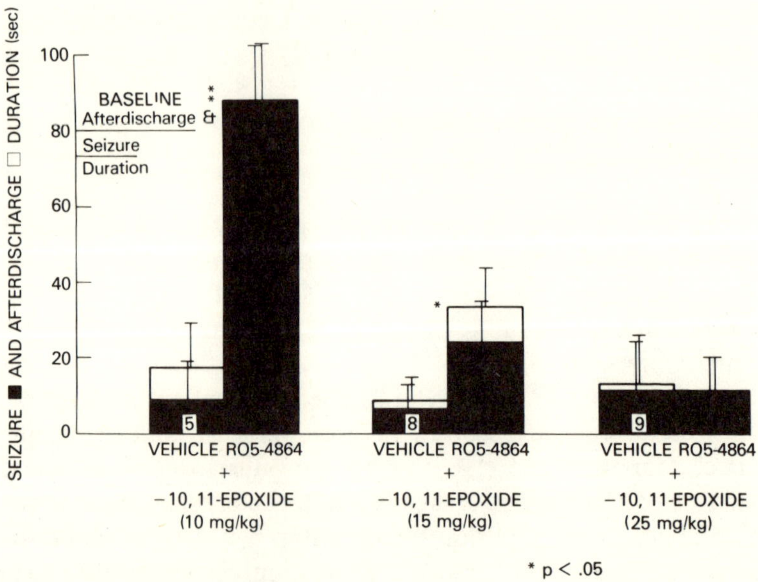

Figure 20. Reversal of the anticonvulsant effects of carbamazepine-10,11-epoxide by Ro5-4864.

the anticonvulsant effects of carbamazepine are not closely related to adenosine binding characteristics. These data are further supported by the lack of significant effects of adenosine antagonists in reversing the anticonvulsant effects of carbamazepine on amygdala-kindled seizures (Weiss et al. 1985a). (See Figure 21.)

One would expect carbamazepine to have a profile opposite to that of caffeine because the latter is a potent antagonist of adenosine receptors and is proconvulsant and anxiogenic; carbamazepine is anticonvulsant and anxiolytic. In some biochemical and physiological tests, however, carbamazepine does not appear to have the predicted adenosine-agonist profile (Table 6). For example, Marangos et al. (in press) found that chronic treatment with carbamazepine, like that with chronic caffeine, significantly increases adenosine-receptor binding, an effect that lasts for several weeks.

Table 6 reviews the differential effects of carbamazepine on adenosine systems, which suggest that it has either agonist or antagonist properties. The mixture and balance of results suggest the possibility that carbamazepine may have mixed agonist–antagonist effects, and the physiological relevance of the potent interactions of carbamazepine on this system remains to be elucidated. Although sedative side effects, anticonvulsant effects, and anxiolytic effects of carbamazepine are potential candidates for adenosine-agonist-like properties, these effects are unlikely to be attributable to pure adenosine properties in light of the lack of potent effects of carbamazepine that might be expected or that occur with other adenosine agonists.

Glutamate

Skerritt et al. (1983a) reported that carbamazepine only weakly affected glutamate binding using (^{3}H)-L-glutamate on frozen and thawed rat brain preparations. S. Nadi (personal communication, 1985), however, reported a more potent effect of carbamazepine on glutamate binding using (^{3}H)-4-aminophosphono butyric acid (New England Nuclear) on freshly prepared rat brain membranes. Vogler and Zieglgansberger (1985) reported that carbamazepine

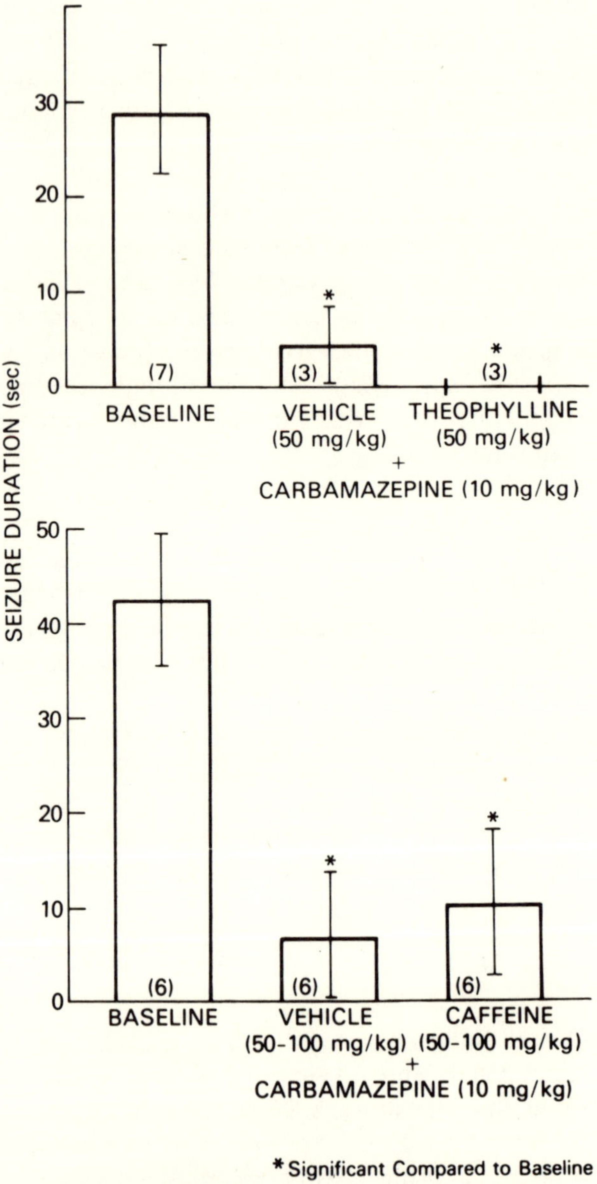

Figure 21. Adenosine antagonists do not reverse the anticonvulsant effects of carbamazepine on amygdala-kindled seizures.

inhibited both spontaneous and L-glutamate-evoked firing in extracellular recordings from single cortical neurons in halothane-anesthetized rats. Other recent physiological evidence suggests that carbamazepine may also alter glutamate efflux. Olpe et al. (1985) reported that carbamazepine reduced (^{3}H)-L-glutamate efflux induced by potassium and veratridine from hippocampal slices with a threshold concentration of 10 μM. The drug again (in concentrations up to 400 μM) failed to affect sodium-dependent binding of (^{3}H)-L-glutamate to hippocampal synaptic membranes, however.

These data suggest that carbamazepine inhibits glutamate release in vitro and may do so in vivo by mechanisms that are not likely to involve a direct effect on glutamate receptors. This inhibition of glutamate release appears to be relatively selective be-

Table 6. Carbamazepine Effects on Adenosine Mechanisms

Agonistlike	Antagonistlike
Sedative; not caffeinelike stimulant; anticonvulsant	More potent on antagonist binding (Marangos et al. 1983; Skerritt et al. 1983a)
Theophylline blocked the inhibition by carbamazepine of guinea pig ileum contractions (Sherritt et al. 1983b)	Affinity for [^{3}H]-PIA or [^{3}H]-CHA; not affected by GTP (Skerritt et al. 1983a; Weir et al. 1984)
Theophylline blocked the anticonvulsant effects of carbamazepine on tonic-extension component of PTZ seizures (Skerritt et al. 1983b)	Inhibits adenosine-mediated c-AMP accumulation (Lewin and Bleck 1977; Skerritt et al. 1983a; Weir et al. 1984)
No potentiation of caffeine-induced running (Weiss et al. 1985a)	Chronic administration causes upregulation of adenosine receptors (Marangos et al. in press)
	Adenosine antagonists do not reverse anticonvulsant effects of carbamazepine on amygdala kindling (Weiss et al. 1985)
	Carbamazepine failed to potentiate adenosine, and high doses (60 mg/kg) weakly blocked adenosine depression of unit firing (Phillis et al. 1981)

Note. [^{3}H]-PIA = ^{3}H-phenylisopropyl adenosine; [^{3}H]-CHA = ^{3}H-cyclohexyladenosine; GTP = guanosine triphosphate; c-AMP = c-adenosine monophosphate; PTZ = pentylenetetrazole.

cause release of GABA and d-aspartate from cerebral minislices is not affected by carbamazepine (Skerritt and Johnston 1983).

Should these data be replicated, it would raise the interesting possibility that inhibition of release of an excitatory neurotransmitter as well as potentiation of inhibitory mechanisms could be involved in the mechanism of action of carbamazepine either in epilepsy or affective illness. This issue should be of considerable import in light of recent evidence linking glutamatergic transmission to seizure processes (Meldrum and Chapman 1983).

Interaction of Carbamazepine With Sodium Channels

Schauf et al. (1974) reported that high concentrations of carbamazepine (0.25 to 1.0 μM) reduced both sodium and potassium conductances of voltage-clamped Myxicola giant axons. These effects were dose dependent and slightly more pronounced than the sodium channel. More recent data (Willow and Catterall 1982) provide additional biochemical evidence of carbamazepine's interaction with sodium channels. These investigators found that phenytoin (IC_{50} = 40 μM) and carbamazepine (IC_{50} = 131 μM) inhibited the binding of (^{3}H)-batrachotoxinin A 20-alpha-benzoate (in addition to veratridine, a marker for type 2 sodium channels, which regulate activation of sodium channels. Type 1, which is marked by tedrotoxin and saxitoxin, inhibits transport; Type 3, marked by scorpion toxin, inhibits inactivation.

The subsequent work of Willow et al. (1985) further supports the physiological relevance of this finding. They showed that half-maximal inhibition of sodium currents in mouse neuroblastoma cells occurred at 30 μM for carbamazepine and phenytoin. The effects of carbamazepine increased under conditions of rapid neuronal firing and depolarization, the effects of each being additive. These situations might be found in nervous tissue involved in epilepsy and trigeminal neuralgia (if not also in affective illness). The voltage-dependent and frequency-dependent effects would, thus, provide a potential basis for specific inhibition of neurons in an epileptic focus (Willow et al. 1985).

Additional confirmation of this suggestion comes from a recent study by MacDonald et al. (1985), working with a preparation involving high-frequency sustained repetitive firing (SRF) in mouse neurons in primary dissociated cell culture. MacDonald and associates found that carbamazepine, phenytoin, and valproic acid limited SRF but did not alter the effects of iontophoretically applied GABA. Thus, the effect does not appear to involve synaptic transmission. They concluded that action-potential repolarization is a combination of inactivation of the sodium current and activation of delayed outward potassium current. The maximal rate of rise of the action potential was modified by carbamazepine only under conditions of a sustained train of action potentials and not following a single action potential. Like Willow et al. (1985), they concluded that this effect of carbamazepine was "use dependent" and "frequency dependent" (occurring only with repetitive activation) as well as time dependent. They, too, noted the voltage dependency of the effect. They reported that this effect of carbamazepine occurred not only in spinal cord neurons but also in cortical and hippocampal neurons, suggesting the generality of this mechanism.

Taken together, the data of Willow et al. (1985) and MacDonald et al. (1985) suggest a mechanism by which the anticonvulsants such as carbamazepine and phenytoin leave normal electrophysiological processes generally unaltered but, under depolarizing and rapid-firing conditions thought to be associated with epilepsy, may be increasingly effective in stabilizing neurons through greater inhibition of sodium fluxes (Willow et al. 1985).

As discussed in detail elsewhere (Post, in press), it remains to be demonstrated whether any aspect of manic–depressive illness is similarly associated with paroxysmal neural firing. To the extent that it is, there remains a possibility that a nonsynaptic stabilization of repetitive neural firing mediated through mechanisms of sodium channels could also be of clinical and physiological relevance in affective dysregulation.

Naylor et al. (1984) suggested that vanadium levels may be raised in manic–depressive illness and, consequently, inhibit sodium potassium adenosine triphosphatase (ATPase) in erythrocytes of patients with affective illness. Naylor et al. (1985) reported that carbamazepine reversed the inhibition of sodium potassium ATPase produced by vanadate. The clinical relevance of this observation remains to be established.

Interaction of Carbamazepine With Cyclic Nucleotides

There is considerable interest in the possible effects of carbamazepine on adenylate cyclase activity, particularly in light of the postulated role of cyclic nucleotides in seizures and affective illness (Palmer 1985) and the potent inhibitory effects of lithium on adenylate cyclase (Belmaker et al. 1984; Zohar et al. 1982). For several animal studies, researchers reported that carbamazepine decreased concentration of cyclic AMP in the brain (Ferrendelli and Kinscherf 1977; Ferrendelli et al. 1979; Lust et al. 1976, 1978; Nistico 1977) or CSF (Myllyla 1976; Myllyla et al. 1976). Palmer et al. (1979) reported that carbamazepine was the only anticonvulsant tested that decreased steady-state levels of cyclic AMP in the cerebral cortex and cerebellum, although all anticonvulsants tested decreased pentylenetetrazole-induced increases in cyclic AMP studied in vivo. In tissue slices from mouse cortex, carbamazepine also decreased cyclic-AMP accumulations following stimulation with norepinephrine, adenosine, potassium, veratridine, and ouabain (Palmer et al. 1979). In a broken cell preparation of mouse and rat cerebral cortex, Palmer (1979) found carbamazepine to inhibit dopamine-induced and norepinephrine-induced accumulations of cyclic AMP. These findings are consistent with those of Lewin and Bleck (1977), who reported that carbamazepine was the most potent anticonvulsant studied in decreasing norepinephrine-induced cyclic-AMP accumulations in rat cortical slices. Ferrendelli and Kinscherf (1979) and Palmer et al. (1981) reported that carbamazepine decreased accumulations of cyclic guanylic acid (GMP) induced by veratridine and ouabain, respectively.

In the only clinical study of which we are aware, we found no significant effect of carbamazepine on basal levels of cyclic AMP and cyclic GMP in CSF of our affectively ill patients, although probenecid-induced accumulations of cyclic GMP were significantly reduced during carbamazepine treatment, compared with medication-free conditions, with a similar trend evident for cyclic-AMP accumulations (Post et al. 1982b).

Taken together, these preclinical and clinical data suggest the possibility that carbamazepine may exert some of its spectrum of therapeutic efficacy by inhibition of cyclic nucleotide formation stimulated by a variety of agents. Because this mechanism has been postulated as important to the antimanic effects of lithium carbonate, this potential mechanism of action of carbamazepine deserves further clinical and basic investigation.

Calcium Channels and Fluxes

We have observed that carbamazepine significantly decreases serum (Joffe et al. in press) but not CSF calcium (Post et al. 1985d), although the mechanism of this effect and its clinical relevance have not been elucidated. Nonetheless, a variety of indirect data suggest that carbamazepine may have important interactions with calcium fluxes. Adenosine, P-type benzodiazepine, and $GABA_b$ receptors (at each of which carbamazepine appears to act as already discussed) have been closely linked to calcium receptors or channel fluxes (Post et al. 1985d). Winkel and Lux (1985) reported that clinically relevant concentrations of carbamazepine reduced calcium currents to 30 percent of normal in voltage-clamped Helix neurons. They did not observe notable effects on sodium or potassium currents in this preparation and suggested that carbamazepine might act through its effects on calcium.

Although carbamazepine does not displace binding at calcium channels (Marangos et al. 1983), its interactions with transmitter systems linked to calcium fluxes (adenosine, P-type benzodiazepine, and $GABA_b$) make this mechanism a potential candidate for the antimanic effects of carbamazepine. Interest in this proposition should also be enhanced by the recent suggestion of the antimanic effects of calcium-channel blockers such as verapamil (Dose and Emrich, 1985; Dubovsky and Franks 1983).

EFFECTS OF CARBAMAZEPINE ON NEUROENDOCRINE AND PEPTIDE SYSTEMS

Effects of Carbamazepine on Opiate Mechanisms

Potential interactions of carbamazepine with endogenous opiate systems in the brain are of focal interest from several different perspectives. Carbamazepine is a potent agent in inhibiting trigeminal neuralgia and other paroxysmal pain syndromes, even though it is not an opiatelike analgetic. Alterations in opiate mechanisms have been postulated as important in affective illness, with many parallels drawn between the euphorogenic and activating effects of opiates and similar alterations in mania (Cohen and Pickar 1981).

Carbamazepine pretreatment has been reported to enhance opiate-induced running activity in mice (Katz and Schmaltz 1979). A similar potentiation of opiate-induced running was also seen with phenytoin and valproic acid. In our basic and clinical studies, we have not found evidence of a direct interaction of carbamazepine with opiate mechanisms. We measured total opiate-binding activity in the CSF of affectively ill patients before and during carbamazepine treatment. There was no effect of carbamazepine on this global measure of CSF total opiate binding in 17 patients (Post et al. 1981).

We also assessed the effects of carbamazepine on the baseline and morphine-induced tail-flick and paw-lick (hot plate) latencies in the rat. Again, no direct effect was observed following either acute or chronic (10 days) administration at doses previously shown to be effective on other measures, such as kindled seizures (see Figure 22). Only at the highest dose of morphine (10 mg/kg i.p.) did carbamazepine significantly potentiate the paw-lick response; this was probably an artifact because the rats were ataxic at this dose combination. Because anticonvulsants particularly effective in the treatment of petit mal epilepsy appear to interact with endogenous enkephalin systems in the brain, further study of the nature of the interaction of carbamazepine with opiate mechanisms appear to be indicated. The potentiation by carbamazepine

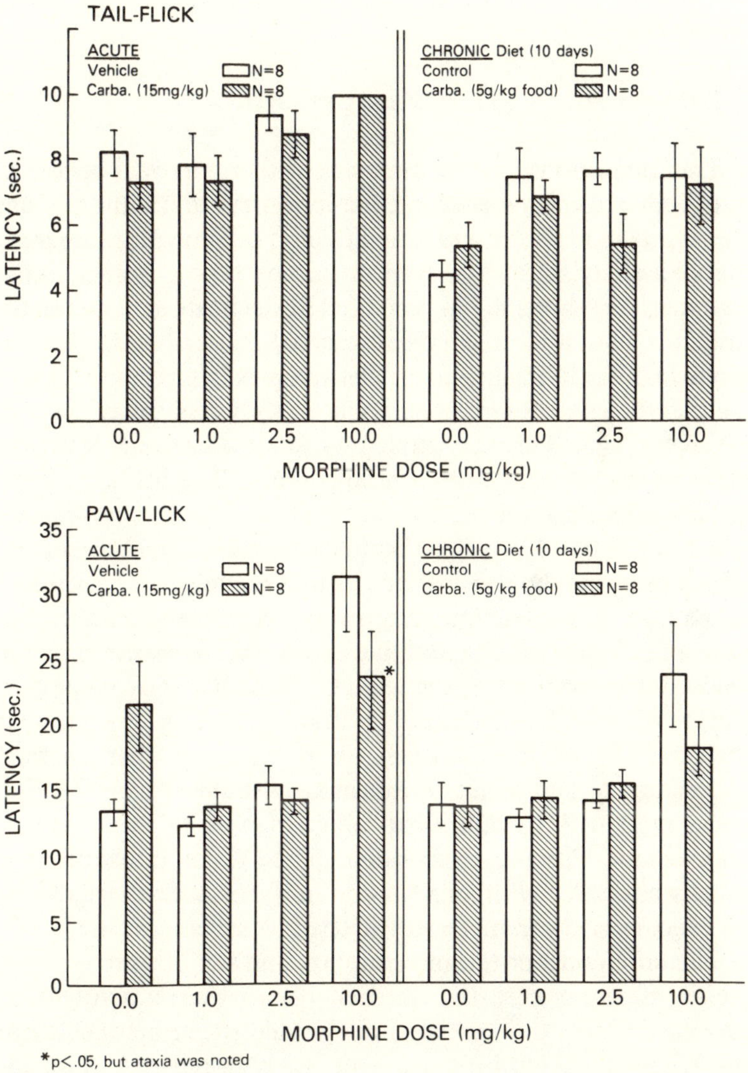

Figure 22. Lack of effect of carbamazepine on morphine-induced analgesia.

of opiate-induced running in the mouse was not paralleled by similar changes in opiate-induced analgesia in the rat, suggesting a complex or system-specific effect of carbamazepine on opiate mechanisms.

Interactions With Vasopressin

The interactions of carbamazepine with vasopressin appear to be of both clinical and basic interest. In contrast to lithium carbonate, which induces diabetes insipidus by inhibition of vasopressin-induced adenylate cyclase, carbamazepine appears to act like a vasopressin agonist and has been used in the treatment of diabetes insipidus. Berrettini et al. (1982) observed that carbamazepine inhibits vasopressin binding to platelet vasopressin receptors, suggesting that the effects of carbamazepine on vasopressin may occur at a receptor level. This may explain why carbamazepine is unable to reverse the effects of lithium on polyuria: The lithium effects are at a sub-receptor level.

Gold et al. (1983) reported that in contrast to lithium carbonate, which increases the response of plasma vasopressin to hypertonic saline load, carbamazepine diminishes the response, possibly because of its vasopressin-agonist-like effects. Because carbamazepine reduced the sensitivity of the response of plasma antiviral protein (AVP) to osmotic stimulation without affecting the osmotic threshold (Gold et al. 1983), it is unlikely that marked hyponatremia and water intoxication (Ashton et al. 1977; Stephens et al. 1977) would occur other than as an infrequent or idiosyncratic response to carbamazepine. Water intoxication is usually associated with an alteration in the osmotic threshold for AVP secretion, a parameter not affected by carbamazepine.

The differential effects of carbamazepine and lithium on vasopressin function raise the question of whether this might be associated with a differential profile of side effects between these two compounds. Lithium carbonate has been reported to impair cognitive function in a variety of tests (Reus et al. 1979), and this is one of the most often cited subjective complaints leading to noncompliance or discontinuation of therapy (Jamison 1982). If this were related to lithium's interference with vasopressin function, it is possible that carbamazepine would not share this problematic side effect because of its agonistlike effects. Preliminary data from Thompson et al. (1980) suggest that carbamazepine shows a lesser degree of cognitive impairment than a variety of other anticonvulsants. Moreover, Mondadori and Classen (1984) reported that carbamazepine is the only anticonvulsant to reverse ECS-induced amnesia in mice. Taken together, these preliminary clinical and basic data suggest the possibility that carbamazepine may not produce the same impairment in cognitive function as does lithium.

In light of the opposite effects of lithium and carbamazepine on vasopressin function, it is difficult to postulate that this system is intimately involved in the antimanic effects of carbamazepine. Gold et al. (in press) hypothesized, however, that alterations in vasopressin function occur in manic–depressive illness and found increases in CSF vasopressin in manic patients relative to depressed patients, although not significantly different from normal, volunteer controls. They suggested that compensatory vasopressin responses to the initial effects of lithium and carbamazepine could account for some of the similar clinical effects of these two agents.

Carbamazepine in the Hypothalamic-Pituitary-Adrenal Axis

Carbamazepine increases excretion of urinary free cortisol in normal volunteers (London 1980) and patients with affective illness (Rubinow et al. in press). Moreover, it induces escape from dexamethasone suppression (Privitera et al. 1982; Rubinow et al. 1984a, 1984b). The mechanism of these effects and the potential relationship to the mechanism of action of carbamazepine in mania remains obscure. It is curious, however, that carbamazepine, with its profile of acute antidepressant effects, in addition to its acute antimanic effects, induces a change in cortisol function that is in the same direction as already exists in depression itself, that is, hypercortisolemia. Effects of carbamazepine on prolactin, growth hormone, and gonadal steroids have been reviewed elsewhere (Joffe et al. in press; Post et al. 1984c).

Hypothalamic-Pituitary-Thyroid Axis

Carbamazepine shares with lithium carbonate some similar effects on thyroid function but exerts a differential effect on the thyroid-stimulating-hormone (TSH) response to thyrotropin-releasing hormone (TRH). The TSH response to TRH is enhanced during treatment with lithium, but it is blunted in response to carbamazepine (Joffe et al. 1985). Both carbamazepine and lithium decrease circulating levels of 3,5,3′-triiodothyronine and thyroxine. In contrast to the clinically relevant increases in TSH observed in many patients during lithium treatment, the TSH increases on carbamazepine are statistically significant but of extremely small magnitude (Roy-Byrne et al. 1984). This also reflects the differential incidence of the necessity to replace thyroid hormone on these two agents. Thyroid replacement is a relatively common need in conjunction with lithium therapy but an extremely rare event with carbamazepine (only two cases in the world literature). Joffe et al. (1984b) recently postulated that the ability of a series of agents to decrease thyroid function (lithium, carbamazepine, and ECS) paradoxically could be related to their psychotropic properties.

Carbamazepine and Somatostatin Function

Rubinow et al. (1985) reported that carbamazepine significantly decreased somatostatin levels in the CSF of manic and depressed patients. This finding is of considerable interest in light of recent data suggesting that somatostatin level is reduced in the CSF of depressed patients, with normalization at recovery and a switch into mania (Rubinow et al. 1984a). In six different studies, reviewed elsewhere (Post et al. in press-d), parallel findings of decreased CSF somatostatin in depression have been reported.

In addition, alterations in somatostatin have been closely linked to convulsant and anticonvulsant mechanisms. Somatostatin is increased in the rat brain following a series of five amygdala-kindled seizures for a duration of at least two months following the last seizure (Kato et al. 1983). Moreover, inhibition of somatostatin function with cysteamine or with the injection of somatostatin antibodies induces an anticonvulsant and antikindling effect on amygdala- and lidocaine-kindled seizures (Higuchi et al. 1983, 1984).

Carbamazepine decreases CSF somatostatin in affectively ill patients, although it does not appear to do so in relation to the degree of psychotropic response. Affectively ill schizophrenic patients who escaped from dexamethasone suppression showed significantly lower levels of somatostatin in their CSF, suggesting that somatostatin alterations might be associated with disinhibition of the hypothalmic–pituitary–adrenal axis (Doran et al. in press). Whether the effects of carbamazepine on somatostatin are related to its antimanic effects is an issue that requires further investigation. It is of interest that lithium does not produce parallel changes in CSF somatostatin (Berrettini et al. 1985; Rubinow et al. 1985), although neuroleptics do suppress somatostatin in CSF, and parallel findings have also been reported in the rat brain (Beal and Martin 1984). Two studies of carbamazepine treatment in rats showed divergent results. In amygdala-kindled animals, carbamazepine significantly decreased brain somatostatin (Higuchi et al. in press), although in naive rats given carbamazepine in their diet for 12 days, Weiss et al. (unpublished, 1986) were unable to show alterations in somatostatin in a variety of brain regions.

CONCLUSIONS

Thus, the emerging clinical data indicate that carbamazepine may be a useful alternative agent in the treatment of manic patients. The clinical predictors of response appear to be partially opposite to those of lithium carbonate. Patients with increased initial severity of mania, more dysphoric mania, and more rapid cycling are among those who respond best to carbamazepine treatment and poorly to lithium carbonate. Thus, although carbamazepine and lithium have similar profiles of efficacy in the treatment of acute mania and longer term prophylaxis of bipolar illness, it is difficult to assess whether one should look for common or differential effects of these two agents relating to their mechanism of action.

In this fashion, more clinical data are required to ascertain whether there are differential subgroups of patients who respond to these two drugs or whether other variables, such as course of illness, may provide the differentiation. As previously noted, lithium and carbamazepine share effects on GABAergic and adenylate cyclase systems. They appear to have differential effects, however, on noradrenergic, serotonergic, dopaminergic, adenosine, somatostatin, vasopressin, and possibly glutamatergic mechanisms.

It is, therefore, premature to decide which of the effects of carbamazepine may be closely associated with its antimanic efficacy. Considerable data, however, suggest that the noradrenergic effects of carbamazepine are associated with its anticonvulsant effects. In a parallel fashion, the data are convincing that P-type benzodiazepine mechanisms may also be related to the anticonvulsant effects of carbamazepine. As such, both of these systems are important candidates for further exploration because they might relate to the mechanism of this drug's action in mania. The effects of carbamazepine on sodium channels also remain important candidates for its anticonvulsant efficacy. In contrast, effects of carbamazepine on $GABA_b$ mechanisms appear to be at least partially implicated in its mechanism of action in trigeminal neuralgia but not in seizures.

Another leverage point in attempting to dissect which mechanisms of carbamazepine may be related to its anticonvulsant efficacy is the comparison of carbamazepine's effects with other anticonvulsants that are not effective in the treatment of mania. Even this approach has become more problematic as valproic acid, clonazepam, and even phenytoin and acetazolamide have been reported to be successful antimanic agents, and each appears to have different mechanisms of action. Clearly, further clinical trials are required to ascertain the relative efficacy of these agents so that further biochemical and pharmacological dissections can be performed.

Lastly, leverage might be obtained by comparing postulated mechanisms of action of carbamazepine with alterations in neurotransmitter and peptide systems found to occur in the manic syndrome. In other words, is there a convergence of evidence based on direct measures in manic patients and indirect reason based on the pharmacological effects of drugs that treat mania. As illustrated in Figure 23 and discussed elsewhere (Post et al. in press-a), considerable evidence links alterations in noradrenergic and dopaminergic function with mania as well as with decreases in CSF calcitonin and oxytocin. Carbamazepine has complicated effects on noradrenergic mechanisms, and this system has been closely linked to its anticonvulsant efficacy. Similarly, carbamazepine appears to decrease dopamine turnover and exert actions on dopaminergic mechanisms that are not similar to those of neuroleptic compounds.

It is hoped that further dissection of the clinical and biological predictors of carbamazepine response in manic illness not only might better delineate subgroups of responsive patients but also may help clarify issues important to the understanding of the pathophysiology of manic syndromes and the mechanisms of action of carbamazepine. Although the advent of lithium carbonate therapy for mania was greeted with the hope that it would rapidly help unravel the underlying biological disturbances of

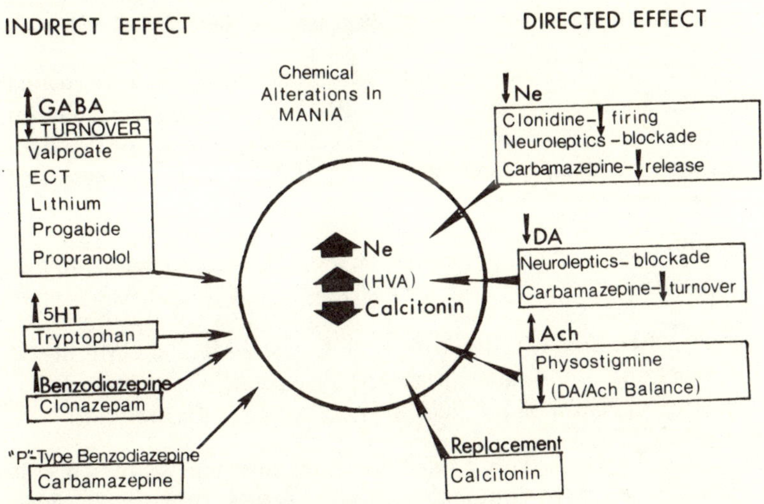

Figure 23. Pharmacology of mania.

mania through an understanding of its mechanism of action, we feel that it is not naive to assume that with the advent of a series of alternative antimanic treatments, greater leverage can be applied in assessing which neurobiological systems are critically involved in the manic syndrome and its effective treatment.

References

Albright PS: Effects of carbamazepine, clonazepam, and phenytoin on seizure threshold in amygdala and cortex. Exp Neurol 79:11–17, 1983

Albright P, Burnham W: Effects of phenytoin, carbamazepine, and clonazepam on cortex- and amygdala-evoked potentials. Exp Neurol 81:308–319, 1983

Ashton MG, Ball SG, Thomas TH, et al: Water intoxication associated with carbamazepine treatment. Br Med J 1:1134–1135, 1977

Ballenger JC, Post RM: Therapeutic effects of carbamazepine in affective illness: a preliminary report. Communications in Psychopharmacology 2:159–178, 1978

Ballenger JC, Post RM: Carbamazepine in alcohol withdrawal syndromes and schizophrenic psychoses. Psychopharmacol Bull 20:572–584, 1984

Baltzer V, Klebs K, Schmutz M: Effects of oxcarbazepine, a compound related to carbamazepine, and of GP47 779, its main metabolite in man, on the evolution of amygdaloid-kindled seizures in the rat. Paper presented at Epilepsy International Congress, Kyoto, Japan, September 1981

Beal M, Martin J: Effects of neuroleptic drugs on brain somatostatin-like immunoreactivity. Neurosci Lett 47:125–130, 1984

Belmaker RH, Zohar J, Rimon R, et al: Cyclic AMP and GMP in the cerebrospinal fluid after high-dose haloperidol treatment. Pol J Pharmacol Pharm 36:217–220, 1984

Bernasconi R: The GABA hypothesis of affective illness: influence of clinically effective antimanic drugs on GABA turnover, in Basic Mechanisms in the Action of Lithium—Proceedings of a Symposium held at Schloss Ringberg, Bavaria, October 4-6, 1981. Amsterdam, the Netherlands, Excerpta Medica, 1982

Berrettini WH, Post RM, Worthington EK, et al: Human platelet vasopressin receptors. Life Sci 30:425–432, 1982

Berrettini WH, Golden LR, Nurnberger JI Jr, et al: Genetic factors in affective illness. J Psychiatr Res 18:329–350, 1985

Bierer LM, Uhde TW, Boulenger J-P, et al: Panic attacks and psychosensory symptoms in patients with affective illness. Abstracts, Society for Biological Psychiatry Annual Meeting, 1985

Cohen M, Pickar D: Pharmacological chalenges to the endogenous opioid system in affective illness. J Clin Psychopharmacol 1:223–231, 1981

Coppola R, Salb J, Chassey J: Topographic analysis of epileptiform discharges. Abstracts, 15th Epilepsy International Congress, Washington, DC, September 1983

Cowdry RW, Gardner DL, de Jong R: Biology and pharmacology of borderline disorders. Proceedings, 137th Annual Meeting, American Psychiatric Association, Los Angeles, May 1984, p. 94

Crunelli V, Bernasconi S, Samanin R: Evidence against serotonin involvement in the tonic component of electrically induced convulsions and in carbamazepine anticonvulsant activity. Psychopharmacology 66:79–85, 1979

Crunelli V, Cervo L, Samanin R: Evidence for a preferential role of central noradrenergic neurons in electrically induced convulsions and activity of various anticonvulsants in the rat, in Neurotransmitters, Seizures and Epilepsy. Edited by Morselli PL, Lloyd KG, Loscher W, et al. New York, Raven Press, 1981

Dalessio DJ: Current concepts. Seizure disorders and pregnancy. N Engl J Med 28:559–563, 1985

DeLorenzo RJ: Calcium-calmodulin protein phosphorylation in neuronal transmission: a molecular approach to neuronal excitability and anticonvulsant drug action, in Status Epilepticus. Edited by Delgado-Escueta AV, Wasterlain CG, Treiman DM, et al. New York, Raven Press, 1983

Doran AR, Rubinow DR, Roy A, et al: CSF somatostatin and abnormal response to dexamethasone administration in schizophrenic and depressed patients. Arch Gen Psychiatry (in press)

Dose M, Emrich HM: Antimanic properties of verapamil. Abstracts, Fourth World Congress of Biological Psychiatry, Philadelphia, September 1985

Dubovsky SL, Franks RD: Intracellular calcium in affective disorders: a review and an hypothesis. Biol Psychiatry 18:781–797, 1983

Elhwuegi A: Antiepileptic drugs and monoamine metabolism in the brain. Br J Pharmacol 64:407P, 1978

Emrich HM, Altmann H, Dose M, et al: Therapeutic effects of GABA-ergic drugs in affective disorders. A preliminary report. Pharmacol Biochem Behav 19:369–372, 1983

Fawcett J, Kravitz DO: The long-term management of bipolar disorders with lithium, carbamazepine, and antidepressants: clinical experience with 90 cases. J Clin Psychiatry 46:58–60, 1985

Ferrendelli JA, Kinscherf DA: Cyclic nucleotides in epileptic brain: effects of pentylenetetrazole in regional cyclic AMP and cyclic GMP levles *in vivo*. Epilepsia 18:525–531, 1977

Ferrendelli JA, Kinscherf DA: Inhibitory effects of anticonvulsant drugs on cyclic nucleotide accumulation in brain. Ann Neurol 5:533–538, 1979

Ferrendelli JA, Gross RA, Kinscherf DA, et al: Effects of seizures and anticonvulsant drugs on cyclic nucleotide regulation in the central nervous system, in Neuropharmacology of Cyclic Nucleotides. Edited by Palmer G. Baltimore, Md, Urban & Schwarzenberg, 1979

Folks DG, King LD, Dowdy SB, et al: Carbamazepine treatment of selected affectively disordered inpatients. Am J Psychiatry 139:115–117, 1982

Fromm GH, Killian JM: Effect of some anticonvulsant drugs on the spinal trigeminal nucleus. Neurology 17:275–280, 1967

Fromm GH, Chattha AS, Terrence CF, et al: Role of inhibitory mechanisms in trigeminal neuralgia. Neurology 31:683–687, 1981

Fujiwara Y, Ebara T, Fukuda K, et al: Prophylactic effect of the combination of lithium carbonate and carbamazepine on bipolar disorder. Folia Psychiatr Neurol Jpn 38:401, 1984

Gastpar M, Kielholz P: Carbamazepine treatment in therapy-resistant patients with manic–depressive psychoses, in Anticonvulsants in Affective Disorders. Edited by Emrich HM, Okuma T, Muller AA. Amsterdam, Excerpta Medica, 1984

Gerner RH, Post RM, Gillin JC, et al: Biological and behavioral effects of one night's sleep deprivation in depressed patients and normals. J Psychiatr Res 15:21–40, 1979

Goddard GV, McIntyre DC, Leech CK: A permanent change in brain function resulting from daily electrical stimulation. Exp Neurol 25:295–330, 1969

Gold PW, Robertson GL, Ballenger JC, et al: Carbamazepine diminishes the sensitivity of the plasma arginine vasopressin response to osmotic stimulation. J Clin Endocrinol Metab 57:952–957, 1983

Gold PW, Robertson GL, Ballenger JC, et al: Plasma and cerebrospinal fluid arginine vasopressin in primary affective disorder. Psychopharmacol Bull (in press)

Greil W, Kruger R, Rossnagl G, et al: Prophylactic therapy of affective disorders with carbamazepine: an open clinical trial, in Anticonvulsants in Affective Disorders. Edited by Emrich HM, Okuma T, Muller AA. Amsterdam, the Netherlands, Excerpta Medica, 1984

Grossi E, Sacchetti E, Vita A, et al: Carbamazepine vs. chlorpromazine in mania: a double-blind trial, in Anticonvulsants in Affective Disorders. Edited by Emrich HM, Okuma T, Muller AA. Amsterdam, the Netherlands, Excerpta Medica, 1984

Hakola HPA, Laulumaa VAO: Carbamazepine in treatment of violent schizophrenics. Lancet 1:1358, 1982

Hernandez-Peon P: Central action of G 32883 upon transmission of trigeminal pain impulses. Med Pharmacol Exp 12:73–80, 1965

Hershkowitz N, Dretchen KL, Raines A: Carbamazepine suppression of post-tetanic potentiation at the neuromuscular junction. J Pharmacol Exp Ther 207:810–816, 1978

Higuchi T, Sikand GS, Kato M, et al: Profound suppression of kindled seizures by cysteamine: possible role of somatostatin to kindled seizures. Brain Res 288:359–362, 1983

Higuchi T, Kokubu T, Sikand G, et al: A study of stomatostatin receptors in amygdaloid-kindled rat brain. J Neurochem 43:1271–1276, 1984

Higuchi T, Kato N, Noguchi T, et al: Kindling and somatostatin, in Kindling III. Edited by Wada JA. New York, Raven Press (in press)

Hitchcock E, Teixeira M: Anticonvulsant activation of pain-suppressive systems. Appl Neurophysiol 45:582-593, 1982

Holm E, Kelleter R, Heinemann HK, et al: Elektrophysiologische analyse der wirkungen von carbamazepine auf das behirn der katze. Pharmakopsychiatr Neuropsychopharmacol 3:187–200, 1970

Inoue K, Arima J, Tanaka K, et al: A lithium and carbamazepine combination in the treatment of bipolar disorder—a preliminary report. Folia Psychiatr Neurol Jpn 35:465–475, 1981

Insel TR, Mueller EA, Alterman I, et al: Obsessive-compulsive disorder and serotonin: is there a connection? Biol Psychiatry 20:1174–1188, 1985

Ito T, Hori M, Yoshida K, et al: Effect of anticonvulsants on cortical focal seizure in cats. Epilepsia 18:63–71, 1977

Jamison KR: Lithium: clinical considerations, in Proceedings of a Symposium, Feb. 2, 1982, UCLA School of Medicine. Edited by Jamison KR. Princeton, NJ, Excerpta Medica, 1982, pp. 52–63

Jimerson DC, Post RM: Psychomotor stimulants and dopamine agonists in depression, in Neurology of Mood Disorders. Edited by Post RM, Ballenger JC. Baltimore, Md, Williams & Wilkins, 1984

Joffe RT, Gold PW, Uhde TW, et al: The effects of carbamazepine on the thyrotropin response to thyrotropin releasing hormone. Psychiatry Res 12:161–166, 1984a

Joffe RT, Roy-Byrne PP, Uhde TW, et al: Thyroid function and affective illness: a reappraisal. Biol Psychiatry 19:1685–1691, 1984b

Joffe RT, Post RM, Roy-Byrne PP, et al: Hematological effects of carbamazepine in patients with affective illness. Am J Psychiatry 142:1196–1199, 1985

Joffe RT, Post RM, Uhde TW: Effects of carbamazepine on serum electrolytes in affective ill patients. Psychol Med (in press)

Julien RM, Hollister RP: Carbamazepine: mechanisms of action, in Complex Partial Seizures and Their Treatment, Advances in Neurology [Volume 11]. Edited by Penry JK, Daly DD. New York, Raven Press, 1975

Kato N, Higuchi T, Friesen HG, et al: Changes of immunoreactive somatostatin and beta-endorphin content in rat brain after amygdala kindling. Life Sci 32:2415–2422, 1983

Katz RJ, Schmaltz K: Facilitation of opiate- and enkephalin-induced motor activity in the mouse by phenytoin sodium and carbamazepine. Psychopharmacology 65:65–68, 1979

Keisling R: Carbamazepine and lithium carbonate in the treatment of refractory affective disorders. Arch Gen Psychiatry 40:223, 1983

Kellner CH, Kling M, Post RM, et al: Intravenous procaine as a probe of limbic activity. APA New Research Abstracts, Annual Meeting, Dallas, TX, May 1985, p. 57 #NR 88

Kishimoto A: A follow-up prophylactic study of carbamazepine in affective disorders, in Anticonvulsants in Affective Disorders. Edited by Emrich HM, Okuma T, Muller A. Amsterdam, the Netherlands, Excerpta Medica, 1984

Kishimoto A, Ogura C, Hazama H, et al: Long-term prophylactic effects of carbamazepine in affective disorder. Br J Psychiatry 143:327-331, 1983

Klein E, Bental E, Lerer B, et al: Carbamazepine and haloperidol vs. placebo and haloperidol in excited psychoses. Arch Gen Psychiatry 41:165–170, 1984

Koella WP, Levin P, Baltzer V: The pharmacology of carbamazepine and some other anti-epileptic drugs, in Epileptic Seizures—Behavior—Pain. Edited by Birkmayer W. Bern, Switzerland, Hans Huber, 1976

Kowalik S, Levitt M, Barkai A: Effects of carbamazepine and antidepressant drugs on endogenous catecholamine levels in the cerebroventricular compartment of the rat. Psychopharmacology 83:169–171, 1984

Kwamie Y, Persad E, Stancer H: The use of carbamazepine as an adjunctive medication in the treatment of affective disorders: a clinical report. Can J Psychiatry 29:605–608, 1984

Lerer B, Moore N, Meyendorff E, et al: A controlled trial of carbamazepine versus lithium in mania. Abstracts, Fourth World Congress of Biological Psychiatry, Philadelphia, September 1985

Lewin E, Bleck V: Cyclic AMP accumulation in cerebral cortical slices: effect of carbamazepine, phenobarbital, and phenytoin. Epilepsia 18:237–242, 1977

Lipinski JF, Pope HG Jr: Possible synergistic action between carbamazepine and lithium carbonate in the treatment of three acutely manic patients. Am J Psychiatry 139:948–949, 1982

Lloyd KG: GABA and the mechanisms of action of antidepressant drugs, in GABA and Mood Disorders: Animal and Clinical Studies, L.E.R.S. Monograph Series. Edited by Bartholini G et al. New York, Raven Press (in press)

London DR: Hormonal effects of anticonvulsant drugs, in Advances in Epileptology, 11th Epilepsy International Symposium. Edited by Carger R, Angeleri F, Penry JK. New York, Raven Press, 1980

Luchins DJ: Carbamazepine for the violent psychiatric patient. Lancet 1:766, 1983

Luchins DJ: Carbamazepine in violent non-epileptic schizophrenics. Psychopharmacol Bull 20:569–571, 1984

Lust WD, Goldberg ND, Passonneau JV: Cyclic nucleotides in murine brain: the temporal relationship of changes induced in adenosine 3′,5′-monophosphate and guanosine 3′,5′-monophosphate following maximal electroshock or decapitation. J Neurochem 26:5–10, 1976

Lust WD, Kupferberg JH, Yonekawa WD, et al: Changes in brain metabolites induced by convulsants or electroshock: effects of anticonvulsant agents. Mol Pharmacol 14:347–356, 1978

MacDonald RL, McLean MJ, Skerritt JH: Anticonvulsant drug mechanisms of action. Fed Proc 44:2634–2639, 1985

Maitre L, Baltzer, V, Mondadori C, et al: Psychopharmacological and behavioural effects of anti-epileptic drugs in animals, in Anticonvulsants in Affective Disorders. Edited by Emrich HM, Okuma T, Muller A. Amsterdam, the Netherlands, Excerpta Medica, 1984

Marangos PJ, Post RM, Patel J, et al: Specific and potent interactions of carbamazepine with brain adenosine receptors. Eur J Pharmacol 93:175–182, 1983

Marangos PJ, Weiss SRB, Montgomery P, et al: Chronic carbamazepine treatment increases brain adenosine receptors. Epilepsia (in press)

Meldrum BS, Chapman AG: Excitatory amino acids and anticonvulsant drug action, in Glutamine, Glutamate, and GABA in the Central Nervous System. Edited by Hertz L, Kwamie E, McGeer E, et al. New York, Alan R. Liss, 1983

Mizoule J, Gauthier A, Uzan A, et al: Opposite effects of two ligands for peripheral type benzodiazepine binding sites, PK11195 and Ro5-4864, in a conflict situation in the rat. Life Sci (in press)

Mondadori C, Classen W: The effects of various antiepileptic drugs on E-shock-induced amnesia in mice: dissociability of effects on convulsions and effects on memory. Acta Neurol Scand 99:125–129, 1984

Morselli PL, Baruzzi A, Gerna M, et al: Carbamazepine and carbamazepine-10, 11-epoxide concentrations in human brain. Br J Clin Pharmacol 4:535–540, 1977a

Morselli PL, Calderini G, Consolazione A, et al: Effect of carbamazepine on brain mediators in control and cobalt-treated rats, in Advances in Epileptology. Edited by Meinardi H, Rowan AJ. Amsterdam, the Netherlands, Swets & Zeitlinger BV, 1977b

Moss GR, James CR: Carbamazepine and lithium carbonate synergism in mania. Arch Gen Psychiatry 40:588–589, 1982

Muller AA, Stoll KD: Carbamazepine and oxcarbazepine in the treatment of manic syndromes: studies in Germany, in Anticonvulsants in Affective Disorders. Edited by Emrich HM, Okuma T, Muller AA. Amsterdam, the Netherlands, Excerpta Medica, 1984

Myllyla VV: Effect of convulsions and anticonvulsive drugs on cerebrospinal fluid cyclic AMP in rabbits. Eur Neurol 14:97–107, 1976

Myllyla VV, Hakkanen E, Nousiainen H, et al: Cerebrospinal fluid cyclic AMP and epilepsy, in Epilepsy, the Eighth International Symposium. Edited by Penry JK. New York, Raven Press, 1976

Naylor G: Reversal of vanadate-induced inhibition of Na-K—a possible explanation of the therapeutic effect of carbamazepine in affective illness. J Affective Disord 8:91–93, 1985

Naylor G, Smith A, Bryce-Smith D, et al: Tissue vanadium levels in manic–depressive psychosis. Psychol Med 14:767–772, 1984

Nelson HB: Cost effectiveness of carbamazepine in refractory bipolar illness (letter). Am J Psychiatry 141:465, 1984

Neppe VM: Carbamazepine in the psychiatric patient. Lancet 2:334, 1982

Nistico G: Effects of GABA, GABOB and some anticonvulsant drugs on dibutyryl cyclic AMP evoked seizures. Int J Clin Pharmacol Biopharm 15:19–22, 1977

Nolen WA: Carbamazepine: an alternative in lithium-resistant bipolar disorder, in Anticonvulsants in Affective Disorders. Edited by Emrich HM, Okuma T, Muller AA. Amsterdam, the Netherlands, Excerpta Medica, 1984

Okuma T: Recent advances in antimanic drug therapy. Abstracts, Fourth World Congress of Biological Psychiatry, Philadelphia, September 1985

Okuma T, Kishimoto A, Inoue K, et al: Anti-manic and prophylactic effects of carbamazepine on manic–depressive psychosis. Folia Psychiatr Neurol Jpn 27:283–297, 1973

Okuma T, Kishimoto, A, Inoue K: Anti-manic and prophylactic effects of carbamazepine (Tegretol) on manic–depressive psychosis. Seishin-igaku 17:617–630, 1975

Okuma T, Inanaga K, Otsuki S, et al: Comparison of the antimanic efficacy of carbamazepine: a double-blind controlled study. Psychopharmacology 66:211–217, 1979

Okuma T, Inanaga K, Otsuki S, et al: A preliminary double-blind study of the efficacy of carbamazepine in prophylaxis of manic–depressive illness. Psychopharmacology 73:95–96, 1981

Olpe H, Jones R: The action of anticonvulsant drugs on the firing of locus coeruleus neurons: selective, activating effect of carbamazepine. Eur J Pharmacol 91:107–110, 1983

Olpe H, Baudry M, Jones RSG: Electrophysiological and neurochemical investigations on the action of carbamazepine on the rat hippocampus. Eur J Pharmacol 110:71–80, 1985

Omura F, Kishimoto A, Tsutsui T, et al: Combined therapy of lithium and carbamazepine in bipolar affective disorders. Folia Psychiatr Neurol Jpn 38:401, 1984

Palmer GC: Interactions of antiepileptic drugs on adenylate cyclase and phosphodiesterases in rat and mouse cerebrum. Exp Neurol 63:322–335, 1979

Palmer GC: Clinical considerations of the cyclic nucleotides in psychiatry and neurology. Integr Psychiatry 3:99-111, 1985

Palmer GC, Jones DJ, Medina MA, et al: Anticonvulsant drug actions on *in vitro* and *in vivo* levels of cyclic AMP in the mouse brain. Epilepsia 20:95–104, 1979

Palmer GC, Palmer SJ, Legendre JL: Guanylate cyclase-cyclic GMP in mouse cerebral cortex and cerebellum: modification by anticonvulsants. Exp Neurol 71:601–614, 1981

Penry JK, Daly DD: Complex Partial Seizures and Their Treatment: Advances in Neurology [Volume 11]. New York, Raven Press, 1975

Phillis JW, Wu PH, Bender AS: Inhibition of adenosine uptake into rat brain synaptosomes by the benzodiazepines. Gen Pharmacol 12:67–70, 1981

Pinel JPJ: Kindling-induced experimental epilepsy in rats: cortical stimulation. Exp Neurol 72:559–569, 1981

Placidi GF Lenzi A, Rampello E, et al: Long-term double-blind prospective study on carbamazepine versus lithium in bipolar and schizoaffective disorders: preliminary results, in Anticonvulsants in Affective Disorders. Edited by Emrich HM, Okuma T, Muller AA. Amsterdam, the Netherlands, Excerpta Medica, 1984

Porter RJ, Penry JK: Efficacy and choice of antiepileptic drugs, in Advances in Epileptology, 1977: Psychology, Pharmacology, and New Diagnostic Approaches. Edited by Meinardi H, Rowan AJ. Amsterdam, the Netherlands, Swets & Zeitlinger, 1978

Post RM: Does limbic system dysfunction play a role in affective illness? in The Limbic System: Functional Organization and Clinical Disorders. Edited by Doane BK, Livingston KE. New York, Raven Press, in press

Post RM, Uhde TW: Treatment of mood disorders with antiepileptic medications: clinical and theoretical implications. Epilepsia 24:S97–S108, 1983

Post RM, Uhde TW: Anticonvulsants in non-epileptic psychosis, in Epilepsy in Psychiatry. Edited by Bolwig TG, Trimble MR. New York, Wiley (in press-a)

Post RM, Uhde TW: Are the psychotropic effects of carbamazepine in manic–depressive illness mediated through the limbic system? Psychiatr J Univ Ottawa (in press-b)

Post RM, Uhde TW: Carbamazepine in the treatment of affective illness, in The Limbic System: Functional Organization and Clinical Disorders. Edited by Doane BK, Livingston KE. New York, Raven Press (in press-c)

Post RM, Ballenger JC, Reus VI, et al: Effects of carbamazepine in mania and depression. APA New Research Abstracts, #7, 1978a

Post RM, Gerner RH, Carman JS, et al: Effects of a dopamine agonist piribedil in depressed patients: relationship of pretreatment HVA to antidepressant response. Arch Gen Psychiatry 35:609–615, 1978b

Post RM, Ballenger JC, Goodwin FK: Cerebrospinal fluid studies of neurotransmitter function in manic and depressive illness, in Neurobiology of Cerebrospinal Fluid, vol. 1. Edited by Wood JH. New York, Plenum Press, 1980a

Post RM, Jimerson DC, Bunney WE Jr, et al: Dopamine and mania: behavioral and biochemical effects of the dopamine receptor blocker pimozide. Psychopharmacology 67:297–305, 1980b

Post RM, Ballenger JC, Hare TA, et al: Lack of effect of carbamazepine on gamma-aminobutyric acid levels in cerebrospinal fluid. Neurology 30:1008–1011, 1980c

Post RM, Pickar D, Naber D, et al: Effect of carbamazepine on CSF opioid activity: relationship to antidepressant response. Psychiatry Res 5:59–66, 1981

Post RM, Uhde TW, Ballenger JC, et al: Carbamazepine, temporal lobe epilepsy, and manic-depressive illness, in Temporal Lobe Epilepsy, mania, and Schizophrenia and the Limbic System, Advances in Biological Psychiatry, Vol. 8. Edited by Koella WP, Trimble M. Basel, Switzerland, S Karger, 1982a

Post RM, Ballenger JC, Uhde TW, et al: Effect of carbamazepine on cyclic nucleotides in CSF of patients with affective illness. Biol Psychiatry 17:1037–1045, 1982b

Post RM, Uhde TW, Ballenger JC, et al: Carbamazepine and its -10, 11-epoxide metabolite in plasma and CSF: relationship to antidepressant response. Arch Gen Psychiatry 40:673–676, 1983

Post RM, Rubinow DR, Ballenger JC: Conditioning, sensitization, and kindling: implications for the course of affective illness, in Neurobiology of Mood Disorders. Edited by Post RM, Ballenger JC. Baltimore, Md, Williams & Wilkins, 1984a

Post RM, Weiss SRB, Pert A: Differential effects of carbamazepine and lithium on sensitization and kindling. Prog Neuropsychopharmacol Biol Psychiatry 8:425–434, 1984b

Post RM, Ballenger JC, Uhde TW, et al: Efficacy of carbamazepine in manic–depressive illness: implications for underlying mechanisms, in Neurobiology of Mood Disorders. Edited by Post RM, Ballenger JC. Baltimore, Md, Williams & Wilkins, 1984c

Post RM, Putnam FW, Contel NR, et al: Electroconvulsive seizures inhibit amygdala kindling: implications for mechanisms of action in affective illness. Epilepsia 25:234–239, 1984d

Post RM, Uhde TW, Joffe RT, et al: Anticonvulsant drugs in psychiatric illness: new treatment alternatives and theoretical implications, in The Psychopharmacology of Epilepsy. Edited by Trimble MR. New York, Wiley, 1985a

Post RM, Rubinow DR, Uhde TW, et al: Effects of carbamazepine on noradrenergic mechanisms in affective ill patients. Psychopharmacology 87:59–63, 1985b

Post RM, Rubinow DR, Gold PW: Neurochemical correlates of mania. Abstracts, Fourth World Congress of Biological Psychiatry, Philadelphia, September 1985c, p 248, #313.2

Post RM, Uhde TW, Rubinow DR, et al: Possible interactions of the anticonvulsant carbamazepine with calcium. Abstracts, Fourth World Congress of Biological Psychiatry, Philadelphia, September 1985d, p 442, #612.11

Post RM, Weiss SRB, Pert A, et al: Chronic cocaine administration: sensitization and kindling effects, in Cocaine: Clinical and Biobehavioral Aspects. Edited by Fisher S. New York, Oxford University Press (in press-a)

Post RM, Rubinow DR, Ballenger JC: Conditioning and sensitization in the longitudinal course of affective illness. Br J Psychiatry (in press-b)

Post RM, Putnam F, Uhde TW, et al: ECT as an anticonvulsant: implications for its mechanism of action in affective illness. Ann NY Acad Sci (in press-c)

Post RM, Rubinow DR, Gold PW: Neuropeptides in manic-depressive illness, in Neuropeptides in Psychiatric and Neurological Disease. Edited by Nemeroff CB. Baltimore, Md, Johns Hopkins University Press (in press-d)

Post RM, Rubinow DR, Uhde TW, et al: Relationship of the efficacy of carbamazepine to dopaminergic mechanisms. Arch Gen Psychiatry (in press-e)

Pratt JA, Jenner P, Johnson AL, et al: Anticonvulsant drugs alter plasma tryptophan concentrations in epileptic patients: implications for antiepileptic action and mental function. J Neurol Neurosurg Psychiatry 47:1131–1133, 1984

Pratt JA, Jenner P, Marsden CD: Comparison of the effects of benzodiazepines and other anticonvulsant drugs on synthesis and utilization of 5HT in mouse brain. Neuropharmacology 24:59–68, 1985

Prien RF: Five-center study clarifies use of lithium, imipramine for recurrent affective disorders. Hosp Community Psychiatry 35:1097–1098, 1984

Privitera MR, Greden JF, Gardner RW, et al: Interference by carbamazepine with the dexamethasone suppression test. Biol Psychiatry 17:611–620, 1982

Purdy RE, Julien RM, Fairhurst AS, et al: Effect of carbamazepine in the *in vitro* uptake and release of norepinephrine in adrenergic nerves of rabbit aorta and in whole brain synaptosomes. Epilepsia 18:251–257, 1977

Quattrone A, Samanin R: Decreased anticonvulsant activity of carbamazepine in 6-hydroxydopamine-treated rats. Eur J Pharmacol 41:333–336, 1977

Quattrone A, Crunelli V, Samanin R: Seizure susceptibility and anticonvulsant activity of carbamazepine, diphenylhydantoin and phenobarbital in rats with selective depletions of brain monoamines. Neuropharmacology 17:643–647, 1978

Quattrone A, Annunziato L, Aguglia K, et al: Carbamazepine, phenytoin and phenobarbital do not influence brain catecholamine uptake, *in vivo*, in male rats. Arch Int Pharmacodyn Ther 252:180–185, 1981

Ramsay RE, Wilder BJ, Berger JR et al: A double-blind study comparing carbamazepine with phenytoin as initial seizure therapy in adults. Neurology 33:904–910, 1983

Reus VI, Targum SD, Weingartner H, et al: Effects of lithium carbonate on memory processes of bipolar affectively ill patients. Psychopharmacology 63:39–42, 1979

Roy-Byrne PP, Joffe RT, Uhde TW, et al: Effects of carbamazepine on thyroid function in affectively ill patients: clinical and theoretical implications. Arch Gen Psychiatry 41:1150–1153, 1984

Rubinow DR, Post RM, Gold PW, et al: Neuroendocrine and peptide effects of carbamazepine: clinical and mechanistic implications. Psychopharmacol Bull 20:590–594, 1984a

Rubinow DR, Post RM, Gold PW, et al: The relationship between cortisol and clinical phenomenology of affective illness, in Neurobiology of Mood Disorders. Edited by Post RM, Ballenger JC. Baltimore, Md, Williams & Wilkins, 1984b

Rubinow DR, Post RM, Gold PW, et al: Effects of carbamazepine on cerebrospinal fluid somatostatin. Psychopharmacology 85:210–213, 1985

Rubinow DR, Post RM, Gold PW, et al: Effect of carbamazepine on mean urinary free cortisol excretion in patients with major affective illness. Psychopharmacology (in press).

Sackeim HA, Decina P, Malitz S, et al: Anticonvulsant and antidepressant properties of electroconvulsive therapy: a proposed mechanism of action. Biol Psychiatry 18:1301–1310, 1983

Sawaya MCB, Horton RW, Meldrum BS: Effects of anticonvulsant drugs on the cerebral enzymes metabolising GABA. Epilepsia 16:649–655, 1975

Schauf CL, Davis FA, Marder J: Effects of carbamazepine on the ionic conductances of myxicola giant axons. J Pharmacol Exp Ther 189:538–543, 1974

Secunda SK, Katz MM, Swann A, et al: Mania: diagnosis, state measurement and prediction of treatment response. J Affective Disord 8:113–121, 1985

Sethi BB, Tiwari SC: Carbamazepine in affective disorders, in Anticonvulsants in Affective Disorders. Edited by Emrich HM, Okuma T, Muller AA. Amsterdam, The Netherlands, Excerpta Medica, 1984

Silberman EK, Post RM, Nurnberger J, et al: Transient sensory, cognitive, and affective phenomena in affective illness: a comparison with complex partial epilepsy. Br J Psychiatry 146:81–89, 1985

Skerritt JH, Johnston GAR: Inhibition of amino acid transmitter release from rat brain slices by phenytoin and related anticonvulsants. Clin Exp Pharmacol Physiol 10:527–533, 1983

Skerritt JH, Davies LP, Johnston GAR: A purinergic component in the anticonvulsant action of carbamazepine? Eur J Pharmacol 82:195–197, 1982

Skerritt JH, Davies LP, Johnston GAR: Interactions of the anticonvulsant carbamazepine with adenosine receptors. 1. Neurochemical studies. Epilepsia 24:634–642, 1983a

Skerritt J, Johnston G, Chow S: Interactions of the anticonvulsant carbamazepine with adenosine receptors. 2. Pharmacological studies. Epilepsia 24:643–650, 1983b

Small IF, Small JG, Milstein V, et al: ECT treatment variables in uni- and bipolar depression and mania. Abstracts, 37th Meeting, Society of Biological Psychiatry, Toronto, Canada, May 1982, #25

Steiner C, Wit AL, Weiss MB, et al: The antiarrhythmic actions of carbamazepine (Tegretol). J Pharmacol Exp Ther 173:323–335, 1970

Stephens WP, Espir MLE, Tattersall RB, et al: Water intoxication due to carbamazepine. Br Med J 1:754–755, 1977

Takezaki H, Hanaoka M: The use of carbamazepine (Tegretol) in the control of manic-depressive psychosis and other manic, depressive states. J Clin Psychiatry 13:173–183, 1971

Terrence CF, Sax M, Fromm GH, et al: Effect of baclofen enantiomorphs on the spinal trigeminal nucleus and steric similarities of carbamazepine. Pharmacology 27:85–94, 1983

Theobald W, Krupp P, Levin P: Neuropharmacologic aspects of the therapeutic action of carbamazepine in trigeminal neuralgia, in Trigeminal Neuralgia: Pathogenesis and Pathophysiology. Edited by Hassler R, Walker AE. Stuttgart, West Germany, George Theime, 1970

Thompson P, Huppert F, Trimble M: Anticonvulsant drugs, cognitive function and memory. Acta Neurol Scand 62:75–81, 1980

Tomson T: Interdosage fluctuations in plasma carbamazepine concentration determine intermittent side effects. Arch Neurol 41:830–834, 1984

Tomson T, Bertilsson L: Potent therapeutic effect of carbamazepine-10,11-epoxide in trigeminal neuralgia. Arch Neurol 41:598–601, 1984

van Praag HM: Depression, suicide, and serotonin metabolism in the brain, in Neurobiology of Mood Disorders. Edited by Post RM, Ballenger JC. Baltimore, Md, Williams & Wilkins, 1984

van Praag HM, Korf J: Central monoamine deficiency in depression: causative or secondary phenomenon. Pharmacopsychiatry 8:322–326, 1975

van Scheyen JD, van Praag HM, Korf J: Controlled study comparing nomifensine and clomipramine in unipolar depression using the probenecid technique. Br J Clin Pharmacol 4:1179S–1184S, 1977

Varotto M, Roman G, Battistin L: Pharmacological influences on the brain level and transport of GABA. 1. Effect of various antiepileptic drugs on brain levels of GABA. (in Italian) Boll Soc Ital Biol Sper 57:904–908, 1981

Vogler J, Zieglgansberger W: Effect of carbamazepine and valproate on cortical neurons of the rat *in vivo*. Abstract, Fourth World Congress of Biological Psychiatry, Philadelphia, September 1985, p 441, #612.5

Wada JA: Pharmacological prophylaxis in the kindling model of epilepsy. Arch Neurol 34:389–395, 1977

Wada JA, Sato M, Wake A, et al: Prophylactic effects of phenytoin, phenobarbital, and carbamazepine examined in kindled cat preparations. Arch Neurol 33:426–434, 1976

Waldmeier PC, Baumann PA, Fehr B, et al: Carbamazepine decreases catecholamine turnover in the rat brain. J Pharmacol Exp Ther 231:166–172, 1984

Weir RL, Padgett W, Daly JW, et al: Interaction of anticonvulsant drugs with adenosine receptors in the central nervous system. Epilepsia 25:492–498, 1984

Weiss SRB, Post RM, Marangos PJ, et al: Adenosine agonists: lack of effect on carbamazepine's inhibition of kindled seizures. Neuropharmacology 24:635–638, 1985a

Weiss SRB, Post RM, Patel J, et al: Differential mediation of the anticonvulsant effects of carbamazepine and diazepam. Life Sci 36:2413–2419, 1985b

Weiss SRB, Post RM, Marangos PJ, et al: "Peripheral-type" benzodiazepines: behavioral effects and relationship to the anticonvulsant effects of carbamazepine, in Kindling III. Edited by Wada J. New York, Raven Press (in press)

Willow M. Catterall WA: Inhibition of binding of [^{3}H] batrochotoxin A 20-alpha-benzoate to sodium channels by the anticonvulsant drugs diphenylhydantoin and carbamazepine. Mol Pharmacol 22:627–635, 1982

Willow M, Gonoi T, Catterall WA: Voltage clamp analysis of the inhibitory actions of diphenylhy dantoin and carbamazepine on voltage-sensitive sodium channels in neuroblastoma cells. Mol Pharmacol 27:549–558, 1985

Willow M, Kuenzel EA, Catterall WA: Inhibition of voltage-sensitive sodium channels in neuroblastoma cells and synaptosomes by the anticonvulsant drugs diphenylhydantoin and carbamazepine. Mol Pharmacol 25:228–234, 1984

Winkel R, Lux HD: Carbamazepine reduces calcium currents in helix neurons. Abstracts, Fourth World Congress of Biological Psychiatry, Philadelphia, September 1985, p 441, #612.6

Wolf P, Inoue Y, Roder-Wanner U-U, et al: Psychiatric complications of absence therapy and their relation to alteration of sleep. Epilepsia 25:S56-S59, 1984

Yassa R: Carbamazepine: an alternative to lithium therapy? Psychiatr J Univ Ottawa 7:252–253, 1982

Zohar J, Ebstein RP, Belmaker RH: Adenylate cyclase as the therapeutic target site of lithium, in Basic Mechanisms in the Action of Lithium. Edited by Emrich HM, Aldenhoff JB, Lux HD. Amsterdam, The Netherlands, Excerpta Medica, 1982

5

Mania: Amines, Symptoms, and Response to Lithium

Alan C. Swann, M.D.
Steven K. Secunda, M.D.
Martin M. Katz, Ph.D.
Stephen H. Koslow, Ph.D.

5

Mania: Amines, Symptoms, and Response to Lithium

Although lithium was discovered to be effective in the treatment of mania almost 40 years ago, the pathophysiologic mechanisms responsible for the symptoms of mania and for their response to lithium are still not clear. In addition, although 20 to 30 percent of manic patients do not respond to lithium treatment (Taylor and Abrams 1981), there is little information about characteristics before treatment that might distinguish subsequent responders from nonresponders (Carroll 1979).

Hypotheses of Mania

A number of hypotheses have been suggested to explain aspects of mania. A successful hypothesis should have a) the ability to account for a maximal number of observations with minimal assumptions, b) the ability to produce experiments that can clearly refute the hypothesis if it is wrong, and c) consequences that are useful in treating patients. These consequences could include a) a means for distinguishing manic patients from other groups, b) a pathophysiologic measure that correlates with severity of the manic syndrome, c) a measure that changes or normalizes with successful treatment, and d) predictors of treatment response.

A caveat related to these considerations is that the mechanism by which symptoms are ameliorated does not have to be the reverse of that by which they were produced. In the case of mood disorders, it is plausible that a number of conditions could produce similar syndromes (Akiskal and McKinney 1973) and that the symptoms, in turn, are complex enough to be modified by a variety of pharmacologic or environmental interventions. That something changes during treatment does not necessarily imply that it was directly related to the cause of the original disorder.

Transmitter Hypotheses

Two developments during the last 20 years have been responsible for the development of neurotransmitter hypotheses for mood disorders. The first was a group of observations, in animals and in man, that pharmacologic reductions in catecholamines or serotonin were associated with behavior resembling depression and that increases in similar substances were associated with amelioration of depression or with mania. These observations were essentially serendipitous. The second was the development of assay methods for monoamines and their metabolites and of evidence relating these metabolites to activity of the underlying transmitter system. Transmitters implicated in the major hypotheses included nonrepinephrine, dopamine, serotonin, acetylcholine, and combinations of these. Techniques for measuring a host of more recently discovered transmitters and peptides have been developed, but none of these has yet supplanted the biogenic amines in research on affective disorders. Whether this is because of a unique role of classical monoamine transmitters in affective disorders or because insufficient time has elapsed since the discovery of the more recent substances remains to be seen. The evidence for involvement of monoamines in mania is reviewed here.

Norepinephrine. The basis of the original catecholamine theory of affective disorders included observations that treatments increasing availability of norepinephrine could precipitate mania of similar states (Schildkraut and Kety 1967; van Praag 1977). In addition, depressive states were associated with reduced norepinephrine. More recently, there have been reports in small numbers of patients that manic patients had elevated concentrations of norepinephrine metabolites in cerebrospinal fluid (CSF) (Shopsin et al. 1973; Wilk et al. 1972), that these metabolites were reduced by treatment in two patients (Shopsin et al. 1973), that urinary excretion of norepinephrine metabolites was reduced in three manic patients treated with lithium (Greenspan et al. 1970), and that treatment with clonidine alleviated manic symptoms (Jouvent et al. 1980).

Dopamine. Studies of animal behavior and observations of drug effects in humans suggest that increased dopaminergic activity is associated with motor hyperactivity, cognitive disorganization, and aggression, all characteristics of mania (Post 1975). Symptoms of mania have been precipitated by 1-Dopa, although more often they have not, and by the specific dopaminergic agonist piribedil (Gerner et al. 1976). In addition, manic symptoms can be treated effectively with antipsychotic drugs, which are dopamine-receptor antagonists (Prien et al. 1972).

Serotonin. Low serotonin is associated with increased aggression and impulsivity (Asberg and Traskman 1981; Asberg et al. 1976a, 1976b), which are frequently characteristics of mania. The possible role of serotonin was emphasized by early reports that lithium, the first modern pharmacologic treatment for mania, might increase or stabilize serotonergic activity (Knapp and Mandell 1975; Mandell and Knapp 1979). Lithium has been reported to stabilize CSF serotonin in depressed patients (Linnoila et al. 1984). Low concentrations of the serotonin metabolite 5-hydroxyindoleacetic acid (5-HIAA) has been reported in the CSF of manic patients (Bowers 1974; Coppen 1972), though Ashcroft et al. (1966) found normal levels. A problem with low-serotonin theories of mania is that for reasons similar to the case with norepinephrine, low serotonin was thought to be associated with depression (Coppen 1972; van Praag 1977), presumably the behavioral opposite of mania.

Serotonin–norepinephrine. The contradiction just mentioned and lithium's appearing to reduce noradrenergic and increase serotonergic function led to the hypothesis that mania consisted of a combination of low serotonergic and high noradrenergic function or possibly an imbalance between the two (Asberg and Bertilsson 1979; Ashcroft and Glen 1974). The general hypothesis was that low serotonin was associated with susceptibility to affective disorder and that the specific disorder depended on whether norepinephrine was high (mania) or low (depression).

Acetylcholine. The possible role of acetylcholine in mania is discussed in the chapter by Dr. David Janowsky in this volume. This hypothesis was based on observations that treatments that increased cholinergic activity reduced manic symptoms (Janowsky et al. 1973). Direct assessment of cholinergic function in mania is more difficult than is the case with catecholamines and serotonin because acetylcholine has no stable or specific metabolites.

Low acetylcholine–high norepinephrine. As was the case with serotonin, the observation that mania was associated with increased catecholamine function was impossible to dismiss and, therefore, has been incorporated into theories that susceptibility to affective disorder is related to the balance between cholinergic and noradrenergic activity (Janowsky et al. 1972). These "balance" hypotheses are attractive in that they acknowledge the complexity of the central nervous system a bit more than the single-transmitter hypotheses do.

Testing transmitter hypotheses of mania. It is unlikely that phenomena as complex as affective disorders can be explained by abnormalities in a few neurotransmitter systems. The purpose of these hypotheses was not, however, to explain mania completely. Instead, these hypotheses were designed to account for as much of the clinically relevant data as possible with the simplest possible assumptions. With the data presented here, we will examine mania and its response to lithium treatment in terms of monoamine function. Consistent with the aims already discussed, we will compare manic patients with age- and sex-matched healthy subjects and with patients with bipolar depressive disorder, examine the correlation between measures of catecholamine function and severity of the manic syndrome, compare responders with nonresponders, and examine the effects of lithium treatment.

National Institute of Mental Health Clinical Research Branch Collaborative Program on the Psychobiology of Depression

Patient Sample

The manic sample consisted of 18 patients meeting Schedule of Affective Disorders and Schizophrenia Research Diagnostic Criteria (SADS-RDC) criteria for a manic episode of major affective disorder (Spitzer and Endicott 1979; Spitzer et al. 1977). There were 11 men (age = 44.8 ± 12.3) and 7 women (age = 43.8 ± 17.1). The demographic characteristics of the group are described in the chapter by Drs. Steven Secunda, Martin Katz, Alan Swann, and Stephen Koslow in this volume (see also Secunda et al. 1985). The patients with bipolar depressive disorder consisted of 31 men (age = 43.9 ± 13.2) and 16 women (age = 42.0 ± 15.8) who met SADS-RDC criteria for major affective episode, depressed, and had met criteria for manic or hypomanic disorder in the past (Secunda et al. 1980). Healthy control subjects were screened with the SADS-Lifetime (Spitzer and Endicott 1979) interview to assure lack of major psychiatric or drug abuse disorders. They included 33 subjects who were hospitalized for the study (15 men aged 47.9 ± 12.5 and 18 women aged 47.8 ± 15.4) and 47 nonhospitalized subjects (23 men aged 43.7 ± 14.6 and 24 women aged 45.1 ± 16.1) who went through a protocol identical to the pretreatment phase of the patients' study. Patients or controls meeting criteria for past or present alcohol or drug abuse disorders or for other major psychiatric disorders were excluded. Clinical characteristics of these patients have been described in detail by Secunda et al. (1985) and Swann et al. (in press-a).

Behavioral Measures

Subjects and controls were behaviorally assessed by nurses on the Affective Disorder Rating Scale (Murphy et al. 1980) and the Global Ward Scale (Burdock et al. 1960) and by physicians on the SADS-Change (Endicott and Spitzer 1978), the Hamilton Depression Scale (HDS; Hamilton 1960), and the Itil-Katz scale (Katz and Itil 1974) and filled out self-rating scales (Symptom Check List 90; Derogatis et al. 1974). These assessments were carried out periodically before and during active drug treatment. A scale for measuring the manic syndrome, called the Mania Diagnostic and Severity Scale (MADS), was developed from these measures as described in an article by Secunda et al. (1985). In addition, a series of behavioral constructs was developed to evaluate drug effects on major psychiatric symptom areas. The development and rationale were described by Katz et al. (1982, 1984). The behavioral constructs consist of depressed mood, anxiety, agitation, retardation, hostility, somatization, distressed appearance, interpersonal sensitivity, positive adaptation, sleep disorder, cognitive impairment, depressed state, and general psychopathology. We will also report separately data from two components of these measures, the HDS and tests of psychomotor speed (Katz et al. 1984; Secunda et al. 1980).

The derivation and validation of these measures was described in detail by Katz et al. (1984). To assure continued consistency of ratings across centers, we held periodic meetings of the physician and nurse raters throughout the study. New raters were also trained in these meetings before being added to the project.

Biochemical Measures

The rationale and procedures for these measures have been described in detail (Koslow et al. 1983; Maas et al. 1980; Secunda et al. 1980). Each biochemical assay was performed in a single designated laboratory. Samples were labeled with computer-generated random numbers and were assayed by personnel who were unaware of their origins as to diagnosis or treatment status. In addition, all assays were performed with blind replicates; that is, identical samples with different random numbers were also assayed. CSF was obtained from lumbar punctures performed as close to 8:30 AM as possible, after at least eight hours of bed rest. Nonhospitalized controls spent the night before the lumbar puncture in the hospital to assure adequate bed rest. Fluid was mixed before appropriate aliquots were mixed with preservatives and internal standards and frozen. Urine collections were obtained on consecutive days, and the averages from the two days were reported. Adequacy of collections was assessed using creatinine excretion and body mass (Bonsnes and Taussky 1945). CSF monoamine metabolites were assayed by gas chromatography–mass spectroscopy (Fri et al. 1974; Swahn et al. 1976). Urinary 3-methoxy-4-hydroxyphenylglycol (MHPG) was measured by gas chromatography (Dekirmenjian and Maas 1970), normetanephrine by spectrophotofluorimetry (Taniguchi et al. 1964), and norepinephrine and epinephrine by an automated spectrophotofluorimetric technique (Anton and Sayre 1962).

Lithium Treatment Protocol

The lithium treatment protocol, which was described in detail by Secunda at al. (1980, 1985), was as follows. Patients were treated with placebo for 16 days, during which they received full behavioral evaluations on Days 3, 10, and 15. Urine was collected on Days 9 and 10, and the lumbar puncture was performed on Day 11. On Day 16, there was a single-dose-lithium pharmacokinetic experiment, and lithium treatment began on Day 17. The dose was titrated in order to obtain a plasma-lithium concentration of between 1.0 and 1.5 as quickly as possible and to maintain it at that level or at the highest feasible level if the concentration were limited by side effects. Behavioral assessments were repeated after 6, 10, 16, and 23 days of treatment. Urine collections were obtained on Days 15 and 16, and the lumbar puncture was repeated on Day 17 of treatment.

Statistical Methods

Before the comparison and correlations reported here were carried out, distribution of data was examined (Shapiro and Wilk 1965); if data were not normally distributed, the natural logarithm was used to improve normality of distribution. Because of reports of age or sex effects or both on some of the measures studied in groups larger than this one (Koslow et al. 1983), for comparisons among groups, we generally used analysis of covariance with age and sex as covariates. In addition, effects of center of origin, weight, and height on the measures studied were examined and found to be nonsignificant (Koslow et al. 1983).

MEASURES OF NEUROTRANSMITTER FUNCTION IN MANIA

Comparison With Healthy Controls and Bipolar Depressed Subjects

Figure 1 shows concentrations of MHPG, homovanillic acid (HVA), and 5-HIAA in the CSF of untreated manic subjects compared to treated manic patients, untreated bipolar depressed patients, and healthy controls. MHPG was higher in manic individuals than in bipolar depressed patients. HVA and 5-HIAA were higher in manic women than in control women, but manic and control groups as a whole did not differ when gender was taken into account. MHPG, the only metabolite that was higher in manics than in either comparison group, regardless of gender, also declined significantly during lithium treatment (Swann et al. in press-b). Figure 2 shows that the excretion of several urinary catecholamine metabolites was higher in manic individuals than in controls, but manics did not differ significantly from bipolar depressed subjects in these measures. Urinary MHPG excretion did not differ significantly among patient groups (Koslow et al. 1983) or change significantly during treatment. The data in Figure 3 show that manic individuals had higher excretion of norepinephrine than either bipolar depressed or healthy control subjects. In addition, norepinephrine excretion in manic individuals was significantly lower during lithium treatment. Excretion of epinephrine was highly variable and did not differentiate manic individuals from the other groups.

Relationship to Outcome

As already mentioned, a means to distinguish subsequent responders from nonresponders would be valuable. Responders did not differ from nonresponders with respect to any of the monoamine measures, however. In addition, comparisons of mixed and pure, predominately irritable–paranoid and euphoric–grandiose, or psychotic and nonpsychotic manic individuals yielded no significant differences.

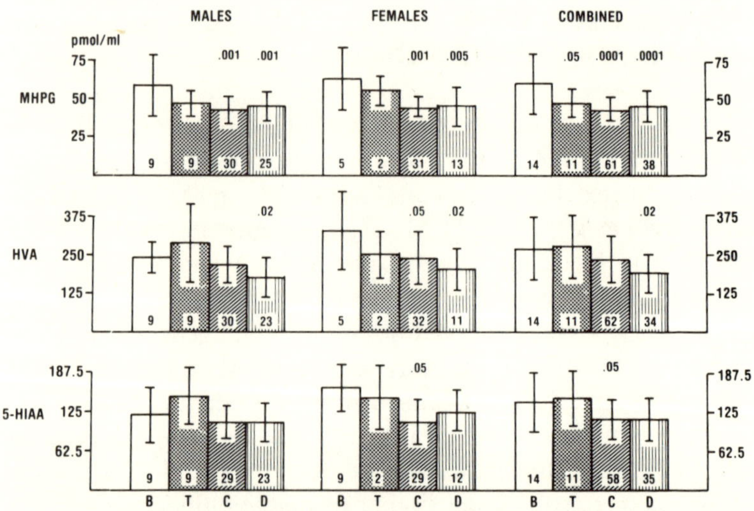

Figure 1. Cerebrospinal fluid monoamine metabolites in treated and untreated manic and comparison subjects. Each metabolite is shown for men and women separately and combined. The order for each set of four is untreated manic (B), treated manic (T), healthy control (C), and untreated bipolar depressed subjects (D). The number is shown in the bar. The error lines give the standard deviations. MHPG = 3-methoxy-4-hydroxyphenylglycol; HVA = homovanillic acid; 5-HIAA = 5-hydroxyindoleacetic acid.

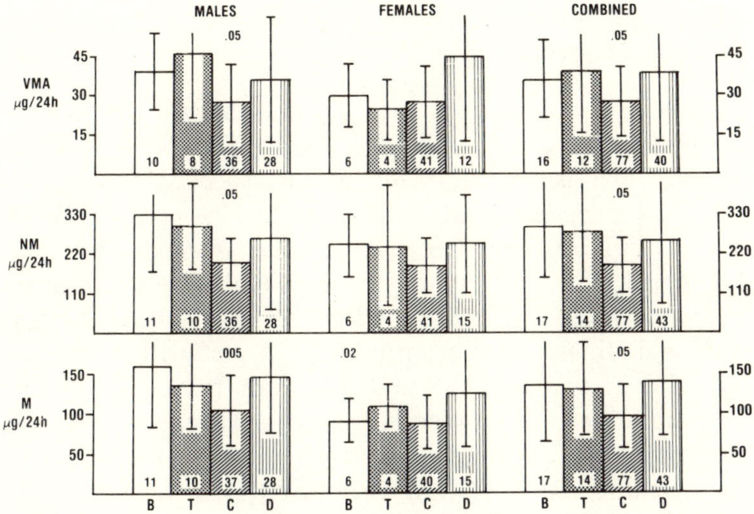

Figure 2. Urinary catecholamine metabolite excretion in treated and untreated manic and comparison subjects. The data are presented as in Figure 1. MHPG = 3-methoxy-4-hydroxyphenylglycol; VMA = vanillylmandelic acid; NM = normetanephrine; M = metanephrine.

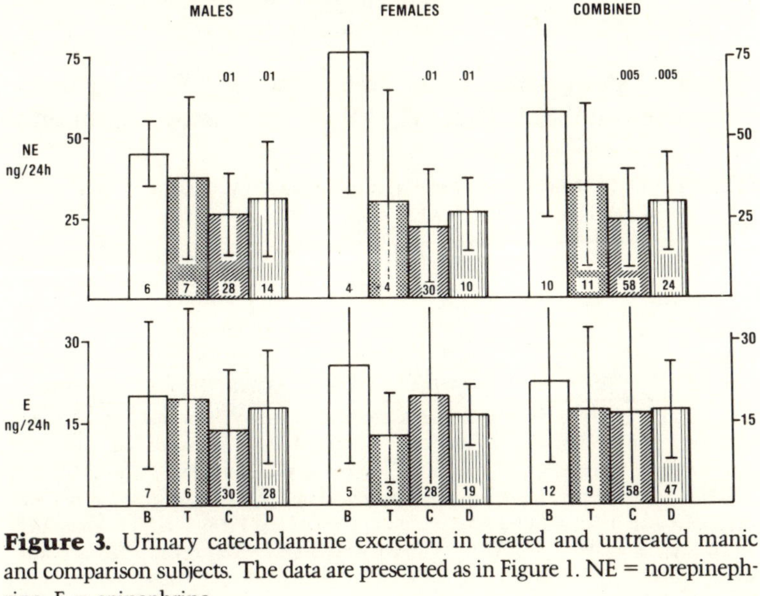

Figure 3. Urinary catecholamine excretion in treated and untreated manic and comparison subjects. The data are presented as in Figure 1. NE = norepinephrine; E = epinephrine.

Change With Lithium Treatment and Outcome

CSF MHPG and urinary norepinephrine changed significantly in manic patients during lithium treatment. These were the same measures that before treatment, distinguished manic patients from bipolar depressed and control subjects. The monoamine effects of lithium were generally similar in responders and nonresponders. In fact, the only changes that were significantly different were larger in nonresponders, CSF MHPG, $t(8) = 2.4, 8$, $p < .05$, and urinary norepinephrine, $t(5) = 4$, $p < .010$. In terms of metabolite measures after 18 days of lithium treatment, the only significant difference between responders and nonresponders was in urinary MHPG excretion (responders, 1.9 ± 0.2 mg/24 hours; nonresponders, 3.0 ± 0.5 mg/24 hours), $t(11) = 2.33$, $p < .05$ (Swann et al. in press-b).

Behavioral Measures in Manic Patients

Correlations Between Behavior and Monoamines

Table 1 summarizes correlations between CSF monoamine metabolites and MADS scores. MHPG correlated significantly

Table 1. Pretreatment Cerebrospinal Fluid Monoamine Metabolites: Correlations With MADS Scores

Scale	MHPG	5-HIAA	HVA
MADS (total)	0.613*	0.171	−0.108
Hostile	0.653*	0.133	−0.115
Elated	0.556*	0.175	−0.140
SADS-GAS	0.114	−0.226	−0.019

Note. All correlations are for 14 subjects (Swann et al. in press-b). The total MADS (Mania Diagnostic and Severity Scale), with the Hostile and Elated subscales, was derived as described by Secunda et al. (1985; see also Chapter 3 in this monograph). The SADS-GAS (Schedule of Affective Disorders and Schizophrenia, Global Assessment Scale) was developed as an index of global severity (Spitzer and Endicott 1978). MHPG = 3-methoxy-4-hydroxyphenylglycol; 5-HIAA = 5-hydroxyindoleacetic acid; HVA = homovanillic acid.

*Pearson r, $p < .05$.

with MADS scores, but the metabolites of dopamine and serotonin did not.

As shown in Table 2, urinary MHPG correlated with MADS ratings, but vanillylmandelic acid and normetanephrine correlated only with the elated component. Table 3 shows that norepinephrine and epinephrine excretion also correlated with MADS scores. These data show that the indexes of noradrenergic function that were elevated in manic patients and altered by lithium treatment also correlated with severity of the manic state (Swann et al. in press-b). Urinary catecholamine excretion also tended to correlate with psychomotor state.

Table 2. Correlations Between Pretreatment MADS Scores and Urinary Catecholamine Metabolites

Scale	MHPG	VMA	NM
MADS (total)	0.513*	0.339	0.340
Hostile	0.440	0.187	0.240
Elated	0.631*	0.613*	0.490*
SADS-GAS	−0.219	0.064	−0.017
Number	17	16	17

Note. The behavioral measures are as described in Table 1. There were no significant correlations with metanephrine excretion (Swann et al. in press-b). MADS = Mania Diagnostic and Severity Scale; MHPG = 3-methoxy-4-hydroxyphenylglycol; VMA = vanillylmandelic acid; NM = normetanephrine; SADS-GAS = Schedule of Affective Disorders and Schizophrenia, Global Assessment Scale.

*Pearson r, $p < .05$.

Table 3. Correlations Between Pretreatment MADS Scores and Urinary Catecholamines

Scale	Norepinephrine	Epinephrine
MADS (total)	0.618*	0.654*
Hostile	0.587	0.541
Elated	0.581*	0.660*
SADS-GAS	0.070	0.084
Number	10	12

Note. Behavioral measures are as in Table 1. MADS = Mania Diagnostic and Severity Scale; SADS-GAS = Schedule of Affective Disorders and Schizophrenia, Global Assessment Scale.

*Spearman r, $p < .05$.

Symptoms Before Treatment and Outcome

Patients with poor outcome tended to have higher MADS ratings before treatment, as shown in Table 4. This was consistent with the report by Prien et al. (1972) that severely ill manic patients responded relatively poorly to lithium alone.

Patients with poor treatment outcome differed from those with good outcome with respect to several measures not considered specific to mania. As summarized in Table 5, these included

Table 4. Correlations Between Pretreatment Urinary Catecholamines and Psychomotor Behavior

Behavior	Norepinephrine	Epinephrine
Retardation	−0.758*	−0.436
Agitation	0.634*	0.587*
Performance retardation	−0.789*	−0.506
Number	10	12

Note. Retardation and agitation were derived from the combination of nurse, clinician, and video ratings and self-ratings as described by Katz et al. (1984).
*Pearson r, $p < .05$.

Table 5. Comparison of Non-manic Symptoms Before Treatment in Patients With Good and Poor Outcome

Symptom	Good	Poor
MADS score	3.77 ± 0.33 (12)	5.42 ± 0.85 (6)**
Depressed mood	1.67 ± 0.41 (12)	2.54 ± 0.55 (5)
Anxiety	2.36 ± 0.32 (12)	3.85 ± 0.55 (5)**
Retardation	1.75 ± 0.11 (11)	1.97 ± 0.22 (5)
Agitation	3.27 ± 0.34 (12)	4.48 ± 0.73 (6)
Hostility	2.40 ± 0.40 (12)	3.59 ± 0.80 (12)
Somatization	1.59 ± 0.20 (12)	2.55 ± 0.66 (5)
Distressed appearance	0.73 ± 0.37 (12)	1.04 ± 0.26 (6)
Interpersonal sensitivity	1.97 ± 0.49 (12)	2.09 ± 0.71 (5)
Positive adaptation	5.89 ± 0.47 (12)	5.59 ± 0.53 (5)
Cognitive impairment	1.91 ± 0.27 (12)	3.08 ± 0.66 (5)*
Sleep disorder	3.00 ± 0.85 (11)	5.34 ± 1.37 (5)
Hamilton score	7.92 ± 1.07 (12)	18.42 ± 3.76 (6)**

Note. Ratings are the averages of Days 10 and 15 of pretreatment. The Hamilton score is based on the Hamilton Depression Scale (Hamilton 1960). MADS = Mania Diagnostic and Severity Scale (Secunda et al. 1985).
*$p = .06$. **$p < .03$.

anxiety, cognitive impairment, and total Hamilton score (Swann et al. in press-a).

BEHAVIORAL CHANGE AND TREATMENT OUTCOME

By definition, patients with good treatment outcome had large changes in MADS scores, and those with poor outcome had little or no change. As previously described, many behavior ratings other than MADS changed during lithium treatment, raising the question of the specificity of these changes with respect to the symptoms of mania. In most cases, changes in behavioral constructs were similar in responders and nonresponders, in contrast to the case with the MADS.

The specific and nonspecific effects of lithium are illustrated in Figure 4. The MADS scores of nonresponders and responders diverged drastically during treatment. By contrast, cognitive impairment in nonresponders improved significantly during treatment.

Characteristics of Patients During Lithium Treatment

Neurotransmitter function in treated manic patients and comparison groups. During lithium treatment, the biochemical measures that were abnormal in manic individuals before treatment no longer differed from those in normal subjects or in untreated bipolar depressed patients. The urinary excretion of catecholamine metabolites was generally higher than in control subjects but similar to bipolar depressed patients, as was the case before treatment (see Figure 2). CSF 5-HIAA and HVA were higher in treated manic patients than in healthy controls or in bipolar depressed patients (Figure 1).

Urinary MHPG excretion during lithium treatment was higher in patients with poor outcome than in responders (see previous text and Swann et al. in press-b). This contrasted with the case before treatment, when there were no differences between subsequent responders and nonresponders. There were no other biochemical differences between treated responders and nonresponders.

Correlations between amines and behavior measures. During lithium treatment, urinary MHPG correlated significantly with MADS scores, but urinary norepinephrine and CSF MHPG did not, as shown in Table 6 (Swann et al. in press-b). Urinary MHPG

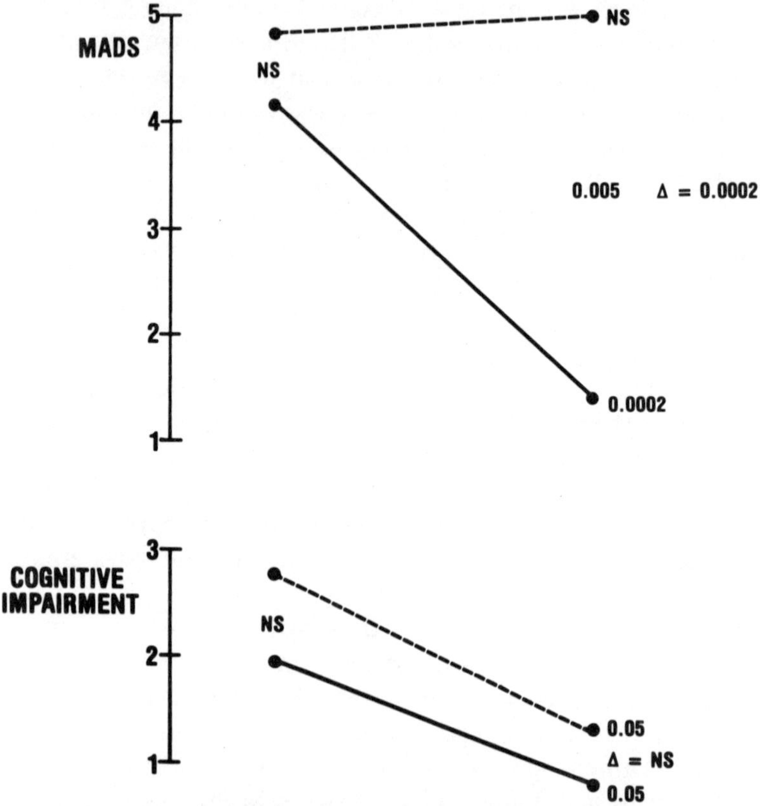

Figure 4. MADS and cognitive impairment ratings in treated and untreated manic patients with good and poor outcome. The MADS is the Mania Diagnostic and Severity score (Secunda et al. 1985); cognitive impairment is a composite score based on patient, clinician, and nurse rating scales (Katz et al. 1982, 1984). Significance of comparisons of untreated and treated subjects within the same outcome group (paired *t*, two-tailed) or of comparisons between treated or untreated patients with respect to outcome is shown by *F* values.

also correlated with other behavioral measures, including cognitive impairment and anxiety. This was consistent with the observation that urinary MHPG during treatment was higher in nonresponders than in responders.

SUMMARY OF RESULTS

To summarize these results in terms of the practical requirements for a useful hypothesis, we found that untreated manic individuals had increased indexes of noradrenergic function that correlated with severity of the manic syndrome and were reduced to normal levels during lithium treatment. There were no differences between untreated responders and nonresponders, however. More important, the abnormal measures appeared to decline during lithium treatment, regardless of outcome.

CONCLUSIONS

Lithium Effects on Noradrenergic Function in Mania

These results are consistent with previous studies reporting that CSF MHPG (Shopsin et al. 1973; Wilk et al. 1972) or norepinephrine (Post et al. 1978) was elevated in manic patients. We recently

Table 6. Correlations Between Behavioral and Transmitter Measures in Treated Manic Patients

Behavior	CSF MHPG	Urinary MHPG	Urinary Norepinephrine
Anxiety	0.294	0.626*	0.562
Agitation	0.344	0.715*	0.401
Hostility	0.459	0.661*	0.579
Cognitive impairment	0.810**	0.840**	0.585

Note. CSF = cerebrospinal fluid; MHPG = 3-methoxy-4-hydroxyphenylglycol. Behavioral measures were derived from clinician, nurse, patient, and video ratings as described by Katz et al. (1984). The Mania Diagnostic and Severity Scale (Secunda et al. 1985) did not correlate significantly with any transmitter measures during treatment (Swann et al. in press-b).

$^*p < .05$. $^{**}p < .01$.

reported that CSF MHPG was correlated with severity of the manic syndrome (Swann et al. 1983 in press-b); the lack of correlation between manic symptoms and 5-HIAA or HVA is consistent with a report by Fyro et al. (1975).

The reduction during treatment in CSF MHPG and urinary norepinephrine were consistent with their elevation in mania and correlation with the manic syndrome. Change in these measures did not correlate with change in MADS scores, however, and the reductions occurred in responders and nonresponders. A similar reduction in CSF MHPG was reported in two patients treated with lithium by Shopsin et al. (1973). Greenspan et al. (1970) reported reduced urinary norepinephrine excretion during lithium treatment in three hypomanic patients. In addition, lithium has been reported to reduce noradrenergic indexes in depressed patients (Linnoila et al. 1983).

Noradrenergic Hypothesis: Pro and Con

These data are consistent with a noradrenergic hypothesis for mania in that noradrenergic indexes were elevated before treatment, correlated with severity, and were reduced during treatment. The reductions were similar in responders and in nonresponders, however, so elevated noradrenergic function is inadequate to explain the effects of lithium in mania. Possible explanations include the following: a) Reduction in noradrenergic activity is necessary but not sufficient for response to lithium; additional changes in some other transmitter system not measured in this study are also required; and b) improvement in manic behavior requires a prolonged reduction in noradrenergic function; biochemical measures were obtained only once during treatment, and the presumed responders may have had a more rapid biochemical response to lithium.

Lithium Effects: Specificity and Nonspecificity

The data raise questions as to the specificity of behavioral effects of lithium relative to the manic syndrome. Lithium improved some aspects of behavior, most notably cognitive impairment, in patients whose mania did not improve. This was similar to the case with indexes of noradrenergic function, which declined whether mania improved or not. Although lithium can have a powerful antimanic effect, this effect does not appear as specific as might be expected. This should not be surprising because the discovery that lithium was effective in mania was serendipitous. The relative lack of specificity of lithium, together with the emerging pattern of relationships between the manic syndrome and measures of transmitter function, suggest strongly that lithium can be improved on as a specific treatment for mania.

References

Akiskal HS, McKinney WT Jr: Affective disorders: toward a unified hypothesis. Science 182:20–29, 1973

Anton AH, Sayre DF: A study of the factors affecting the aluminum oxide trihydroxyindole procedure for the analysis of the catecholamines. J Pharmacol Exp Ther 138:360–375, 1962

Asberg M, Bertilsson L: Serotonin in depressive states, in Neuropsychopharmacology. Edited by Saletu B. New York, Pergamon, 1979

Asberg M, Traskman L: Studies of CSF 5-HIAA in depression and suicidal behavior. Adv Exp Med Biol 133:739–752, 1981

Asberg M, Thoren P, Traskman L, et al: Serotonin depression: a biochemical subgroup within the affective disorders? Science 191:478–480, 1976a

Asberg M, Traskman L, Thoren P: 5-HIAA in the cerebrospinal fluid: a biochemical suicide predictor? Arch Gen Psychiatry 33:1193–1197, 1976b

Ashcroft FW, Glen AIM: Mood and neuronal functions: a modified amine hypothesis for the etiology of affective illness. Adv Biochem Psychopharmacol 11:335–339, 1974

Ashcroft GW, Crawford TBB, Eccleston D, et al: 5-hydroxyindole compounds in the cerebrospinal fluid of patients with psychiatric or neurologic diseases. Lancet Vol. no. ii:1049–1952, 1966

Bonsnes RW, Taussky HH: On the colorimetric determination of creatinine by the Jaffee reaction. J Biol Chem 158:581–591, 1945

Bowers MB Jr: Lumbar CSF 5-hydroxyindoleacetic acid and homovanillic acid in affective syndromes. J Nerv Ment Dis 158:325–330, 1974

Bowers MB Jr: Clinical measurement of central dopamine and serotonin metabolism: realiability and interpretation of cerebrospinal fluid acid monoamine metabolite measures. Neuropharmacology 11:101–110, 1972

Burdock EI, Hakesem G, Hardesty AS, et al: A ward behavior rating scale for use with mental hospital patients. J Clin Psychol 16:246–247, 1960

Carroll BJ: Prediction of treatment outcome with lithium. Arch Gen Psychiatry 36:870–878, 1979

Coppen A: Indoleamines and affective disorders. J Psychiatry Res 9:163–171, 1972

Dekirmenjian H, Maas JW: An improved procedure of 3-methoxy-4-hydroxyphenylethylene glycol determination by gas–liquid chromatography. Anal Chem 35:113–122, 1970

Derogatis LR, Lipman MS, Rickels K, et al: The Hopkins Symptom Checklist (HSCL): a measure of primary symptom dimensions, in Psychological Measurements in Psychopharmacology: Modern Problems in Pharmacopsychiatry (Vol 7). Edited by Pichot P. Basel, Switzerland, Karger, 1974

Endicott J, Spitzer RL: The schedule for affective disorders and schizophrenia. Arch Gen Psychiatry 35:837–844, 1978

Fri CG, Wiesel FA, Sedval G: Simultaneous quantification of homovanillic acid and 5-hydroxyindoleacetic acid in cerebrospinal fluid by mass fragmentography. Life Sciences 14:2469–2480, 1974

Fyro B, Petterson U, Sedvall G: The effect of lithium treatment on manic symptoms and levels of monoamine metabolites in cerebrospinal fluid of manic-depressed patients. Psychopharmacologia 44:99–103, 1975

Gerner RH, Post RM, Bunney WE Jr: A dopaminergic mechanism in mania. Am J Psychiatry 133:1177–1180, 1976

Greenspan K, Schildkraut JJ, Gordon EK, et al: Catecholamine metabolism in affective disorders. III. MHPG and other catecholamine metabolites in patients treated with lithium carbonate. J Psychiatr Res 7:171–183, 1970

Hamilton M: A rating scale for depression. J Neurol Neurosurg Psychiatry 23:56–62, 1960

Janowsky DS, El-Yousef MK, Davis JM: Parasympathetic suppression of manic symptoms by physostigmine. Arch Gen Psychiatry 28:542–547, 1973

Janowsky DS, El-Yousef MK, Davis JM: A cholinergic–adrenergic hypothesis of mania and depression. Lancet ii: 632–635, 1972

Jouvent R, Lecubier Y, Peuch AJ, et al: Antimanic effect of clonidine. Am J Psychiatry 137:1275–1276, 1980

Katz MM, Itil TM: Video methodology for research in psychopathology and psychopharmacology. Arch Gen Psychiatry 31:204–210, 1974

Katz M, Robins E, Croughan J, et al: Behavioral measurement and drug response in unipolar and bipolar depression. Psychol Med 12:25–36, 1982

Katz MM, Secunda S, Koslow S, et al: A multivantaged approach to measurement of behavioral and affect state for clinical and psychobiological research. Psychol Rep 55:619–671, 1984

Knapp S, Mandell AJ: Effects of lithium chloride on parameters of biosynthetic capacity for serotonin in the rat. J Pharmacol Exp Ther 193:812–823, 1975

Koslow SH, Maas JW, Bowden CL, et al: CSF and urinary biogenic amines and metabolites in depression and mania: a controlled, univariate analysis. Arch Gen Psychiatry 40:999–1010, 1983

Linnoila M, Kasoum F, Rosenthal N, et al: Electroconvulsive treatment and lithium carbonate: their effects on norepinephrine metabolism in patients with primary, major depressions. Arch Gen Psychiatry 40:677–680, 1983

Linnoila M, Miller TL, Bartko J, et al: Five antidepressant treatments in depressed patients: effects on urinary serotonin and 5-hydroxyindoleacetic acid output. Arch Gen Psychiatry 41:688–692, 1984

Maas JW, Koslow SH, Davis JM, et al: Biological component of the NIMH Clinical Research Branch Collaborative Program on the Psychobiology of Depression: I. Background and theoretical considerations. Psychol Med 10:759–776, 1980

Mandell AJ, Knapp S: Asymmetry and mood, emergent properties of serotonergic regulation. Arch Gen Psychiatry 36:909–916, 1979

Murphy DL, Pickar D, Alterman IS: Methods for the quantitative assessment of depressive and manic behavior, in Quantitative Techniques for the Evaluation of the Behavior of Psychiatric Patients. Edited by Burdock EI, Sudilovsky A, Gershon S. New York, Marcel-Dekker, 1980

Post RM: Cocaine psychoses: a continuum model. Am J Psychiatry 132:225–231, 1975

Post RM, Lake CR, Jimerson DC, et al: Cerebrospinal fluid norepinephrine in affective illness. Am J Psychiatry 135:907–912, 1978

Prien RF, Caffey EM, Klett CJ: Comparison of lithium carbonate and chlorpromazine in the treatment of mania. Arch Gen Psychiatry 26:146–153, 1972

Schildkraut JJ, Kety SS: Biogenic amines and emotion. Science 156:21–30, 1967

Secunda S, Koslow S, Redmond DE Jr, et al: Biological component of the NIMH Clinical Research Branch Collaborative Program on the Psychobiology of Depression: II. Methodology and data analysis. Psychol Med 10:777–703, 1980

Secunda S, Katz M, Swann A, et al: Mania: diagnosis, state measurement and prediction of treatment response. J Affective Disord 8:113–121, 1985

Shapiro SS, Wilk MB: An analysis of variance test for normality (complete samples). Biometrika 52:591–611, 1965

Shopsin B, Wilk S, Gershon S, et al: Cerebrospinal fluid MHPG: an assessment of norepinephrine metabolism in affective disorders. Arch Gen Psychiatry 28:230–233, 1973

Sjostrom R, Roos BE: 5-hydroxyindoleacetic acid and homovanillic acid in cerebrospinal fluid in manic depressive psychosis. Eur J Clin Pharmacol 4:170–176, 1972

Spitzer RL, Endicott J: Schedule for Affective Disorders and Schizophrenia (Third Edition). New York State Psychiatric Institute Biometrics Research Division, 1978

Spitzer RL, Endicott J, Robins E: Research Diagnostic Criteria for a Selected Group of Functional Disorders (Third Edition). New York State Psychiatric Institute Biometrics Research Divison, 1977

Swahn OG, Sandgarde B, Wiesel FA, et al: Simultaneous determination of three major monoamine metabolites in brain tissue and body fluids by a mass fragmentographic method. Psychopharmacology 48: 147–152, 1976

Swahn OG, Sandgarde B, Wiesel FA, et al: Simultaneous determination of the three major monoamine metabolites in brain tissue and body fluids by a mass fragmentographic method. Psychopharmacology 48:147–152, 1976

Swann AC, Secunda S, Davis JM, et al: CSF monoamine metabolites in mania. Am J Psychiatry 140:396–400, 1983

Swann AC, Secunda SK, Katz MM, et al: Lithium treatment of mania: clinical characteristics, specificity of symptom change, and outcome. Psychiat Res, in press-a

Swann AC, Koslow SH, Katz MM, et al: Lithium treatment of mania: CSF and urinary monoamine metabolites and treatment outcome. Arch Gen Psychiatry, in press-b

Taniguchi K, Kainoto Y, Armstrong MD: Quantitative determination of metanephrine and normetanephrine in urine. J Lab Clin Med 64:469–484, 1964

Taylor MA, Abrams R: Prediction of lithium response in mania. Arch Gen Psychiatry 38:800–803, 1981

van Praag HM: Significance of biochemical parameters in the diagnosis, treatment, and prevention of depressive disorders. Biol Psychiatry 12:101–131, 1977

Wilk S, Shopsin B, Gershon S, et al: Cerebrospinal fluid levels of MHPG in affective disorders. Nature 235:440–441, 1972